What People Are Saying

What a lovely way to begin each day... ...ning our hearts in prayer! Mary DeMuth goes first, drawing from a deep well of honest self-disclosure and hard-earned wisdom as she puts into words the soul long-ings we all share. The verses are perfectly chosen, unfolding God's love story from Genesis to Revelation, and the single-word titles capture the essence of each passage. A truly original and beautiful devotional.

Liz Curtis Higgs, bestselling author of *31 Verses to Write on Your Heart*

Mary's heart for Jesus and people is contagious. These prayers reflect those passions and will remind you how fleeting this life can be and how much hope we have in the one to come. Enjoy!

Jennie Allen, author of *Nothing to Prove* and IF:Gathering founder

So many of us feel clumsy and unsure when we approach God in prayer, but in *Jesus Every Day*, Mary takes our hand and serves as a loving guide. These prayers not only illumine Scripture in fresh and powerful ways, but they will undoubtedly transform the prayer life of every reader. This book is a treasure!

Sharon Hodde Miller, author of *Free of Me*

In *Jesus Every Day* Mary DeMuth is a tender and compassionate guide who steps me through the Bible and leads me to God's heart. I feel as if Mary is by my side, helping me to open up an authentic conversation with God. Her words are a beautiful start, helping me to continue the conversation with my Savior. I cannot wait to share this book with friends, especially the young moms I mentor who often ask, "How do I pray? What do I pray?" What a beautiful book!

Tricia Goyer, author of 70 books, including *Walk It Out*

As a real-life friend, I have personally been the recipient of Mary DeMuth's faithful prayer life. So to see her prayers touch paper and go out into the world for we, the readers, to pray as well is truly a gift. Out of all the books Mary has written, this is her most important. May the prayers of this beautiful servant inspire and ignite the prayer lives of us all as we experience *Jesus Every Day*.

Lisa Whittle, Speaker, Bible teacher, author of *Put Your Warrior Boots On*

This book is an incredible tool written by an incredible author that could help you begin a journey that will transform your life and walk with God. I wholeheartedly with much enthusiasm encourage you: *Use this book and watch your walk with God flourish!*

Bob Roberts, senior pastor Northwood Church, Keller, Texas, and author of *Lessons from the East*

This devotional is a gem! The powerful scriptures and poignant prayers meld seamlessly, giving voice to our deepest longings and offering rich and intimate times with our Lord. You won't want to miss the boundless blessings of this exceptional book!

Judy Gordon Morrow, author of *The Listening Heart*

Talk about fresh, deep, and authentic! I found myself a bit breathless as I read through *Jesus Every Day*, eager to pray through the Bible with Mary. The life-changing petitions probe real stuff and offer real grace.

Paula Moldenhauer, author of the Soul Scents devotional series

Imagine this: 366 beautifully written prayers. Now imagine these prayers are based on selected scriptures from Genesis to Revelation. That's what Mary DeMuth does in *Jesus Every Day*. That's the gift she has given us. It is a guide for praying through the Bible. Thank you, Mary, for connecting two such powerful elements—daily prayer and God's Word.

Will Davis Jr., author of *Pray Big!*

I knew when I prayed the very first prayer in this book that I was holding something incredibly special. I found myself in the presence of God with a lump in my throat, and I experienced something completely new: The deep things in my heart were beautifully written on the page in front of me. If you are serious about going deeper with God, *Jesus Every Day* is for you.

Cheryl Weber, *100 Huntley Street* cohost and senior executive producer

Jesus Every Day is a powerful book of beautiful prayers to Jesus based on His Word. Mary's life journey fuels these prayers with an exquisite honesty, vulnerability, and hope. The prayers in this marvelous book remind us that whether we are struggling in the valley or partying on the mountaintops, the Jesus celebration is ongoing and we are His honored guests.

Boz Tchividjian, executive director of GRACE and law professor, Liberty University School of Law

It's hard to put prayer into words at times. It's hard to see how our small, insignificant stories could ever be part of the glorious story God's writing on eternity. In *Jesus Every Day*, Mary DeMuth shows us how to make ourselves available to Him, wrapping prayers around key moments in the Bible. What a lovely companion to a surrendered life.

Joanna Weaver, author of *Having a Mary Heart in a Martha World*

Mary has a unique way of unlocking each verse, opening her heart vulnerably, and leading you, the reader, to that "ah ha" moment when *your* heart opens and *you* begin to worship and say "Yes, yes, yes" along with her. Each prayer is deeply personal to Mary, yet is such a mirror image of our own struggles that we can pray with her, finding real help for entering God's presence.

Aldyth Thomson, director of Beauty for Ashes, South Africa

Mary DeMuth writes in a very authentic way, making you feel as if she's sitting across from you in a coffee shop. *Jesus Every Day* isn't your typical daily devotional, Mary doesn't use Sunday school answers; she gets real, taking you straight to authenticity with Jesus. Just what I needed.

Becky Shaffer, executive director of Saving Grace, NW Arkansas

None of us knows what the next year holds for our health, finances, or family. That's why we need *Jesus Every Day*. Written for your heart from a fellow traveler and prayer warrior, these 365 prayers offer just the right mix of the practical and the eternal.

Allen Arnold, author of *The Story of With*

In *Jesus Every Day*, Mary helps us pray honest and bold prayers. This journey she takes us on through the Bible will give you the words to take your prayer life to the next level. I encourage everyone to pick up a copy and make these prayers a part of your daily life!

Aaron Graham, lead pastor, The District Church, Washington, DC

This Book Belongs To:

_____

_____

They delight in the law of the LORD,
meditating on it day and night.
They are like trees planted along the riverbank,
bearing fruit each season.
Their leaves never wither, and they prosper in all they do.

PSALM 1:2-3

Mary DeMuth

JESUS EVERY DAY

HARVEST HOUSE PUBLISHERS
EUGENE, OREGON

Cover design by Emily Weigel

Interior design by Janelle Coury

Mary E. DeMuth is represented by David Van Diest from the Van Diest Literary Agency, 34947 SE Brooks Road, Boring, OR 97009.

JESUS EVERY DAY
Copyright © 2018 by Mary DeMuth
Published by Harvest House Publishers
Eugene, Oregon 97402
www.harvesthousepublishers.com

ISBN 978-0-7369-7101-0 (pbk.)
ISBN 978-0-7369-7102-7 (eBook)

Library of Congress Cataloging-in-Publication Data

Names: DeMuth, Mary E., 1967- author.
Title: Jesus every day / Mary DeMuth.
Description: Eugene, Oregon : Harvest House Publishers, 2017. | Description based on print version record and CIP data provided by publisher; resource not viewed.
Identifiers: LCCN 2017023229 (print) | LCCN 2017028140 (ebook) | ISBN 9780736971027 (ebook) | ISBN 9780736971010 (pbk.)
Subjects: LCSH: Devotional calendars.
Classification: LCC BV4811 (ebook) | LCC BV4811 .D46 2017 (print) | DDC 242/.2—dc23
LC record available at https://lccn.loc.gov/2017023229

Printed in the United States of America

17 18 19 20 21 22 23 24 25 / VP-JC / 10 9 8 7 6 5 4 3 2 1

To Judy Douglass,
a person of great prayer.
And to my Restory tribe
who asked for and inspired this devotional.

An Invitation...

I don't remember when I started writing, "Mind if I pray for you?" at the end of my monthly newsletters, but I do remember the frequent response: Thank you; I needed that. In this busy and broken world, we casually throw out, "Hey, I'll be praying for you," but so often the sentiment is as far as we get. (I've done it too.) Having the opportunity to pray for the people I'd come to love felt like joy and breathing all wrapped together. As I typed my prayers, I asked God to please infuse my small words with his majesty and comfort. A lot of my prayers reflected my current worry or struggle or victory or grief. And what I found was this: My own life in its vulnerable form connected with my readers, and my written prayers represented the cries of so many hearts.

I've often said that four words inform my life, particularly as an author and speaker.

Go first.

Me too.

I believe God calls us to authenticity, to share our worlds with one another. We do that so that others no longer feel alone. We dare to go first so that someone who's struggling can remark, "Me too." These 366 prayers are my go first, and it's my hope that you'll find yourself in between the lines so you can say, "Me too."

We may not see our way around the next unknown bend in the road. But Jesus does. He walks alongside us every day, giving us the hope we need to make the next decision, love the people in front of us, forgive those who have hurt us, let go of the control that makes us twitchy, and practice the art of gratitude. He is with us in the heartache, the questions, the dreams, and the frailty of life. And he longs for our hearts to unfold before him, trusting him to act in his perfect (yet sometimes slow) timing. Prayer is that intersection between an almighty God and our all-encompassing need. It's how we connect with God—not merely listing off our wants and needs like a child on Santa's lap, but sharing our bruises, joys, hopes, and bewilderments. Prayer is the language of a close relationship.

I've taken a pilgrimage of prayer to discover the nearness of Jesus. As I mature in my relationship with him, I find myself becoming more and more content with simply praying for people. I pray for strangers. I pray for friends. I pray for my family constantly, like breathing. I ask permission to pray for someone and then place my hand on a shoulder. In that circle of two, I ask Jesus to please help us all face our lives, to find peace in our trials. I pray bold prayers, seeking healing and health. I pray timid prayers, full of ifs and maybes. I pray wordless prayers, those times when our words can't seem to form at the enormity of what we face. And through it all, Jesus hears. He sees. He receives. And he intercedes. Closer than our breath.

You're holding this book because some of my prayers made it into print and a gaggle of people emailed me asking me to please write a book full of them. I shopped *Jesus Every Day* for several years, hoping and praying it would find a home. I'm utterly grateful that it has—it's a dream come true.

This is a unique devotional because you can start it on March 3 or October 21. Just begin on Day 1 and begin the journey. The book moves through every book of the Bible, from Genesis to Revelation, so that by the time you close the book, you'll have an overarching understanding of the heart of God—his great redemptive story. You'll read a scripture and then pray through it—simple as that. It's my sincere hope that my words will echo your heart and that your own prayer life will deepen each day as a result. By year's end, you'll have prayed through the entire Bible.

It seems fitting to end this introduction with this:

Mind if I pray for you?

Jesus, I pray for the dear person reading this prayer. Would you woo them to yourself? Would you bring peace into whatever chaos they face today? Would you show them how deeply and widely (and wildly) you love them? Remind them in this sweet circle of two that you are there. You are available. You offer grace to approach you—no stern looks, no sighs of disappointment, no tsking or shaking of the head. Your arms, they are wide open, and your embrace is always available. Take my friend on a journey through this book. Deepen their relationship with you. Empower them to run to you when life careens or hope wanes. Invigorate their prayer life. Move mountains. Unleash freedom. Heal wounds. Restore what's been lost. Demonstrate your love in them-shaped ways. Thank you that you're the empathetic savior who understands what it's like to walk this dusty earth, clay-footed. Thank you for making a way for them to be safe, forgiven, and welcomed—all because you left the glory of heaven for earth's sin-scarred shore. Oh, how you love them. Oh, how they need you. Do something new in the heart of the one reading these words. May spiritual growth and freedom spring forth, a new river through a wild land. Amen and amen.

Mary DeMuth

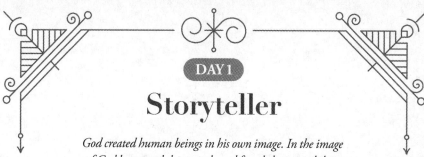

Storyteller

God created human beings in his own image. In the image
of God he created them; male and female he created them.

GENESIS 1:27

Jesus, you made everything from nothing. What a surprising Creator you are. All our creativity has its origin in you.

I acknowledge that every gift of inspiration originates from you. So forgive me for hoarding it, displaying it for my glory, dismissing it, wasting it.

I confess that I have tried to manufacture a life in my small strength. Left to my devices, Lord, I fail, grow prideful, and forget the kingdom.

You, who are the Word, are the one I worship with my words. You are the Storyteller of my life, but I have settled for a lesser story of stuff, recognition, and power. Forgive me.

Everything I do, Jesus, I do now because I love you and want my life to count for your kingdom. Any fame that comes my way is a trifle offering, and it becomes a platform to make you famous and proclaim your radical story of redemption to a dying, storyless people. I give you permission to write my story however you see fit. I hand the pen back to you. I no longer want to dictate to you what I want my story to be. I choose now to surrender my story wholly, fully to you.

Take the pen, Lord Jesus. And write. Amen.

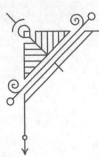

Detailed

*Two by two they came into the boat, representing
every living thing that breathes. A male and female
of each kind entered, just as God had commanded
Noah. Then the LORD closed the door behind them.*

GENESIS 7:15-16

Jesus, I love that you are concerned about every detail of my life,
just as you were in Noah's time. You gave him specific instructions.
You warned him about what would come. You blessed him with skills
and knowledge and guts to carry out the preservation of everyone. You
didn't leave him alone, scratching his head, wondering where you were.

I love that you shut the door behind him and his family. Because
who else could? Every last detail, you took care of—in person this time.

Help me remember your attention to minutiae when my mind
wanders toward thousands of worries. Show me the picture of you
shutting the door behind Noah as the waters erupted from the sky
and ground. You know the big stresses in my life—but more than that,
Jesus, you know the smallest bothersome thoughts. You know what
niggles me at night. You know me intimately.

So today I choose to worship you for remembering small things, for
taking care of pesky details, for loving me in big and small ways. Help
me to rest safely behind the door you close after me. Amen.

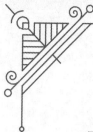

Fame

*They said, "Come let's build a great city for ourselves with
a tower that reaches into the sky. This will make us famous
and keep us from being scattered all over the world."*

GENESIS 11:4

Jesus, I confess that I long to be noticed. I want to make a name for myself, for others to see me, applaud my unseen efforts, and recognize me publicly. I may say this isn't true, but deep down, I struggle to base my identity on you, not on what I accomplish.

Thank you for this verse today that reminds me that all my tower building ends in confusion. I'm sorry that I've worshipped my own name, wanting to curry my own fame instead of reorienting my life toward your renown on this earth.

You are the famous one, O Lord. You are the one worth worshipping. I want to become more like what I worship. But when I worship myself, my life becomes shrunken and me-centric. Teach me to worship you so I become more like you—bigger hearted, full of love for those who differ from me, a person of forgiveness and grace.

I tend to build towers to myself. But today, stop me short, Jesus. Remind me that anything I build on this earth will only tumble and ultimately fail. Oh, how I need your perspective today. Amen.

Between

*Abram traveled south and set up camp in the hill country, with
Bethel to the west and Ai to the east. There he built another altar
and dedicated it to the LORD, and he worshiped the LORD.*

GENESIS 12:8

Jesus, thank you for the story of Abram, how he left everything comfortable and cozy, dared to trust you fiercely, and lived a life of faith-inspired adventure. Oh, how I want to live that way too. Teach me that kind of grit, Jesus. (And thank you for making the same kind of sacrifice, leaving the pristine fields of heaven to come to earth to willingly die for us. How can I thank you?)

In some ways, I don't relate to Abram, but in this one I truly can. He pitched his camp between two worlds—Bethel (house of God) and Ai, the "heap of ruins" that was a Canaanite stronghold. What a picture of my life on this earth.

Help me understand the pull of both—of spending time in the house of God, yet venturing out into the world to be a beacon of your light. Help me to worship you in the in-between places—where you aren't named, where others blame you, dismiss you, rail against you, or flat out don't believe you exist.

Thank you that, through the Holy Spirit, I have the house of God inside me, wherever my feet take me. Help me rest in that today, trusting that you will always be with me. I choose to worship you wherever I find myself today. Amen.

Promise

*Some time later, the LORD spoke to Abram in a vision
and said to him, "Do not be afraid, Abram, for I will
protect you, and your reward will be great."*

GENESIS 15:1

Jesus, I love that you understand just how scared I can be. Because you walked this earth, experiencing mockery, storms, hunger, homelessness, and ridicule, I know you offer me sympathy when I struggle with fear.

Thank you for this example of your Father caring about the deepest parts of Abram. He must've been bewildered at the journey before him—with a promise of offspring, a barren wife, and no homeland yet to call his own. He lived by the skin of his obedience, and oh, how I want to live that same way.

Even though Abram believed, he worried too. And you offered him sweet assurance that you saw him and knew his struggles. You didn't simply acknowledge that he struggled; you spoke into the situation with words of life.

That's where I am right now, Jesus. I am struggling. Fear has become my companion for the next scary steps. And I need you to intervene with words. Speak protection over me. Help me to know you see me today—broken, needy, worried.

I trust that you will protect me. All things that come my way sift through your sovereign embrace. Help me not to dictate what my reward will be, but to trust you for the reward you will bring. Amen.

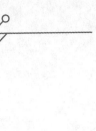

Sees

*Thereafter, Hagar used another name to refer to the
LORD, who had spoken to her. She said, "You are the God
who sees me." She also said, "Have I truly seen the one
who sees me?" So that well was named Beer-lahai-roi
(which means "well of the Living One who sees me").*

GENESIS 16:13-14

Jesus, thank you for the example of Hagar. There have been times when I've felt just like her—forgotten and fleeing from people and circumstances that have leveled me flat. She was forsaken by the very one who forced her into her circumstance, and she found herself alone in the wilderness.

And yet...you saw her. You noticed her there at the well she named. You intervened. And I love that she also gave you a name, the "the Living One who sees me."

Thank you that you are living. You're not a statue. Instead, you're a vibrant well—a fountain of never-ending, thirst-quenching nourishment. You sustain me. You provide everything I need.

I need to know, in whatever small way you want to show me, that you notice me today. Please be the God who sees me as I wrestle with my own shame and inadequacies. I need to know you're acquainted with my weakness, and that you don't hold it against me. Meet me in the wilderness I find myself in today, and pour your refreshing water over me. Amen.

Word

*The LORD kept his word and did for
Sarah exactly what he had promised.
She became pregnant, and she gave birth to
a son for Abraham in his old age.
This happened at just the time God had said it would.*

GENESIS 21:1-2

Jesus, sometimes it's hard to trust you. It's difficult to realize that you really are a God who keeps his promises. Remind me of your faithfulness so I don't faint under the weight of my fears and unmet expectations. Refresh my memory of how you kept your word to me just as you kept it to Abraham and Sarah. In retrospect your timing makes beautiful sense, but when I'm in the middle of my circumstances, it feels arbitrary or late.

Give me patience as I wait for your promises to me to unfurl. I need a persevering spirit, a tenacious bent. Honestly, sometimes I give in to weariness, especially when I've prayed for something for several years and have not seen an answer. I don't want to be a prayer-quitter, but the day-to-day trusting makes my heart heavy.

I choose right now to reignite, by the power of the Holy Spirit within me, my prayers for those things in my life that need changing. I pray again for that friend who is far from you. I lift up the prodigals who seem so content to be far from you. I give you the grief I carry as I wait. And I ask that you would please show me afresh that you've got all this, and I don't need to fret any longer. Amen.

Provide

Abraham named the place Yahweh-Yireh (which means "the
Lord will provide"). To this day, people still use that name as a
proverb: "On the mountain of the Lord it will be provided."

GENESIS 22:14

Jesus, I realize that I'm so much more joyful when I number my blessings, when I reflect on the many beautiful ways you've provided for me. Keep my heart in that contented place. I want to live today in anticipation of what you will do next instead of constantly complaining about what isn't pristine in my life.

You will provide. It's a bedrock truth. You love the birds, the cattle on a thousand hills, the ants, the world you created. You provide clothing and shelter and food. Help me be truly content with every provision, and please don't let me become complacent, forgetting all the amazing ways you've sustained me.

Show me where my mountain is today, Jesus. Where do I need to lay my Isaac down? What do I trust in more than I trust in you? What is keeping me from fully, wholeheartedly following you and obeying your voice? Show me, even if I tremble as I ask this.

Thank you that Abraham's surrender resulted in peace and provision. I pray the same for myself today. Amen.

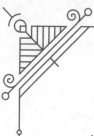

Camp

As Jacob started on his way again, angels of God came to
meet him. When Jacob saw them, he exclaimed, "This
is God's camp!" So he named the place Mahanaim.

GENESIS 32:1-2

Jesus, I haven't seen an angel, but I can only imagine what it would be like to encounter one. And yet, when you walked the earth, you were much greater than angels, but folks missed your significance. I don't want to do that. I don't want to miss you. Keep my eyes wide open to the spiritual dimension all around me. I want to be fully alive in every moment today, able to see your dealings throughout the day.

Help me be like Jacob when I encounter you. He gave you credit when you sent angelic visitors. He named the place where you visited. He stopped and didn't move forward without first acknowledging and praising you.

Jesus, I live in a crazy world right now. I'm constantly bombarded with images, words, moving pictures, sounds. Forgive me for being so distracted by busyness and tasks. I want to become like Jacob, wholly interruptible, able to stop and worship you in the midst of my day.

I long for my life to be your camp, Lord—the place where you dwell. As I venture into today, heighten my awareness of your presence, and go with me. I love you. Amen.

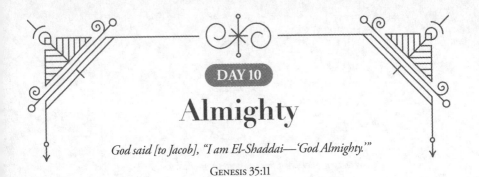

Almighty

God said [to Jacob], "I am El-Shaddai—'God Almighty.'"

GENESIS 35:11

Jesus, there are days (most days!) when I feel ill-equipped to live the Christian life. My weakness is ever before me, and I can't see my way out. And when I focus on all my lack, I forget (forgive me!) that you are the almighty one, and you never asked me to be strong, but dependent.

I confess I'm incapable of running my own little universe, let alone the entire cosmos. But you capably hold both in your hands as if they were nothing. Help me remember that nothing is too difficult for you. Nothing is too perplexing. Nothing is insurmountable. You are El-Shaddai, God Almighty.

Forgive me when I forget that. Forgive me when I desperately try to be almighty in my own small strength. Forgive me when I worship at the altar of controlling-everything-in-my-life. I don't want to do that anymore. I am tired, Jesus. Tired of trying to manufacture mightiness.

I surrender. I choose to trust your power. I relinquish control to you today, and I ask that you enable me to see this paradox: that when I'm weak, you have the opportunity to be mightily strong. Amen.

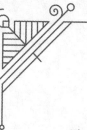

Success

*The LORD was with Joseph, so he succeeded in everything
he did as he served in the home of his Egyptian master.
Potiphar noticed this and realized that the LORD was
with Joseph, giving him success in everything he did.*

GENESIS 39:2-3

Jesus, I love that Joseph thrived as a slave. He chose to do the right thing, honoring you when his life was no longer his own. Although he could've silently rebelled because of his brothers' betrayal and treachery, he chose to honor rather than blame you.

I want to be more like that today, Jesus. Show me the places in my life where I've allowed circumstances to dictate my mood and alter my faithfulness. Show me the excuses I've used to disobey you when life's become tough.

I also love that Joseph didn't do the right thing in order to get blessings. The blessings were simply a by-product of his faithfulness. Oh, how I want to live like that too. I want to be honorable, faithful, diligent, and kind—even when my circumstances stretch my resolve and depression lurks. Help me to obey you simply because I love you—not to get things from you.

As I pray, reinforce this Joseph-idea. I don't want my prayer life to simply be an endless list of things I want from you. Instead, let it be a time where I worship you, revere you, and strive to praise you despite my circumstances. Amen.

Filled

Joseph's suggestions were well received by Pharaoh and his officials. So Pharaoh asked his officials, "Can we find anyone else like this man so obviously filled with the spirit of God?"

GENESIS 41:37-38

Jesus, I want others to ask this question of me. I want to be "obviously filled" with your Spirit and overflow you wherever I go. I want it to be evident, noticeable—not for my own glory, not so I can boast about my capabilities at living the Christian life, but so I can boast solely in your ability to do good work through me.

I face this day with uncertainties looming before me. I have no idea what will happen or how I will react. But you are there. You are with me. You will strengthen me. Right now I choose to reorient my heart toward you and the whispers you send my way. Help me become responsive to your voice, to obey when it seems strange or counterintuitive. To care more about your glory and your way than my story and my way.

I can't manufacture your presence, nor do I want to try. I surrender my agenda today and humbly, wholly ask that you would flood me with your Holy Spirit in a noticeable way, for the sake of your kingdom. Amen.

Pain

*[Joseph] turned away from them and began to weep.
When he regained his composure, he spoke to them again.*

GENESIS 42:24

Jesus, there are days when I feel like Joseph, so bound up in pain that weeping leaks out. It's real. It's honest. It doesn't demonstrate a lack of faith to feel sad, to embrace pain in the moment. What does show faithlessness is pretending pain doesn't exist, shoving it way down deep into the recesses of my soul so that I become robotic—unscathed by pain, yet walled off from joy.

Help me be human—to be real, to weep when weeping is called for, to laugh wholeheartedly when life throws curveballs, to be angry and yet not sin in that anger. Help me to shake hands with everyday emotions, not relegating them to the basement of my soul but allowing them fresh air in the moment.

Oh, Jesus, I want to inhabit every sacred moment today. I want to feel again. I long to heal from all the pain I've shoved into carefully locked closets. Instead of hiding from ghosts who haunt me, I choose right now to hand you the key to the locked places. Open the doors wide, Jesus, and let the sunshine make the dust particles of my past emotions dance and live. I'm afraid to feel pain, but I understand that you are well acquainted with grief, and that you'll hold me as I do. Free me. Unleash me. Heal me. Amen.

Sovereign

I am Joseph, your brother,
whom you sold into slavery in Egypt.
But don't be upset, and don't be angry with
yourselves for selling me to this place.
It was God who sent me here ahead of you to preserve your lives.

GENESIS 45:4-5

Jesus, I want this kind of perspective. Instead of making it my aim to punish the perpetrators in my life, let me see my story through the filter of your dynamic, expanding kingdom. I want to move from the punishment phase to the praise place—entrusting my anger to you.

I choose to forgive those who have hurt me deeply. Not because it's easy, but because you ask me to. In light of that choice, please grant me your perspective on the past suffering I've endured. Open my eyes to see two things: that my enemy is not people, but the evil one who comes to steal, kill, and destroy; that you have woven a beautiful narrative of my life that includes heartache—even when I don't understand why.

Bring me to a new place of freedom where I can boldly say this in the aftermath of a painful story: "It was God who sent me here." Amen.

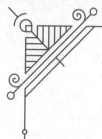

Honor

The scepter will not depart from Judah,
nor the ruler's staff from his descendants,
until the coming of the one to whom it belongs,
the one whom all nations will honor.

GENESIS 49:10

Jesus, you are the fulfillment of this verse, gloriously so. The scepter of Judah is yours. The ruler's staff too. At the end of the age, every knee will bow and every tongue will confess that you are Lord. In light of all this, help me remember my tiny piece in your grand redemptive story—a story you started weaving before time began.

I'm humbled and grateful that you welcome me to participate in this redemption—that you rescued me on that terrible, beautiful cross. Your resurrection astounds me, silences me, makes me sing too. Help me rest my wayward mind on that truth—that you are not solely about ruling and reigning and reaping honor, but you're also about redeeming all of us so we can participate alongside you.

To honor you with my life seems like such a small sentiment in light of your perfection, life, death, and resurrection, but it's what I bring to you today. I love you. I need you. I honor you.

I may not know what today holds for me, but I know you are with me, holding me through whatever storm crashes my way. I want to be ready, but more than that, I want to honor you. Amen.

Claimed

Say to the people of Israel: "I am the LORD. I will free you from your oppression and will rescue you from your slavery in Egypt. I will redeem you with a powerful arm and great acts of judgment. I will claim you as my own people, and I will be your God. Then you will know that I am the LORD your God who has freed you from your oppression in Egypt."

EXODUS 6:6-7

Jesus, I am so grateful that you are a God of freedom for many—including me. Thank you for freeing me from the oppression of the sin that surrounded my heart and marred my view of you and myself. Thank you for rescuing me from the power of the enemy who wanted me enslaved and destroyed.

Today keep me mindful of the ways you've redeemed me in the past. Help me to spend a little time recounting how you've rescued me from so much. I confess that I often get mired in today's to-do list, and my personal failure taints my joy. Instead of concentrating on the ways I've fallen short, redeem the way I view my life. I want to boast about the amazing things you have done instead.

So replace my overwhelmed thoughts with reminders of your provision. And as you do that beautiful work in my mind today, I will settle into the truth that you have claimed me as your own. I'm stunned about your kind affection and rescue, Jesus. Let me live in wholehearted gratitude today. Amen.

Listen

Moses told the people of Israel what the Lord had said,
but they refused to listen anymore. They had become
too discouraged by the brutality of their slavery.

Exodus 6:9

Jesus, in the center of my stress lives this word: *worry.* It's easy for me to mock the Israelites being faithless, but as I look into my own life, I see bits and pieces (and whole sections) of my heart reflected in theirs. So, blinded by my own fear, I often choose to close my ears to your encouragement.

But not today. I want to hear from you—about who I am in you, about how you run the universe with love at the center, about how much you love those people in my life who are far from you. Today I want to see my worries as small and you as larger than a mountain. Forgive me for reversing that, Lord.

Encourage me specifically today, Jesus. Show me that you see the little things as well as the big. And please do this not because I'm the center of my universe, but because you are. Your kindness toward me reflects your glory and character. And your glory and character are traits you possess that empower your love for all this world.

Enlarge my view of the people in the world you've placed me in. Help me to see the brutality of their slavery. I want to hear your encouraging voice not simply to be whole myself, but to impart that wholeness to the rest of the world. Amen.

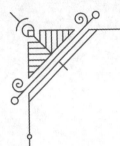

Guide

With your unfailing love you lead
the people you have redeemed.
In your might, you guide them
to your sacred home.

EXODUS 15:13

Jesus, I need a guide to my sacred home, and this verse reminds me that it's you. You lead with love, not with shame or petty anger. You are not the wrathful parent in the sky, waiting for my failure in order to snuff me out—banishing me from hearth and home. But sometimes I rely on my warped view of you, shaped by years of pain on this earth. Explode my wrong perceptions today, Jesus.

Today I am choosing to rest in the steadiness of your love. Thank you that it's not reliant on my merit or power or failure. Thank you that your love is foundational and true, unshaken and longstanding. I can camp on it, build an edifice upon it, stomp my feet and find it firm.

I need you to guide me today through your beautiful Holy Spirit, to whisper instructions as I make decisions small and large. I want to do small things with great love, but I can't without your guidance and power.

Oh dear Jesus, I rest in the word *unfailing* right now. Because that is who you are—a Savior who does not fail to love me, who leads me onto amazing new paths, who flat out loves me, brokenness and all. Amen.

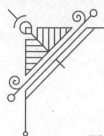

Worn

"This is not good!" Moses' father-in-law exclaimed. "You're going to wear yourself out—and the people, too. This job is too heavy a burden for you to handle all by yourself."

EXODUS 18:17-18

Jesus, thank you for Moses' wise father-in-law, Jethro, who uttered these seasoned words to a worn-out leader. I am worn out too. I carry burdens way too heavy for me to handle. I try so hard to be all things to all people, to work hard at proving my usefulness in this earth, in my family, in my community—only to come to the end of myself far too many times.

Problem is, I work like crazy, then blame you for my burnout. Forgive me for that. I realize now that I need to rest in my worth—secured profoundly and beautifully by you on the cross. And when I nestle into my worthiness, I no longer need to burn out for you.

Place Jethros in my life, Jesus—those who can gently warn me when I get close to the edge of collapse. And in that sending, would you prepare my heart to hear their counsel? Help me to know that it's not failure on my part when I can't carry a burden—it's simply a signal that it's time again to surrender. Thank you for your example of profound surrender as you pursued the cross. In light of that, I surrender to you, and I ask you to carry the burdens that overwhelm me today. Your shoulders are so much more capable of carrying them than mine are. Amen.

"gods"

God gave the people all these instructions: "I am the Lord your God, who rescued you from the land of Egypt, the place of your slavery. You must not have any other god but me."

Exodus 20:1-3

Jesus, when I read this commandment, I confess I often gloss over it. Of course I've had no other gods I've devoted myself to. I have not followed any other god except you. But then I remember that a god is anything you give your full attention and affection to. It's what you spend your time, talent, and treasure honoring above anything else. And I have to hang my head and sigh.

Forgive me for chasing my reputation as if it were a god to be pursued. Forgive me for serving my safety and currying favor with comfort. For all those times I've trusted in almighty money instead of running after you, forgive me. When I've centered my life on making a specific relationship fit my heart perfectly, remind me that I'm created solely to be occupied by you in that sacred space. Forgive me for worshipping at the altar of control.

In this space of you and me, with everything laid bare, open my eyes to the ways I have fashioned other gods and pursued them rather than you. I know my life has deep joy and peace when I serve only you. So restore me to that place of dependence today. Amen.

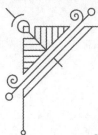

Covet

You must not covet your neighbor's house. You must not covet your neighbor's wife, male or female servant, ox or donkey, or anything else that belongs to your neighbor.

Exodus 20:17

Jesus, I wish I could say I've never coveted what someone else had, but I'd be lying. Our world system is built on coveting things. The advertisements that constantly berate me remind me that I don't have enough, that what I do have is inadequate. None of that is true, yet I've fully bought into the lie that if I could just have what she has or what position he holds, I would finally be happy—only to get that thing or achieve that status, and find myself empty and wanting again.

This is a terrible treadmill of expectations I've been on, Lord. I never reach the end of it, and all this chasing just leaves me exhausted and spent.

But deeper than that is this idea that maybe you love everyone else far more than you love me. Coveting what someone else has is an indictment against your care for me. I sometimes feel like you care for others, give gifts to them, answer their prayers, give them good relationships, bless them financially, and bring them position and power—all while ignoring my pleas.

Remind me afresh that I actually don't know what's best for my soul—that you have me on a me-shaped journey that doesn't involve the same favor or money or possessions that others have. I want to rest in my journey, finding true contentment while I applaud the journeys of others. Amen.

Speak

Burnt offerings are to be made each day
from generation to generation.
Offer them in the Lord's presence at the Tabernacle entrance;
there I will meet with you and speak with you.

Exodus 29:42

Jesus, thank you that when you died on the cross, the Father ripped the veil in the Temple in two, from top to bottom—a final welcome party to your presence. This holy rending is final and for all eternity. Where the Israelites had to make continual offerings and sacrifices to be clean enough to hear from you, your offered life and beautiful sacrifice ushered in your presence once and for all.

I'm so grateful.

Speak, Lord, your servant is listening. Sometimes I strain my heart toward heaven to hear from you, only to realize that you've profoundly relocated the Tabernacle/Temple from a physical place on earth to an entirely different physical place—inside me. Your Spirit not only enlivens me, but he speaks with me, offering the daily encouragement I need.

Gratitude seems like a small offering in light of this. You paid the price for my continual access to your presence. Forgive me for forgetting your sacrifice. Forgive me for taking your presence for granted. Help me to live joyfully, fully pursuing conversation with you throughout the day. What a privilege! Amen.

Meeting

Inside the Tent of Meeting, the LORD
would speak to Moses face to face,
as one speaks to a friend.
Afterward Moses would return to the camp,
but the young man who assisted him, Joshua son of Nun,
would remain behind in the Tent of Meeting.

EXODUS 33:11

Jesus, I want to experience the Tent of Meeting right now in my life—finding a place of solitude and silence to hear your voice and spend time with you. Forgive me for the rush-rush of my life that leaves little room for your whispers.

Thank you for providing a way for me to commune with the Father through your sacrifice. While just Moses and Joshua had the privilege of meeting with you intimately, I now have divine access because of the cross. May I never take that lightly.

You have called me friend, and for that I thank you. You are my friend, my constant companion, the one who lifts my head when I'm sad or afraid. Oh, how I need your steadfast ways in my life, especially today.

When life gets crazy, remind me of Joshua who stayed behind to spend time and be present with you. I want to pause. I want to be interruptible. I want to settle my soul long enough to hear from you. Amen.

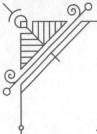

Cloud

The cloud covered the Tabernacle, and the glory of the
LORD filled the Tabernacle. Moses could no longer enter
the Tabernacle because the cloud had settled down over
it, and the glory of the LORD filled the Tabernacle.

EXODUS 40:34-35

Jesus, settle down over me like a cloud today—your presence permeating me like dense fog. I want to revel in the mystery of it, even when I don't completely understand the width, depth, and strength of your love.

Honestly, there have been other things clouding my life lately—in the form of voices that shout my smallness. They disempower my vision, keep me wandering in confusion. Voices like "You'll never accomplish what you want out of life," and "You always mess things up," and "You deserve to be treated poorly." For so long I've entertained those voices, thought they were the truth.

But I'm learning that your voice is far different. It doesn't smother with condemnation and anger. No, it welcomes me with grace. Let that grace seep into me so much so that the voices in my head become smaller than a pinprick and your voice of encouragement drowns out all those lies.

Fill me as you filled the Tabernacle—with your power and weight of glory. I'm utterly grateful that you haven't abandoned me to my pain-inducing thoughts. Amen.

Near

*Then Moses said to Aaron, "This is what
the LORD meant when he said,
'I will display my holiness through those who come near me.
I will display my glory before all the people.'" And Aaron was silent.*

LEVITICUS 10:3

Jesus, I understand that your nearness is what makes my heart thrill. But so often I am wayward, wandering into places I shouldn't go, wondering about your goodness when I've ventured far, far away. Your promise here says that your holiness is displayed in me when you're near. So I want you near.

That seems easy to pray but so hard to actually do. I am a person of unclean lips. My heart is fickle, bent toward the world's ways. Prone to wander, as the hymn says, oh, how I feel it.

Today I want to be like Aaron. Silent. Pondering. Quiet in my heart. Because when your glory is displayed for everyone to see (even in me!), the only right response is awe-filled silence. I choose to take my eyes off the things that distract and woo me and instead place them firmly on the glory all around me.

I choose to see that glory in the shape of a leaf, the heart of a child, the way my food tastes in my mouth, the smell of the air. Oh, to be silent and wide awake to your glory, dear, dear Jesus.

Display your glory through me. Help me to see it not only outside myself, but also within myself through the evident presence of the Holy Spirit in my life. Amen.

Fair

*Do not twist justice in legal matters by favoring the poor or being
partial to the rich and powerful. Always judge people fairly.*

LEVITICUS 19:15

Jesus, I live in an unfair world. And as I scan the headlines, I realize there are other places on earth where justice seems obliterated. It can overwhelm me. It's easy for me to rail against injustice over there without looking to myself to see how I'm living a just life here in my corner of the world.

Empower me to be wise, to intervene in convoluted situations all for the sake of justice and being fair. If it means I suffer, give me grace to do the right thing even when no one is looking. If it means rescuing those who can't rescue themselves, enable me to be inconvenienced for their sake. If it means I write or say words that highlight the plight of the downtrodden, help me to do so with grace and strength, no matter how others might respond

Instead of staying safely on the sidelines of human history, give me the guts and grit I need to step in and rescue as you lead. I don't want to give great favors to the rich, proud, smart, and powerful. I want to see this world with your eyes, bent toward the poor, humble, broken, and needy. I know I'm more like you, Jesus, when I consider the least of these. Today please open my eyes to those who need to be treated fairly. Amen.

Grudge

*Do not seek revenge or bear a grudge against a fellow
Israelite, but love your neighbor as yourself. I am the LORD.*

LEVITICUS 19:18

Jesus, I don't like myself when I'm full of vengeful plans or grudge nursing. I don't want to be a bitter, closed-off person, always waiting for the next relationship to disappoint me. I want to be carefree in the way I love others—healed from past wounds and ready to be open to new friendships.

But sometimes reminders come up—fragments of memories that reignite past pain and make me wonder if I actually have forgiven my foe. Instead of camping in the land of beating-myself-up over this, help me remember that normal forgiveness is layered—not simply a one-time decision. Next time a memory assaults me, help me be matter-of-fact about it, doggedly choosing to forgive another layer, another memory. I know that when I do that, my desire for revenge lessens, and my ability to love my enemy from afar increases.

I'm grateful that you love me enough to give me wise counsel like this from your Word. Teach me what it means today, what it tangibly looks like to love my neighbor (friend, family member, spouse, child, difficult relationship) as much as I love myself. And as I ponder that, help me to truly understand that you love me well, and I need to extend that same grace to myself.

You are a good God. I will choose to leave room for your justice in my relationships where justice hasn't yet prevailed. In the meantime, I choose love. Amen.

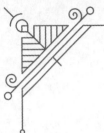

Smile

May the LORD bless you and protect you.
May the LORD smile on you and be gracious to you.
May the LORD show you his favor and give you his peace.

NUMBERS 6:24-27

Jesus, yes to this prayer of blessing! Yes! Because I need blessings from you. I revel in your perfect protection. I'm humbled that you look upon me with a smile, not a grimace. I'm grateful for your graciousness that enables me to find joy in the midst of pain. I do long for your favor and rest in your peace.

As I consider your smile, help me to place a difficult person's name into this blessing, replacing "you" with their name. Would you please bless and protect my wayward friend? Would you smile upon the person who gossiped about me? Would you be gracious to my prodigal child? Would you show favor on my disgruntled spouse? Would you bring peace to that broken friendship?

Give me the gumption to pray this blessing over those who occupy negative space in my mind—as a means of surrendering them to you.

Jesus, I'm amazed at your amazing love. And I so need to know today that you are aware of me and you're for me. In the same way, help me to see my difficult relationships as people beautifully loved by you. Amen.

Unlike

God is not a man, so he does not lie. He is not human, so he does
not change his mind.
Has he ever spoken and failed to act? Has he ever
promised and not carried it through?

NUMBERS 23:19

Jesus, you are so completely other than me. And the Father is not like me either—he is utterly different. The Spirit does things I cannot fathom or understand. You as Trinity are beautifully different, utterly consistent, and fully powerful. Thank you that you are bedrock. You do not change. You carry out your plans because your promises are true.

I choose to settle into that today. Because when I chase after my own fear, and I look at the world around me, I can give in to panic. I tend to forget that you are big and the world's problems are microscopic in comparison.

Elevate my gaze above my stress today. Remind me afresh that you have an amazing plan no man can thwart. Even the most evil people bent on destroying others cannot ruin your perfect, sovereign plan. I can't pretend that I understand it all, and I still wrestle with the evil in the world, but today I choose to rest in this verse that reminds me of your capability, your glory, and your steadfast, reliable work on behalf of humanity.

No matter what may ruffle the feathers of my life today, no matter what trials escalate, I am choosing to trust you, the one who never changes, the one who never fails to act. Amen.

Obey

*Remember how the LORD your God led you through the
wilderness for these forty years, humbling you and testing you
to prove your character, and to find out whether or not you
would obey his commands. Yes, he humbled you by letting
you go hungry and then feeding you with manna, a food
previously unknown to you and your ancestors. He did it to
teach you that people do not live by bread alone; rather, we
live by every word that comes from the mouth of the LORD.*

DEUTERONOMY 8:2-3

Jesus, help me remember your faithfulness to me throughout my life. In fact, today I choose to look over every decade, recounting how you provided for me, led me, taught me your truth, brought strategic and beautiful relationships into my life, healed me, and set my feet upon the rock of your truth. Oh, how faithful you have been to me.

I choose today to thank you for the trials, the deprivation, the times when all I could do was feed off your Word for my sustenance. It was during those times of subtraction that you added character to my life. You taught me how to rely on you during lean times, inaugurating a grateful heart.

Show me today what it is you want me to obey. What next adventure do you have for me? Thank you that everything that's occurred in my life so far—trials, relationships, living without—has prepared me for new obedience today. I want to boldly obey you. Amen.

Fame

Do not forget that he led you through the great and terrifying wilderness with its poisonous snakes and scorpions, where it was so hot and dry. He gave you water from the rock! He fed you with manna in the wilderness, a food unknown to your ancestors. He did this to humble you and test you for your own good. He did all this so you would never say to yourself, "I have achieved this wealth with my own strength and energy." Remember the LORD your God. He is the one who gives you power to be successful, in order to fulfill the covenant he confirmed to your ancestors with an oath.

DEUTERONOMY 8:15-18

Jesus, I live in a world of accomplished people—folks who have clambered up the ladder of success, who can point to their degrees and pedigrees and boast of their abilities. It's tempting to do that in my own life. And yet, I'm reminded from this passage today that nothing I have today can be fully attributed to my effort. You are the one who gave me the energy to work, the ability to think, the power to do the next thing.

Forgive me when I live as if everything is up to me. Forgive me for becoming a practical atheist—one whose actions indicate there's no need for you. I need you. I cannot do this life on my own. I acknowledge your hand in my life.

So Jesus, when the scorpions and snakes of life invade mine, remind me that you are my deliverer. When I'm hungry and thirsty, quench and feed me. I am profoundly grateful for your faithfulness. You truly have given me the power to find success. In that achievement, I bow to my knees and give you all the glory. Amen.

Walking

Now listen! Today I am giving you a choice between life and death, between prosperity and disaster. For I command you this day to love the LORD your God and to keep his commands, decrees, and regulations by walking in his ways. If you do this, you will live and multiply, and the LORD your God will bless you and the land you are about to enter and occupy.

DEUTERONOMY 30:15-16

Jesus, there are days I'd rather do things my way. My heart is terribly fickle, chasing comfort rather than communion with you. When I choose my own selfish journey, my heart grows small, and my world shrinks. It cannot be all about me. Because when life is all about my selfish desires, others suffer, and I decrease my heart's capacity for you.

Show me three choices I can make today that bend me away from self-centeredness toward your dynamic kingdom. I want to walk in your ways, not my own—because my ways are not profitable, and yours lead to blessings and soul prosperity.

Help me align myself with your way of life—noticing the unnoticed, choosing the unchosen, loving the unlovely, forgiving the reckless, giving to the ungrateful. I realize as I pray this that I cannot carry it out in my own strength. Jesus, revive my desire to follow you through the Holy Spirit within me. Empower me to walk your way with your heart. Amen.

Personally

*Do not be afraid or discouraged, for the LORD will
personally go ahead of you. He will be with you;
he will neither fail you nor abandon you.*

DEUTERONOMY 31:8

Jesus, I have often been afraid. I worry about this world. I fret about the unfaithful ones who steal, kill, and destroy. I sometimes think the enemy, Satan, has won far too many victories, and I've been a casualty of evil.

Discouragement has haunted me as well. It's become oppressive, weighing me down in the dark of night, poisoning my resolve to follow you.

Oh, how I need guts and encouragement today, Lord. Your Word promises that you personally go ahead of me. Knowing you exist outside of time, this makes sense to me. You're the God of the past—even my past full of regrets. You're the great I Am, the God of the present tense, empowering me in this moment. And you surprisingly occupy the future—my future, which lies before me in pristine potential.

Even when darkness threatens to win the battle, remind me afresh that you ultimately win the war. I choose to rest in knowing you are with me right now, and that it's never in your nature (never!) to fail or abandon your children. Good fathers are faithful, and you are my good Father. Thank you for your constancy, the *hesed* so evident throughout the Hebrew Scriptures, that means "loyal love." Amen.

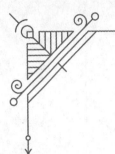

Forgot

You neglected the Rock who had fathered you;
you forgot the God who had given you birth.

DEUTERONOMY 32:18

Jesus, I have been in this place before, where I've lived as if you didn't care for me. I've made all sorts of vows about being in control and protecting myself, running on a treadmill of my own self-sufficiency. Oh, please forgive me. Because it's not up to me. Life is not even about me. It's about you and your ability to love your children.

You are my Rock. You are the one who has fathered me. I am your child. I am not abandoned or orphaned on this lonely planet, destined to fight and scrap to protect myself.

That may have been how I felt growing up, but you have been writing my story all along, chock-full of twists, turns, enemies, friends, valleys, and mountain passes. You are my Author—the perfecter of my faith. Forgive me from grabbing the pen from you and trying to write my own story in my own strength, with my small imagination.

Enlarge my imagination for the ways you'll be writing my story today. Help me to weather conflicts and challenges like a main character whose hero is you.

I love you. I need you. I don't want to forget you. I don't want to be separated from you, angry at your ways that didn't align with my expectations. No, Jesus, I want to rest in your embrace. Amen.

Courageous

*Be strong and very courageous. Be careful to obey all
the instructions Moses gave you. Do not deviate from
them, turning either to the right or to the left. Then
you will be successful in everything you do.*

JOSHUA 1:7

Jesus, the fact that the Father instructed Joshua to be strong and courageous meant that this was not an impossible task. I admit, though, that I often feel weak and fearful, and to somehow muster power and courage seems impossible. Give me a greater vision—the kind of overarching story that beckons me toward heroism. Maybe the strong and courageous command seems impossible because my vision of what's next is too small.

So steep me in your Word that it becomes instinctive for me to know your will and obey it with joy. I choose to fix my mind on you, not becoming distracted by the wooing world or the lust for more and more and more. I'm tired of spiritual ADD, jumping here and there onto bandwagons and grabbing spiritual snow cones, when you offer meat and sustenance in your Word. Help me not to chase the culture's fluff, but instead to find all my satisfaction in you and your bedrock instructions for me.

Show me where I've deviated from the straight and narrow. Reorient my heart toward longing to obey you. I am through with lackadaisical faith—it wearies me and shrinks my heart. Instead, may today be a day when I'm deeply connected to you, listening for your voice, and joyfully obeying in small and big ways—full of your strength and courage. Amen.

Meditate

*Study this Book of Instruction continually. Meditate on it day
and night so you will be sure to obey everything written in
it. Only then will you prosper and succeed in all you do. This is
my command—be strong and courageous! Do not be afraid or
discouraged. For the LORD your God is with you wherever you go.*

JOSHUA 1:8-9

Jesus, I don't always study your Word carefully. I know other things really well—and social media has often captured my imagination more than your words to me. Forgive me for pursuing temporary things more than the permanent truth you offer.

Not only that, I have a hard time slowing my brain down long enough to really think about the Bible and its message. I don't know what it means to meditate on your words. Please teach me. Enable me to quiet my racing, thought-filled mind long enough to breathe you in deeply.

I acknowledge that I much prefer the end of this verse—the part where you prosper me and bring me success—where you are with me wherever I plant my feet. But I'd rather have all that without sacrifice. I'm sorry.

I choose to fix my mind on the commands you have for me in these verses: study, meditate, obey, be strong, be courageous. These aren't my natural tendencies, but I want them to be. Today I choose to write some lists—to highlight the habits I'd like to create around this truth today. Empower me to be deliberate about studying your Word, and quicken my heart to obey what I study, meditate on, and read. Amen.

Never

So the sun stood still and the moon stayed in place until the nation of Israel had defeated its enemies. Is this event not recorded in The Book of Jashar? The sun stayed in the middle of the sky, and it did not set as on a normal day. There has never been a day like this one before or since, when the LORD answered such a prayer. Surely the LORD fought for Israel that day!

JOSHUA 10:13-14

Jesus, you defy logic. As the triune God—Father, Son, Holy Spirit—you trump the laws of nature and physics. You can do impossible feats. You major in *never*. You are more powerful than the rising of the sun or the way of the moon across a night sky. And you act in supernatural ways on behalf of those you love. I am amazed.

Right now I list the *nevers* in my life—those prayers that seem like they'll never receive answers, the ones I've grown tired and weary of praying. People who have strayed from you, breaking my heart—I lift them up to you, oh God of the unmoving sun. My financial messes, Lord, I gladly hand over to you. Those dreams I can't seem to let go of, but seem impossible—please take them into your capable hands for safekeeping. My twin needs for home and hearth, I give them to you.

Elevate my view of you. Remind me afresh that you are so much bigger than my small view of your capabilities. Wow me with your power. Take my *nevers* and bring new possibilities. I trust you again. Amen.

Cling

So be very careful to follow everything Moses wrote in the Book of Instruction. Do not deviate from it, turning either to the right or to the left. Make sure you do not associate with the other people still remaining in the land. Do not even mention the names of their gods, much less swear by them or serve them or worship them. Rather, cling tightly to the LORD your God as you have done until now.

JOSHUA 23:6-8

Jesus, I don't live in an overtly pagan culture where gods are worshipped in little spirit houses at everyone's doorway. And yet, I'm surrounded by gods everywhere I go. Open my eyes to the things people worship—but more than that, show me where I am pursuing other gods, making idols, and becoming conformed to the image of the culture I'm steeped in.

Your Word in Romans 12 reminds me that the way to shed this culture conformity is to renew my mind. I love how Joshua harmonizes this thought. To renew my mind is to keep my mind on you, your ways, choosing not to deviate toward the easy way everyone else does things.

I don't want fame. I know prestige emaciates my soul. Wealth, when pursued at any cost, will make my heart poor. Accumulating things on earth robs from the treasure you want me to store up in heaven. Having the perfect body is a vain, crazy-making pursuit that can only end in heartache as I age. All these things my culture worships. But I want to worship you and you alone. Today I choose to run from those entangling things and, instead, cling to you. You are my everything, Jesus. Amen.

But

But if you refuse to serve the LORD, then choose today whom you will serve. Would you prefer the gods your ancestors served beyond the Euphrates? Or will it be the gods of the Amorites in whose land you now live? But as for me and my family, we will serve the LORD.

JOSHUA 24:15

Jesus, I'm grateful I have the choice to serve you. You don't force yourself on me like a dictator or maniacal king. You welcome me through the blood you shed on the cross, beckoning me toward relationship with you.

While others may run a million miles away from you toward all this world has to offer, how I long for my heart to be faithful to you. Like Joshua, I choose today to serve you. Media may offer a banquet feast of other people, projects, or pride, but in the quiet of my day I choose you. I serve you.

You are the only one who satisfies me. Forgive me when I've lived for lesser things, pursuing them in vain, believing wrongly that a person will fill my heart, or a position would finally make me stop searching for meaning. When I chase after these things—money, power, "perfect" relationships—my heart becomes a sieve, and all they have to offer is water pouring through, spilled on the ground.

But you are the water well that never runs dry. You provide me with living water every single day. In you, I stop thirsting, striving, pursuing. I can rest. Because you are everything my heart needs. Amen.

Personally

*The people of Israel served the LORD throughout the lifetime
of Joshua and of the elders who outlived him—those who had
personally experienced all that the LORD had done for Israel.*

JOSHUA 24:31

Jesus, I want this to be said of me. Help me look at this walk with you as an ultramarathon, not a sprint—a daily connection to you over the years. I choose today to serve you, and by your grace, I will serve you as long as I have breath. What I need right now is endurance. True, long, lasting endurance.

I have a feeling that kind of perseverance comes in between sweet times of experiencing you personally—just when I need to know you see me. Sometimes those stretches feel too long, and I want to stop running, walking, stepping.

In times like those, Jesus, give me the insight to remember how you've dealt with me in the past. I want to be someone who remembers your bounty, the way you've heard and responded to my prayers and given me the courage I needed when life felt dangerous and impossible.

With you all things are possible. With your Spirit's presence imbedded deep within my soul, I can find joy in this moment. No matter where today's journey takes me, Jesus, I choose to take a breather and listen for your voice. You're all I need. You're all I want. You're the one for whom I live. Amen.

Sing

Listen, you kings! Pay attention, you mighty rulers!
For I will sing to the LORD.
I will make music to the LORD, the God of Israel.

JUDGES 5:3

Jesus, there are days when singing is the last thing on my mind. I see broken relationships, and I cave in to despair. I read about atrocities, and my heart faints within me. Instead of focusing on who you are and the beauty you readily create, I camp in the land of discouragement, preferring to keep my mind on this broken world than to make music in my heart because of your abilities.

Retune my heart today, Jesus, to hear from you, to make it a discipline (a joyful one!) to sing away my worries—not because they don't exist, but because they do, and you've promised to overcome the world.

Lift my eyes from the dangers and snares. Raise my gaze to the heavens that you created, and may a melody birth in me, a song of praise to you who are more worthy than anything I can imagine.

Help me to remember that the devastation and dilapidation of this earth are not the end of the story. You will set things aright. You will make things new. You will do a new thing. I choose to sing about that now. Amen.

Weakest

"But Lord," Gideon replied, "how can I rescue Israel? My clan is the weakest in the whole tribe of Manasseh, and I am the least in my entire family!" The LORD said to him, "I will be with you. And you will destroy the Midianites as if you were fighting against one man."

JUDGES 6:15-16

Jesus, I feel like Gideon so often. I look at the pedigrees of other believers, those who seem to tackle spiritual mountains with gusto, who have connections and privilege aplenty, and I cry out because of my lack. I can't do this. I can't seem to get my life together, let alone fight for others.

Thank you for the reminder you gave Gideon. He may be small. He may come from a humble background. He may be the runt of the litter, but that matters little to you. In fact, it's his humble recognition of his weakness that you find endearing. I love that you do your best work through the weak ones.

I am weak today, so please act as you did on Gideon's behalf. Be with me. Help me to understand that this is not my fight, but yours. And your abilities far surpass my own—they are miraculous, powerful, and completely outside my capacity.

When I feel small, I choose to remember your greatness. When I feel weak, I choose to focus on your strength. When I feel overlooked, I choose to meditate on your fame and glory. Just as you were faithful to weak Gideon, you have been kindhearted and available to me. Amen.

Facedown

Then Manoah took a young goat and a grain offering and offered it on a rock as a sacrifice to the LORD. And as Manoah and his wife watched, the LORD did an amazing thing. As the flames from the altar shot up toward the sky, the angel of the LORD ascended in the fire. When Manoah and his wife saw this, they fell with their faces to the ground.

JUDGES 13:19-20

Jesus, I can't imagine what it must have been like to see your glory and power in such a tangible way. I know I'm guilty of reading passages like this and thinking that you can only be miraculous in the pages of the Bible.

You are the miracle, Jesus. You are fire and water and redemption. You are greater than angels. You ascended into heaven in much the same way, but not before completing the work your Father asked you to do—to innocently die for the sake of the world mired in sin. You breathed your last in this rescue mission. And then, by the power of your Father, you rose again to new, vibrant life.

As Manoah and his wife fell facedown in the presence of miraculous power, I choose today to lower myself to the ground, face to the floorboards, acknowledging just how amazing and powerful you are. Keep me in that posture of reverence and awe as I move throughout my day. You are the miracle, and I'm utterly grateful to be the recipient of your redemption. How can I possibly thank you enough? Amen.

Seemed

In those days Israel had no king; all the people did
whatever seemed right in their own eyes.

JUDGES 21:25

Jesus, I live in "those days." Everywhere I look, people are creating their own religions, codes of personal conduct based on nothing but feelings and entitlement. Truth only exists as each individual person believes it. And often that truth centers on selfishness and the desire to be seen and honored. We don't want to honor others; instead, we demand honor—which also means we expect others to applaud every decision we make, or they're being unloving.

That's a perfect picture of living under cheap grace, and I want nothing to do with it, Jesus. Holiness has become passé, cliché. It's been replaced by situational ethics and relativism.

But you have a better way, the way to genuine, meaningful life. Though people who want to invent their own morality don't see it this way, you promise to give us the abundant life we've longed for.

It's counterintuitive. It means denying myself, taking up my cross daily, dying to my selfish wants, and pursuing you wherever you lead me. I want to do what's right in your eyes, not my own—because left to myself, my vision is clouded. Amen.

Devoted

But Ruth replied, "Don't ask me to leave you and turn back. Wherever you go, I will go; wherever you live, I will live. Your people will be my people, and your God will be my God. Wherever you die, I will die, and there I will be buried. May the LORD punish me severely if I allow anything but death to separate us!" When Naomi saw that Ruth was determined to go with her, she said nothing more.

RUTH 1:16-18

Jesus, I'm grateful for Ruth's faithful example of *hesed*—so reflective of your loyal, covenant-keeping love. She, like Abraham, left her homeland for the sake of relationship. You left heaven for the sake of rescuing us.

Thank you that Ruth's fierce determination to be with her mother-in-law shouts of who you are. Wherever I go, you will be with me. Wherever I live, you dwell inside me. The people of God are my people—because of you I have deep community. And because of you, the Father accepts me into this messy-but-beautiful family of God-lovers.

Nothing separates me from your loyal love, Jesus. Nothing. You doggedly pursue my heart and the hearts of everyone in this world because you are a relational God, loving us with strength and determination. I'm so grateful. How can I thank you enough?

In light of all you've done, enable me to be Ruth to someone today. I want to be a loyal friend, family member, parent, spouse—one who walks through valleys and mountains, one who suffers alongside. By your strength help me to be you to those I love. Amen.

Reputation

"Yes, I know," Boaz replied. "But I also know about everything you have done for your mother-in-law since the death of your husband. I have heard how you left your father and mother and your own land to live here among complete strangers."

RUTH 2:11

Jesus, I love that Ruth's reputation was evident. She may have thought that all her gleaning and faithful work on Naomi's behalf was simply unnoticed obedience. And yet, her constancy brought recognition.

In light of that, help me remember that those who are faithful in small things will be entrusted with much more. Just as Ruth's stature and stage started out miniscule, they expanded in light of your elaborate, beautiful plan. She played a key role in ushering you into the world, Jesus. She started faithfully small, but ended stunningly large.

Oh, how I need this example in my life as I labor on your behalf in obscurity. Help me to joyfully do small things with great care because you are watching. You see. I want my work to glorify you, even when no one else is watching.

You promise that my work in the secret place will be rewarded. Oh, how I want my reputation to be good—a disciple who simply does what is asked, but with wholehearted joy and perseverance.

And any reputation I may garner through faithfulness, I recognize that it's you who gives me the ability to live for your reputation. Amen.

Fame

So Boaz took Ruth into his home, and she became his wife.
When he slept with her, the LORD enabled her to become
pregnant, and she gave birth to a son. Then the women of the
town said to Naomi, "Praise the LORD, who has now provided a
redeemer for your family! May this child be famous in Israel."

RUTH 4:13-14

Jesus, you are my Redeemer. You have taken me from being lost, forgotten, and sin-entrenched to being a child of yours, wholly free, truly accepted and graced. Thank you, too, that you have a plan beyond my life, just as you did with Ruth.

I love that the women of the town praised you, hinting at the importance of Ruth's offspring. She didn't live to see her great-grandson's ascension to the throne of Israel—Obed, Jesse, King David. Her faithful devotion extended beyond her generation, ushering in the reign and rule of the man after your heart. And David's lineage eventually became yours, Jesus.

Forgive me for thinking my small obedience matters nothing in your kingdom. In fact, it reverberates beyond my death. Every choice I make today for your kingdom shakes the kingdom of darkness.

Because of that, I wait in silence for your direction. I choose to be faithful to you, to worship you, to do the next thing you ask. Help me live in holy anticipation of how my obedience (by your strength!) changes the landscape of the kingdom forever. Amen.

Rock

Then Hannah prayed: "My heart rejoices in the LORD!
The LORD has made me strong.
Now I have an answer for my enemies;
I rejoice because you rescued me.
No one is holy like the LORD! There is no one besides you;
there is no Rock like our God."

1 SAMUEL 2:1-2

Jesus, I want to be like Hannah. I want my heart to rejoice in you because it is completely true that you have made me stronger than I ever thought possible. This is a paradox because, left to myself, I am weak. In your upside-down kingdom, you promise that my weakness is the avenue for your strength to perform its best.

I take time right now to recognize your rescue. You shook the heavens and came down, away from the pristine beauty of heaven to this sin-carved earth on a rescue mission. You died for me, for them, for all of us. And you came to abolish and nullify the works of the enemy, Satan. You silenced and disempowered him, Jesus. I'm grateful.

In my own strength, my life shifts like mud underfoot. But you are my Rock. You are the place I can go that will not shake or move beneath me. When life wavers and shimmies today, I run to you, my Rock, my place of rescue and refuge. Amen.

Order

He lifts the poor from the dust and
the needy from the garbage dump.
He sets them among princes, placing them in seats of honor.
For all the earth is the LORD's, and he has set the world in order.

1 SAMUEL 2:8

Jesus, the whole world is yours. Nothing escapes your notice. You created it, know every nook and cranny, and before you everything is laid bare. No one can deceive you because you perceive everything correctly. I'm grateful for that because that means you truly are in control of the chaos in my life.

In my life full of complicated relationships, would you lift me from the dust of other people's reactions? There have been times when the pain has been so great that I feel like I live in a garbage dump—the stench of other people's betrayal assaulting me. Rescue me from that place. Help me to forgive others.

And beyond that, remind me when my actions have placed others in dust and dumps. Give me the courage to ask forgiveness, to say, *I'm sorry* and to try to make things right. That's hard, Lord. So hard to do. It's easy for me to see how others have hurt me, harder to admit that I've hurt others.

Order the chaos of my emotions today. Help me to see them as you do. I choose to not let them overtake my joy or my resolve to do the right thing. Amen.

Listening

And the LORD came and called as before, "Samuel! Samuel!"
And Samuel replied, "Speak, your servant is listening."
Then the LORD said to Samuel, "I am about
to do a shocking thing in Israel."

SMALL CAPS 1 SAMUEL 3:10-11

Jesus, this is a loud world I live in. Everyone's shouting and hollering and sharing and revealing themselves every minute of every day. There is seldom any mystery left. And yet I let all that over-sharing overcome my life. I look at other people's picture-perfect lives and want what they have. I flood my mind with the negative thoughts of others, preferring their angst to the sweet peace you offer.

So I am grateful for Samuel who heard his name being called and was curious enough about it to inquire what it all might mean. He learned you were calling his name, and then he welcomed your response.

Thank you for calling my name. Thank you for speaking to me. Like Samuel, I choose to say, "Speak, your servant is listening." The truth is, I'm tired of the shrill cacophony of the media. I'm wearied by my own cluttered mind. I cannot seem to stop the noise all around me. So I choose today to settle my ears, to be quiet enough to hear your voice. Jesus, I'm listening. Amen.

Fear

But be sure to fear the LORD and faithfully serve him. Think
of all the wonderful things he has done for you.

1 SAMUEL 12:24

Jesus, because you are so different from me, so holy, so completely
amazing, forgive me for treating you like a casual acquaintance. You're
so much more than a friend whom I call on the weekends to hang out.
You're the God of the universe, and you paid the highest price to secure
my future. I don't want to take you lightly.

So much is said these days about friendship with you. I'm grateful
for that, but I fear I've lost some reverence along the way. In my familiar treatment of you, I've forgotten to stand, sit, and kneel in awe of
you—your goodness, power, and grace.

You have done wonderful things. As I trace your fingerprints
throughout my life, I see faithfulness poking through. I see so many
dangers you've saved me from. I remember relationships I pined over
that you mercifully let end. I ponder the many times you've healed my
heart from wounds that wept from my soul.

You are my best friend.

You are the Lord of all—holy, shining, almighty.

Both these truths I hold in tension. Oh, how I love you, Jesus.
Reframe my day so I experience you more, turn to you in every moment,
and remember to thank you for all you've done. Amen.

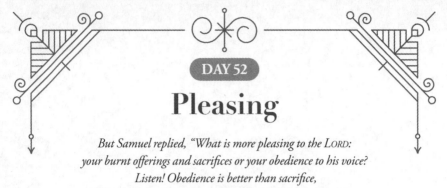

Pleasing

But Samuel replied, "What is more pleasing to the Lord:
your burnt offerings and sacrifices or your obedience to his voice?
Listen! Obedience is better than sacrifice,
and submission is better than offering the fat of rams."

1 Samuel 15:22

Jesus, I want to be pleasing to you, but so many times I get it wrong. I think you're impressed by my pointed-to sacrifice, my token religious to-do list—those things I do when my heart is unengaged with you, when I'm doing church activities by rote. I can playact my relationship with you, but you are not fooled.

I'm tired of superficial relationship. And I'm sorry I've perpetrated it. Instead let me live the truth of these verses. Obedience requires engagement. It means I press in to hear your voice, forsaking all other voices. It means I die to myself, take up my cross, and, by your Spirit, follow in your footsteps. It means I walk where you walked, among the poor, needy, and broken, seeking to alleviate suffering.

Teach me what it means to submit to you. And elevate my clouded understanding of that word *submission*. At first glance, it doesn't seem joyful, but burdensome. But submitting has everything to do with the character of the one I'm submitting to, and your character is beautiful, grace-embodied, and encouraging. Today, I choose to listen to you, then obey whatever you say because I want to honor you with my life. Amen.

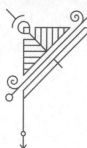

Heart

But the LORD said to Samuel, "Don't judge by his
appearance or height, for I have rejected him. The LORD
doesn't see things the way you see them. People judge by
outward appearance, but the LORD looks at the heart."

1 SAMUEL 16:7

Jesus, I'm so grateful that you see everyone—not by their fancy facades, but by their hearts. That both relieves and terrifies me because it reminds me of how you see everything in me—the bad and the good. And yet, because of you, I have unfettered access to the Father, and I am well loved, fully forgiven, and walk daily in newness of life. The old is gone; the new awaits.

Help me to live in joyful anticipation. The fact that you see me is great comfort, but it also motivates me to follow you closely.

I give you permission today to do the necessary heart surgery my soul needs. Where have I been jealous? Petty? Vengeance-consumed? Wrathful? Mean? Impatient? Worrisome? Harsh? Uncontrolled? Root out those traits, Lord. I don't want them to be a part of me anymore.

On the other hand, would you also show me what I'm doing right? When have I been patient? Kindhearted? Sacrificial? Servant-minded? Self-controlled? I want these traits to become so entrenched in my heart that they're a reflexive habit. Amen.

Unique

How great you are, O Sovereign LORD! There is no one like you.
We have never even heard of another God like you!

2 SAMUEL 7:22

Jesus, forgive me for making you out to be just like me except a little better. You are so unlike me. Every part of you is utterly holy and unique, sinless, powerful. Unlike the enemy of my soul who cannot create but only destroys, you are creative, the ultimate generator of new things. You are constantly spinning new stories, new pathways—all while holding the universe together.

I am in awe.

Even so, my mind sometimes strays to other gods—ones that offer quick relief from my daily stress. Food can satisfy for a moment, but it cannot be the Bread of Life. Fame might fill a hole in my soul, but it cannot satisfy the deeper longings of my heart to be noticed and loved by the one who created me. The god of comfort beckons me to lay down my will, embracing lethargy and self-satisfaction—and to be honest, I like that.

But you, Lord, are utterly unique. Only you can satisfy me to my bones. Only you understand me. (I don't even know myself!) Only you are the truly famous one who deserves my breath, my allegiance, my praise.

Today remind me to pull away from my pursuit of lesser things so I can revere you, recognizing you for who you are—the God of all creation. Amen.

Enemies

*I called on the L*ORD*, who is worthy of praise,
and he saved me from my enemies.*

2 SAMUEL 22:4

Jesus, I am helpless here. I cannot rescue myself from those who are stronger than me. I cannot resurrect my reputation when others have marred it. I cannot make people like me. I can't force someone to reconcile with me. I can't create peace or harmony, no matter how hard I try.

So I sit in silence, waiting for you.

I call on you, you who are fully worthy of my affection. I entrust every relationship to you today. I list each name, pausing, asking your will to be done on earth as it is in heaven—in their lives, in the circle of our relationship. I stop when I reach a difficult name—someone who acts like an enemy in my life—and I ask you for a new perspective.

Your Word says I need to forgive, that if I have an enemy who persecutes and maligns me, I should turn the other cheek. My occupation as a follower of you is to pray for my enemies. So I do that right now. Would you give my enemy a good day? Would you turn their heart toward you? Would you rescue them? Would you enable them to forgive me (if that's necessary) so they won't be saddled with bitterness the rest of their life? Set me free from trying to force this all to work. I trust you. Amen.

Fame

God's way is perfect. All the LORD's promises prove true.
He is a shield for all who look to him for protection.
For who is God except the LORD? Who but our God is a solid rock?

2 SAMUEL 22:31-32

Jesus, I have to be honest. I think my way is perfect. Many of my prayers are asking you to please adhere to my good plan. Bless me! Do what I want! Bring success! When I do this, I see my plan as superior to yours. Help me to pray openhandedly, letting you orchestrate my life instead of me trying to force you to bend to my will. I'm so sorry, Lord.

Your Word promises that your way is absolutely perfect. And you are a God who fulfills promises. You are not fickle. You are tender-hearted and dedicated to helping your children fulfill their unique mission on this earth.

And not only that, you provide protection, often unseen. I breathe because you give me breath. I live and move because you have allowed me a place in this world. Your angels have intervened in unseen accidents. And I sit here in awe, realizing that your goodness is so far beyond what I have witnessed.

I love you. I need you. I bow before you today, repenting of my need for control, and relinquishing that tightfisted way of living to you. You are a good God who is best able to orchestrate my life. Amen.

Meeting

God is my strong fortress, and he makes my way perfect.
He makes me as surefooted as a deer, enabling me to stand on
mountain heights.
He trains my hands for battle; he strengthens
my arm to draw a bronze bow.

2 SAMUEL 22:33-35

Jesus, today I'm not sure-footed. I stumble and slip on the slopes of this life. So I do need your supernatural strength to make me like a deer, clambering over rocks and pitfalls to reach the next mountain you've put in front of me.

I'm tired of the valley, the long, arduous trek that seems to stretch before me for hours, days, years. That prayer I've been praying for so long in the valley? I need to know you are hearing my prayer and that you are acting on my behalf. I pray I won't be immobilized from taking the next step of faith you have for me, but that I'd welcome my deer transformation, no longer afraid of attempting new things, new prayers, new ways of living this life.

Life has felt like a battlefield of late. So I'm grateful you train me for battle. When I am weak, you strengthen me, empowering me to keep walking forward, advancing against the enemy's plans.

I choose to rest in the fact that you will make my way perfect in your timing. Whether I find myself mired in the muck of the valley or smelling the fresh air of timbered heights, I will follow where you lead. Amen.

Charge

I am going where everyone on earth must someday go. Take courage and be a man. Observe the requirements of the LORD your God, and follow all his ways. Keep the decrees, commands, regulations, and laws written in the Law of Moses so that you will be successful in all you do and wherever you go.

1 KINGS 2:2-3

Jesus, help me to realize the fleeting nature of this life—that tomorrow is not guaranteed. It is a vapor, a fleeting wisp. I pray today I would capitalize on the time given to me, fully alive in each moment, loving the people you've put in my path.

Thank you for these words from King David to his son Solomon as the king prepared for death. I will internalize his advice for my life today. I will take courage. I will observe your laws. I will follow your ways. I will keep the decrees written in the Word of God.

Your promise is that when I live this way, as David instructed, I will find success in what I do and where I go. I love that David didn't say exactly what tasks Solomon should do, nor did he prescribe the places Solomon should go. Your will does not necessarily lie in occupation or place. Your will lies in simple obedience to the truths I already know.

Teach me to number my days, to revel in this moment, to value your nearness. Steep me in your presence and perspective. Constantly remind me of the truth of your Word. Amen.

Wholehearted

O LORD, God of Israel, there is no God like you in all of heaven above or on the earth below. You keep your covenant and show unfailing love to all who walk before you in wholehearted devotion.

1 KINGS 8:23

Jesus, I am so easily distracted by this life. My heart is fractured in so many different pieces, pursuing one hundred things, majoring on minors, and minoring on majors. I am scattered.

But your desire is that I would be wholehearted, and that I'd channel my heart in complete devotion to you. You long for me to be faithfully focused on you, not chasing after every shiny object. In this world, it's hard to stop the chase. It's hard to pursue only you.

I'm reminded, though, that you model who I'm to become. Because you are faithful, I can live a life of faithfulness. Because you keep your covenantal promises, I can live a trustworthy life. Because you are utterly holy, I can live a set-apart life, available to do whatever it is you call me to do.

In short, your abilities and power inform and influence my life for good. Thank you for being a beautiful example of what love is.

Remind me of your love today. Show me in small ways and big demonstrations that you care for me. And as I settle into your embrace, help me to be like you in this world starved for love. Amen.

Rest

Praise the LORD who has given rest to his people Israel,
just as he promised. Not one word has failed of all the
wonderful promises he gave through his servant Moses.
May the LORD our God be with us as he was with our ancestors;
may he never leave us or abandon us.
May he give us the desire to do his will in
everything and to obey all the
commands, decrees, and regulations that he gave our ancestors.

1 KINGS 8:56-58

Jesus, I love that you gave Israel the rest you promised them. And I love that you ushered in ultimate rest in the aftermath of your death, burial, and resurrection. Because of you, I no longer have to strive to prove my worth. Instead, I can rest in knowing I'm well loved, forgiven, and set free to follow you for the rest of my life. Thank you.

Even though there have been times I have been fickle and unfaithful to you, even though I have forsaken others, you are not like me. You were with the Israelites. You nurtured and cared for them through slavery, wars, and exile. And you kept your promises to them even when they were unfaithful. What an encouraging picture for me whose heart is prone to meander away from you.

Thank you for never abandoning me. Thank you for being the God who never dies. Thank you for continually reaching out to your children and showing your favor and presence. I'm astounded that you rescued me. Amen.

Harp

"Now bring me someone who can play the harp." While the harp was being played, the power of the LORD came upon Elisha.

2 KINGS 3:15

Jesus, I don't pretend to understand how your power is connected to music, but I do know that when I worship you in song, my spirit lifts. I do know I begin to elevate you and see my problems as small. I realize that this life is not all about me or my selfish desires, but it's about your kingdom coming to earth as it is in heaven. It's about your fame and power covering the earth like the oceans. It's about your majesty and strength.

There are a few situations in my life over which I feel powerless. Instead of worrying about them, I choose to sing away my fears. Help me choose songs of praise and reflection that aptly focus me on you—what you can do when I can't do anything more.

You are big. You are glory. You are might. You are strength. You are capable. You are intelligent. You are wise. You are hope. You are listening. I sing about you with the breath you've supplied, trusting you again. In that song, I entrust my niggling worries, choosing to place each one like an offering into your capable, strong hands.

Oh, Lord Jesus, how I need to know you have me in the palm of your hands today. I sing because you are good. I sing because you are sovereign. Amen.

Rescue

You must worship only the LORD your God.
He is the one who will rescue you from all your enemies.

2 KINGS 17:39

Jesus, I have to admit that sometimes I wrestle with the idea that you are a rescuing God. There have been several times looking back where I wasn't rescued from a harmful situation. I understand that you will work out everything for your good purposes, but it's hard sometimes to understand why you permit pain on this earth.

There are times I let these mental meanderings sidetrack my faith because I don't understand. Your Word says you rescue, but you don't always rescue. And 100 percent of the people on this earth will die, so ultimately you don't rescue any of us—at least in the physical sense. So what does it mean? Should I pray for rescue? Do you always rescue people? What about martyrs? How do I view this verse?

I come back to realizing again that I am small, and my mind cannot fathom your perfect plan. I choose to believe these questions will be answered in eternity, and for today I must have faith. Enlarge my view of you. Expand my understanding of your Word.

Keep me close to you so I will trust you wholeheartedly, even in times of calamity. More than answers, Jesus, I want your presence in the midst of my pain. And maybe that's the answer right there: You don't deliver me from pain, but you are my Deliverer in the midst of it. Amen.

Remnant

For a remnant of my people will spread out from Jerusalem,
a group of survivors from Mount Zion.
The passionate commitment of the LORD of
Heaven's Armies will make this happen!

2 Kings 19:31

Jesus, in light of the craziness of this world, this idea of a remnant resonates with me. It seems like people are doing whatever they want with no mooring, and calling their faith *Christianity.* But your Word says that the way is narrow that leads to life, and so few find it. Those of us who are left are part of your remnant, a ragtag group of followers who truly want to see your kingdom on this earth.

Encourage me as I walk the lonely path of a remnant. Help me to be an encourager of the other pilgrims on this journey. Would you show me someone today who truly needs to know you love them? That you see them as one of the "group of survivors"?

I can't live this life of faith without you, Jesus. And I'm grateful beyond words that you are passionately committed to be with me every day of my life. I'm humbled that you, the Lord of Heaven's Armies, fight on my behalf.

Help me to live in a way today that makes you smile, that brings your heart joy. Oh, how I want to be part of your holy remnant. Amen.

Never

Never before had there been a king like Josiah, who
turned to the LORD with all his heart and soul
and strength, obeying all the laws of Moses.
And there has never been a king like him since.

2 KINGS 23:25

Jesus, when I read about King Josiah, I am both encouraged and discouraged. Encouraged because he lived a life of integrity before you. Discouraged because he was unique—the only king who truly obeyed and loved you with all that was within him.

I am distracted today—by tasks and news and interruptions. I often turn my heart toward those distractions. But right now I stop. I turn. And like King Josiah, I ask that your Holy Spirit would empower me to turn wholeheartedly toward you and your agenda for the day.

I give you my heart—all the past pain that needs to be mended, all the relationships that have wowed or wounded. I give you permission to remodel my heart, helping me choose forgiveness over bitterness.

I give you my soul—all the broken places where I chase after reputation or control. Settle my soul into your embrace today. Help me know my worth apart from my work.

I give you my strength—and it seems so small. But I'm grateful your power is made perfect in my weakness. Amen.

Exult

Exult in his holy name; rejoice, you who worship the LORD.
Search for the LORD and for his strength; continually seek him.
Remember the wonders he has performed, his
miracles, and the rulings he has given.

1 CHRONICLES 16:10-12

Jesus, I want to live an exulting life. To be jubilant, to rejoice exceedingly, to possess lively joy—all because of what you have done. I'm tired of living with deadened desires and emotions. I want to live in elation over what you have done in my life and in the lives of my family and friends. Awaken me to your Word! Enliven me again so I can perceive your greatness in the midst of my life.

Instead of focusing all my energy today on what I don't have, I choose to become alert to your ways. I choose to remember all you've done. You've saved me from myself. You've rescued me from the power of sin. You've walked with me through deep waters. You've been with me in the fiery furnace of trials. You are present in my life.

Today I choose to search for you—both in the past landscape of my life and in the present journey you have for me. By your power, I will continually seek you because you alone give me worth and peace.

I give you my mood today, Lord, and ask you to lift it in your perfect timing. I want to rejoice again. I want to find meaning and hope. Revive me, Lord. Amen.

Good

Give thanks to the LORD, for he is good!
His faithful love endures forever.

1 CHRONICLES 16:34

Jesus, so little is good these days. But you are the personification of goodness. You are wholly kind, fully grace-filled, completely holy, and full of love. Your love endures forever. But mine doesn't always do that. I give up on people. I fret about their antics. I think of ways not to be good.

So please help me mimic your goodness in this world. Thank you that I don't have to create my own good traits, but that because of the Spirit within me, I have direct access to goodness all day long. Because of this, I can love those who hurt me, turn the other cheek, walk another mile, and pray for those who persecute me.

Thank you for the example of enduring love, of faithfulness that extends beyond today to forever. I'm grateful you were good when I was small, learning to navigate this world. I'm humbled that you continue to show me your goodness today. I feel such peace knowing that tomorrow won't erase your kindness, that you will endure with me until the end.

Today I choose to think of twenty ways you've been good to me. And then remind me of twenty ways you've been good to someone I'm struggling with. Let that be the fuel to my prayer on their behalf today. Amen.

Everything

*Who am I, and who are my people, that
we could give anything to you?
Everything we have has come from you, and we
give you only what you first gave us!*

1 Chronicles 29:14

Jesus, what a beautiful passage about a truth I've found in my own life: You own it all and bless your children with abundance. Everything I have is a gift from you. Everything. That includes the people you've placed around me. It encompasses my health, mental state, lodging, and daily food. You hold my world together. You give me breath and life.

Because of that, all I have today I choose to fling heavenward—back to you as the only right offering. I give you my worries over finances. I hand you my most satisfying relationships, thanking you for them. I hand my plans back to you, giving you full reign to change them as you see fit. I place my health and welfare in your capable hands, asking for perspective.

I surrender me. It's all I have.

I do that because you surrendered you. You gave everything for the sake of a wayward world. You gave it all, so my response is to give you my all. Thank you, Jesus. Those words seem small, but today I want to thank you with my surrendered life. Amen.

Greatness

Yours, O LORD, is the greatness,
the power, the glory, the victory, and the majesty.
Everything in the heavens and on earth is yours, O LORD,
and this is your kingdom.
We adore you as the one who is over all things.

1 CHRONICLES 29:11

Jesus, forgive me for elevating my problems above your majesty. You are big, and I choose to believe the things that worry me are small in light of your grandeur. All glory belongs to you. I desire to worship you in tangible ways today. Please show me what that means.

The world I live and breathe and move in is not my kingdom, though sometimes I live as if it were. No, my little patch of earth is yours, as is every landmass, every mountain, the oceans, the stars, and the distant galaxies. You are master of atom and sun, bacteria and asteroid. I can scarcely take it all in.

Your ownership over it all humbles me. Your creativity in making the heavens and earth and animals and people and trees and fish keeps me remembering my smallness.

And yet...

You love me.

You dignify me.

You give me purpose.

I do adore you. You are the King of all things, and the King of my heart. Amen.

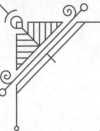

Examine

I know, my God, that you examine our hearts and
rejoice when you find integrity there. You know
I have done all this with good motives,
and I have watched your people offer their
gifts willingly and joyously.

1 Chronicles 29:17

Jesus, sometimes I'm worried about your tests. I fret about an examined life. Because when I look back at my choices, I'm not always proud. I see all the flaws, all the wayward thinking, and the small and big ways I have strayed from your path. My mind is darkened by my sins and regrets.

But you also see everything about me. Your affection is not discolored by my sins. Because of your sacrifice on the cross, you view me as a loved, saved child of yours. And you find integrity in my heart—the good things I often dismiss or overlook. Thank you for finding the good parts (no matter how small!). Thank you for uncovering my motives. (It's so hard for me to even discern them!)

Your overarching kindness makes me love you even more. I don't want to view my relationship with you as a checkoff list. It's not rote tasks I do to appease an angry deity. It's not about polishing up my outsides.

No, this is about spontaneous response—an inward glee that comes from knowing I'm deeply loved. You have transformed me from the inside out, and I'm so grateful. Remind me today that I don't have to perform Christianity. Instead, it's about your internal transformation. Amen.

Rewarded

*But as for you, be strong and courageous, for
your work will be rewarded.*

2 Chronicles 15:7

Jesus, I have spent a lot of time laboring for your kingdom in unnoticed ways. The hours I've spent praying in secret places, the gifts I've given without thought of reciprocity, the relationships I've pursued even when the favor's not returned—all these can lead to burnout or discouragement. Sometimes the road feels overlong, and I let discouragement seep into my soul.

But you remind me to stay strong in the midst of my quiet work. You encourage me to do things anyway, with courage and conviction. Not because this world will applaud my efforts, but precisely because it won't. What the world values has virtually nothing to do with what you value.

So today lift my gaze heavenward. Remind me that nothing done with the kingdom in mind, and with the strength you graciously provide, is done in vain. You see it all. You will reward me for unrewarded work. You will right the wrongs and settle the judgments. You will make everything beautiful, come what may.

I give you my burnout, my discouragement as I work without being seen. I give you my fear that I won't matter on this earth. And I ask you to show me afresh that everything done for your sake matters for eternity. Amen.

Fully

*The eyes of the LORD search the whole earth in order to
strengthen those whose hearts are fully committed to him.*

2 CHRONICLES 16:9

Jesus, this is exactly what I want. And it's everything I need from you. I'm utterly thankful your eyes are roaming this sin-scarred earth searching for and seeking after those who want to wholeheartedly follow you. I so want to be that person!

But I stumble. I fall. I wrestle. I break. I commit myself to my plans, my health, my worth, my way of life. I run after reputation to the demise of my pursuit of you. I so much need to be noticed that I sacrifice my allegiance to you in order to be fully committed to being praised by others.

Please forgive me for wrong-way pursuits, for distractions that seem shiny in the moment but ultimately fizzle and burn, leaving me feeling restless and needy again. Why do I keep thinking that this next thing will finally fill me, only to be disappointed over and over again? When will I learn?

My weakened heart needs your strengthening. I can't love well without the empowered presence of the Spirit. I cannot follow you singlemindedly when my mind is occupied with only satisfying myself. Rescue me from me, Jesus.

I choose today to rest in the promise of this verse, that as I seek you, you will strengthen me. Amen.

Justice

*Fear the LORD and judge with integrity, for the LORD our God does
not tolerate perverted justice, partiality, or the taking of bribes.*

2 CHRONICLES 19:7

Jesus, I'm so grateful you aren't swayed by bribes or trickery. No
one can pull the wool over your eyes. You see everything. You know
intentions, motives, and secret sins. You see when someone's benevolence is a ploy to look good for other people's opinions. I'm heartened
that you hold justice in the midst of all this knowledge, Lord. You will
do what is right—by you, by me, by them.

No one can buy your favor—you offer it freely. No one can pur-
chase your pardon—you secured it through your costly death on the
cross. And because of all that, I am free to be your loved child, settled
in my worth right now.

Because of all you've done and how much you value justice on this
earth, open my ears to the cries of the poor. Open my eyes to the plight
of the broken. Open my heart to the oppressed living nearby.

Help me remember the book of James, where it's clear that showing favoritism to rich folks and disdain for the weak and needy is a sin
in your eyes. I want to look on the people you place in my life with
fairness and love. Forgive me for favoritism. Forgive me for overlook-
ing. I pray you'd gift me with your beautiful compassion today. Amen.

Looking

*O our God, won't you stop them? We are powerless against
this mighty army that is about to attack us. We do not
know what to do, but we are looking to you for help.*

2 Chronicles 20:12

Jesus, it would be easy for me to look at this verse and think it's not for me. After all, this is a prayer shouted on the battlefield, fear infused way down deep because of an imminent attack. But the last part echoes how I feel about life these days: I don't know what to do, but I'm looking to you for help.

Today I turn my attention away from what looms in front of me. I choose to look away from problems, worries, fretting, and obstacles and face you—the one who is bigger than any conflict I face. Please intervene in big and small ways, Lord. I want to live submitted and surrendered to you.

And for those in my life who are experiencing the reality of a battle, I choose to stand in the gap for them. I intercede for those who face battles too big. I place each person facing hardship in your sweet hands, entrusting their journey to you. I can't solve their problems. I can't make them change. I can't prevent the onslaught that might come. I can do the best thing possible for them—get on my knees and ask for your intervention.

Whenever I feel powerless (oh, how many times that happens!), remind me of this verse. Remind me of your faithfulness. Remind me that you will fight the battle for me. Amen.

Greater

*"Be strong and courageous! Don't be afraid or discouraged because
of the king of Assyria or his mighty army, for there is a power
far greater on our side! He may have a great army, but they are
merely men. We have the LORD our God to help us and to fight our
battles for us!" Hezekiah's words greatly encouraged the people.*

2 CHRONICLES 32:7-8

Jesus, when life overwhelms and my relationships are broken, I
choose to remember that you are alongside me, and your power is as
near as my breath. Thank you for sending the Holy Spirit after Pentecost to your followers—as a comforter and your empowering presence. With your Spirit settled in me, I don't need to shake and fear. I
can trust instead.

So please replace my trepidation with confidence. Substitute my
worry with a warrior's heart. Take my perspective and replace it with a
kingdom one—where you are greater than any problem, and you work
on behalf of those who fear you.

Forgive me when I fear the opinions of others, when they immobilize me. Instead, Lord, I want to live for your reputation, unashamed
of your activity in my life. I don't need to give in to feelings of helplessness. I simply need to rest in your accomplished work.

I love you today. I choose to follow after you. I want to be a person after your heart, settled in my worth, ready to be empowered to
do your work. Amen.

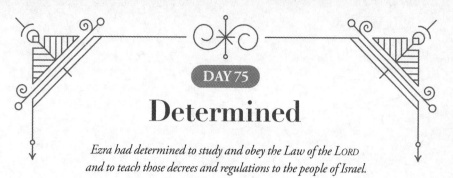

Determined

*Ezra had determined to study and obey the Law of the LORD
and to teach those decrees and regulations to the people of Israel.*

EZRA 7:10

Jesus, I want to be like Ezra. But first I need to value your Word, making it a priority in my life. Steep me in it. Give me a deep-seated passion for everything written in its pages. Teach me to not only know, memorize, and meditate on it, but to also internalize, then obey it joyfully. I will truly know your Word when doing what it says is a priority in my life.

Study and obey—it's how I want to be known. Teach me to value what you value. May your Word become my greatest standard, how I measure everything. May it become the filter by which I see my world, regardless of the opinions of others. I'm grateful it never changes, never wanes, and always points to you and what you've done.

Show me people in my life (or bring new folks) to whom I can teach your Word. I confess I am afraid to do that. I don't feel qualified or ready. But I do know that people are starving, that biblical literacy is waning, and so I choose to raise my hand and volunteer. Reveal the *who* and the *when* of this important task.

Your Word is truly a spotlight on my heart, a beacon highlighting the next steps you want me to take, a measuring stick of my outward behavior, and the most amazing love story about a God who pursues his people. I love it, and I love you. Amen.

Relief

*We have been given a brief moment of grace, for the LORD our God
has allowed a few of us to survive as a remnant. He has given us
security in this holy place. Our God has brightened our eyes and
granted us some relief from our slavery. For we were slaves, but
in his unfailing love our God did not abandon us in our slavery.
Instead, he caused the kings of Persia to treat us favorably. He
revived us so we could rebuild the Temple of our God and repair its
ruins. He has given us a protective wall in Judah and Jerusalem.*

EZRA 9:8-9

Jesus, help me to see the "brief moment of grace" you've given me
this week. I want to look back on your faithfulness with discernment
and awe at all the ways you led me and helped me see you. In my insecurity, you became my secure Rock. In my darkened view of life, bor-
dering on sad pessimism and despair, you brightened my eyes, my
vision. I was enslaved to myself, to the sin that so easily entangled my
heart, but you died on the cross to rescue me.

Today I am set free because of you in my life. I sing for joy because
you didn't abandon me to wander around in my loneliness and aim-
lessness. Just as you were faithful to the exiled Israelites, you have been
faithful to me. You have revived me, and you will revive me again.

I confess I can't revive myself today. I tend to jump to sadness. But
you are the lifter of my head, the one who protects my heart, the God
who has beautifully rebuilt my ruins. Amen.

Confess

O LORD, God of heaven, the great and awesome God who keeps
his covenant of unfailing love with those who love him and
obey his commands, listen to my prayer! Look down and see me
praying night and day for your people Israel. I confess that we have
sinned against you. Yes, even my own family and I have sinned!

NEHEMIAH 1:5-6

Jesus, while I am quite familiar with my own sins, particularly the ones that mess with me constantly (oh, please set me free!), it's not often that I confess other people's sins to you as Nehemiah did. As a leader of a nation, he confessed the collective faithlessness of his people to you.

In that spirit, I confess the sins of my city and country. We have let you down, Lord. We have followed after other gods, preferring the security of money more than serving you wholeheartedly. We have called sin freedom and freedom sin. We have marginalized the aging population while elevating the young. We have chased after shiny things and forsaken faithfulness in small things. We live as if we don't believe the way is narrow—instead, we think everyone is part of your family, and we applaud everyone's sin, calling it their identity, something not to be messed with. We love appearances, but we don't care about integrity. We say one thing, yet do another. We oppress the poor and pay homage to those who exploit them.

Forgive us, Jesus. Reorient our hearts. Revive us again. Bring your light to bear on our nation. We've gotten it wrong for so long, building sand-castle kingdoms while neglecting you, our rock. Amen.

Bring

Please remember what you told your servant Moses:
"If you are unfaithful to me, I will scatter you among the nations.
But if you return to me and obey my commands and live by them,
then even if you are exiled to the ends of the earth,
I will bring you back to the place
I have chosen for my name to be honored."

NEHEMIAH 1:8-9

Jesus, you promise to bring back those who are exiled. So I pray that promise over the people in my life who used to be close to you, but now are very far away—content in their exile, happy in Babylon. I pray you would make their captivity evident, that their eyes would be open to the slavery of sin and self-centeredness. They've grown accustomed to their chains, so please make those chains uncomfortable and confining.

You are the one who made each person's heart. You best know how to woo those who are straying. You are the Shepherd who leaves the 99 for the one. I implore you to please remain faithful to those you have called, to those who have walked away from you. It breaks my heart, Lord, and I so want to see them reconciled once again with you.

Bring them to the bottom of their journey, so all they can do is look up and ask for your rescue. Keep me alert to continually intercede on their behalf. Amen.

Will

I replied, "The God of heaven will help us succeed.
We, his servants, will start rebuilding this wall.
But you have no share, legal right, or historic claim in Jerusalem."

NEHEMIAH 2:20

Jesus, help me to make decisions to act deliberately today. I love that the word *will* is peppered throughout this verse about the rebuilding of Jerusalem's wall. God *will* help bring success. We *will* start rebuilding. Thank you for empowering me and inviting me to be a part of your work. I'm grateful that Christianity is not passive, where I sit back and let things happen. No, with your power, I get to participate in rebuilding this world, in bringing your kingdom to bear.

The enemy of my soul, the prince of the power of the air, says he lays claim to your world, Lord. But that's simply a lie. This is your world, and I know your heart is to bring your kingdom to earth just as it is in heaven. So please show me today what that tangibly looks like. Who needs your love today? Who needs to know that you see them? How can I pray in a kingdom-centered way? In what ways do I need to die to myself and carry your cross? How can I serve the underserved?

All these tasks, when done with your power, are bricks in the wall of your kingdom. Thank you for inviting me to be a part of this building effort. Thank you for loving this world enough to pursue it, recruiting your church to love the unlovely and be a light in the darkness. When I live in light of your work, I know I will discover kingdom-centered success. Amen.

Bold

As I looked over the situation, I called together the nobles and the
rest of the people and said to them, "Don't be afraid of the enemy!
Remember the Lord, who is great and glorious,
and fight for your brothers, your sons, your
daughters, your wives, and your homes!"

NEHEMIAH 4:14

Jesus, I'm tired of living scared. I don't want to cower and live small anymore. My fear serves no one. I know you've given me a spirit of power. So why do I shrink back from the next faith adventure you're beckoning me to? I don't want to stay here, safe. I want to live dangerously in your hands.

So, like Nehemiah, help me to remember your greatness. Help me to bask in your glory. Give me the guts I need to fight on behalf of my family and the family of God. Instead of concentrating on the mountain ahead of me and cowering beneath its peak, teach me to focus on the one who made the mountains, the sea, the dry land, the earth, the skies, the cosmos. When I think of you, the way you flung the stars into existence, suddenly the obstacles before me shrink, and my fear emaciates.

Empower me, through your Holy Spirit, to be bold in my generation, to be gutsy. I want to follow you down whatever scary path you call me to, forsaking fear and embracing a new perspective—that you are big, and the problems in my life are small by comparison. Amen.

Celebrate

*Go and celebrate with a feast of rich foods and sweet
drinks, and share gifts of food with people who have nothing
prepared. This is a sacred day before our Lord. Don't be
dejected and sad, for the joy of the LORD is your strength!*

NEHEMIAH 8:10

Jesus, worry saps me of strength. Fretting empties me of vitality.
Fear drains me of my vitality. But joy? Because true joy comes from you,
it is the backbone of my strength. I choose to celebrate that joy today,
even if it doesn't feel like joy. I know joy is not an emotion, but a choice
to feast on the presence of God even in the midst of stress.

In the Shepherd's Psalm you prepare a table in the presence of my
enemies. That's a beautiful picture of joy—a banquet in the middle of
a conflict—and one I didn't prepare at that. So I keep that kind of cel-
ebratory feasting at the top of my mind today. I want to pull away from
my pity party, sit down at your banquet, and ingest your goodness.

There are days when I am dejected and sad. There are weeks when
I'm mowed over by too many tasks, not enough time, and worries
stacked high. Even so, give me the grit I need to look beyond those
trials to you—the one who prepares a feast, the one who died for me.

Your joy is my strength, Jesus. Your life gives me life. You defeated
sin and death so I could feed on forgiveness and life. Oh, how I love
you today. Amen.

Praise

The leaders of the Levites—Jeshua, Kadmiel, Bani, Hashabneiah,
Sherebiah, Hodiah, Shebaniah, and Pethahiah—called out to the
people: "Stand up and praise the LORD your God, for he lives from
everlasting to everlasting!" Then they prayed: "May your glorious
name be praised! May it be exalted above all blessing and praise!
You alone are the LORD. You made the skies and the heavens and
all the stars. You made the earth and the seas and everything in
them. You preserve them all, and the angels of heaven worship you."

NEHEMIAH 9:5-6

Jesus, I do want to stand up and praise you because you do live from everlasting to everlasting. You are forever; I am finite. You are all powerful; I am weak. You are all knowing; I see in a mirror darkly. You are full of covenantal love; I break my promises.

I love that the people in Nehemiah's day exuberantly praised you. They said you were better than your blessings. You're better than the kind words you speak over us. You're better than your creation because you originated everything—flowers, rivers, otters, pastures, space, time, butterflies. All those amazing creatures and land features came from your mind.

Your Word reminds us that you made everything, and you hold the cosmos together. Everything orbits and lives because you created it. You not only shaped it all, but you empower our universe to keep working—giving us life and breath to praise you.

It's a beautiful truth, Lord. Help me remember today just how amazing you are. Amen.

This

Mordecai sent this reply to Esther: "Don't think for a moment that because you're in the palace you will escape when all other Jews are killed. If you keep quiet at a time like this, deliverance and relief for the Jews will arise from some other place, but you and your relatives will die. Who knows if perhaps you were made queen for just such a time as this?"

ESTHER 4:13-14

Jesus, when I see how you orchestrated the deliverance of the Jewish people through Queen Esther, I am reminded again that you have a plan. I may not always understand the plan in the moment, and I might be afraid to do my part in the plan, but nonetheless, your purposes prevail.

I look around at my life—my station in life, the friends and family you've placed in my path. I see where I live, my neighbors, my job, and my work friends. I notice where you've allowed me to travel. I see my church. All these are in your hand and part of a plan. You have placed me here. For such a time as this. I want to be like Esther, choosing to do the right thing no matter how it may affect me.

Jesus, ignite in me a holy hunger for integrity. I want to bloom where you've rooted me, firm in the soil of my worth and acceptance by you. I want to choose to do the right thing whether people see me or not. I choose to revere you, holding your opinion of me over my own desire for reputation or a godly appearance.

None of that! I don't want to simply appear one way; I want to *be*—to exist from the center of my soul as a disciple of yours, ready to obey no matter what you ask. I may not understand the plan you're enacting today, but I do understand this: Obedience is important to you, so I choose to obey. Amen.

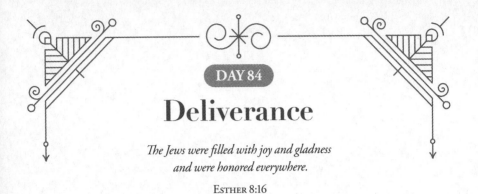

Deliverance

The Jews were filled with joy and gladness
and were honored everywhere.

ESTHER 8:16

Jesus, remind me what it means to be delivered from an enemy today. You delivered me from the one who wanted to steal from me, kill me, and destroy my soul. He lied to me, over and over again, called me worthless scum. He obliged me to sin, made sin attractive and alluring, and then condemned me for partaking.

This enemy laughed gleefully when I fell facedown in the dirt. He rejoiced when I thought of death. He celebrated when I gave in to despair and overworry. He meant evil for me, sent people my way who were bent on hurting my soul.

But he does not get the final say. You came to earth to utterly destroy his works, his insidious words, his uncreative schemes to mar humanity. When you were on the cross, Satan must've thought he'd snatched victory, but you had the last word as you forgave the people who put you there. Your blood poured out, welcoming us to your Father for the first time. With the Temple veil torn, we were no longer separated from the one who loved us.

You have inaugurated me into your family, and in that act on the cross, you sounded the death knell for Satan through your resurrection. Because of your clear victory, he will spend the rest of his time on earth as a defeated foe.

So, Jesus, in light of your redemption, I'll choose rejoicing. Like you delivered the Jews from certain death, you rescued me from life without you. I don't know how to thank you adequately other than to, once again, surrender my life to you. Amen.

Naked

*He said, "I came naked from my mother's womb, and I will be
naked when I leave.
The LORD gave me what I had, and the LORD has taken it away.
Praise the name of the LORD!"*

JOB 1:21

Jesus, oh, to have faith like Job. When everything was stripped from him—his relationships and wealth, all he had worked for through integrity and sweat—he still remembered you. He understood that everything he had remained in your hands, and that you had the power to give or take away. He didn't merely love you during the times of blessings, but he chose to revere you in times of destitution.

I want to be more like that.

Help me remember that I brought nothing into this world except my howl and newborn skin. And when I return to the earth, my howl will silence and my skin will decay. I won't hold my loved ones, nor will I ask that they put trinkets in my coffin. Naked I came; naked I leave.

So everything I have right now is a gift. Instead of fretting about what I don't have, or looking at that person and wishing I had what they had, help me to live in light of today with contentment as my guide. All that I have is from you. I am grateful. But I want to live in such a way that I'm openhanded, ready for whatever may befall me.

I can rejoice because you are better than anything else I chase on this earth. You fill me more than my relationships do. You provide your presence—and it's better than wealth or security. I hold my life loosely and praise you right now. Oh, how I love you. Amen.

Foolish

*Job replied, "You talk like a foolish woman. Should we
accept only good things from the hand of God and never
anything bad?" So in all this, Job said nothing wrong.*

JOB 2:10

Jesus, sometimes I think I have to be nice all the time to represent you. But in this exchange with Job's wife, he speaks the truth to her and yet doesn't sin. I pray that kind of gutsy boldness would permeate my own life today. Help me to speak the truth in love to the people in my life—not just to vent because I'm frustrated, but because I am simply obeying your prompting.

But first let me examine my own heart because, like Job's wife, I'm prone to foolishness too. I like to have my life ordered and perfectly in line with my expectations. I don't like it when things explode or change. And it's hard for me when you allow frustrating, painful things in my life. Jesus, please remove the log from my eye before I dare to help someone with their own little speck.

I want to live openhearted. I want to be willing to praise you when the situations in my life turn out horribly. I confess, it's not my first instinct to praise you. It's to question your goodness.

So today, as I rest in your love, remind me again of your goodness despite my circumstances. Remake my heart so that I willingly accept difficulties as if they were presents from you. And help me to speak the truth to those I love. Amen.

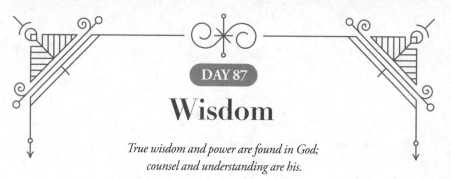

Wisdom

True wisdom and power are found in God;
counsel and understanding are his.

JOB 12:13

Jesus, I've searched this earth for wisdom. I've read widely, interacted with people's opinions, asked a lot of questions. And I realize now that, while it's good to seek wise counsel, it inevitably won't work if I don't first seek you. You are the originator of wisdom. By wisdom you created everything I see. I cannot mine the depths of your intelligence. You know everything.

Forgive me for chasing people's approval rather than settling myself into you. Teach me what it means to think in terms of your kingdom, because it's often completely different from the world's point of view. I confess I've steeped myself in the constant braying of the world—big is better; youth trumps old age; life's all about getting my needs met; money equals true power—so much so that I've forgotten your kingdom ways.

Your kingdom is built on wisdom. It praises the small, obedient act over the large, flashy show. It seeks out those whom others scorn, listening to the voice of the voiceless. It dignifies what our world marginalizes.

Today I slow down enough to listen to your voice. Teach me to be wise like you are. Impart your guidance as I seek to love the people in my life, chase the dreams I feel you've put before me, and give of myself in sacrifice. I cannot do this life without your counsel, nor would I want to. Please come near, dear Jesus. Amen.

See

I know that my Redeemer lives,
and he will stand upon the earth at last.
And after my body has decayed, yet in my body I will see God!
I will see him for myself. Yes, I will see him with my own eyes.
I am overwhelmed at the thought!

JOB 19:25-27

Jesus, I long for the day I will see you face-to-face, but for now, I content myself by knowing someday it will happen. You live. You are not dead. You are blessedly, most assuredly alive, and by your life, I have life. Thank you for leaving the sweetness of heaven for the broken earth, and dying for broken me.

I appreciate that Job said these words in the midst of terrible trials, ones that threatened his very life. He chose to see your life amidst deathly circumstances. Oh, how I need that kind of mind shift today. I need to filter the things dying in my life with the life you are living through me today.

I am overwhelmed at the thought that you love me, that you see me, that you are working on my behalf, even when I sleep. You gracefully run the universe without my help. I cannot intervene in human history, nor can I change any person's heart, but you are in this world spinning beautiful stories of redemption from ashes and death.

Give me a new perspective on my life today, I pray. I want to see aging as a gift—a journey closer to seeing you face-to-face rather than an inevitability to dread. Help me to live an anticipatory life today. Amen.

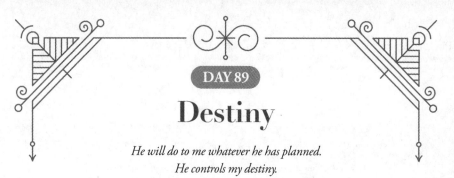

Destiny

He will do to me whatever he has planned.
He controls my destiny.

Job 23:14

Jesus, you controlled Job's destiny, though it didn't always seem rosy, and there were times when Job gave full vent to his despair. I have been in that place, and I understand. I want to ask, "Where were you when I was weeping into my pillow and no one seemed to notice my panic?"

But then I remember the patience of Job, how he endured the loss of so much—family, friends, farm, and nearly his faith. How he sat haggard, picking at his sores, bereft of hope, aching and longing.

Oh, I have been there. Not in the same Job-like way, but there have been times where I felt you didn't see me, didn't notice my plight, when heaven seemed terribly silent. Those were the times my faith was stretched beyond what I thought it could bear. And I worried that I'd snap. But you grew me, moved me beyond immaturity, and taught me to trust in the darkness. What I learned there cannot be replaced. The wisdom was hard-won, but worth it.

So I rest and nestle in your embrace today, Jesus, knowing full well that I may never understand my destiny, but trusting that it's safe and secure in your embrace. Amen.

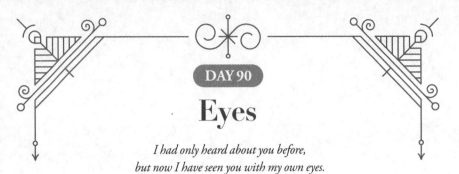

Eyes

I had only heard about you before,
but now I have seen you with my own eyes.

Job 42:5

Jesus, help me to realize that my best growth in you emerges from the darkest places of my soul. Job's journey of extreme loss and subtraction began with him knowing you pretty well. He heard your voice. He had integrity and honor. And yet, after enduring trials upon trials, he not only heard you, but he *saw* you.

Move me from hearing to seeing, Lord. Give me a new perspective on my current level of suffering—that it will be the very means to usher me from knowing you pretty well to knowing you deeply and intimately. I confess that I often want to grow deep in easy times. I want a simple pathway to spiritual maturity. But you do your best work in crucibles, in the refining fire of furnace trials.

As I look back on my life and trace my greatest growth curves, they correspond directly to my darkest trials. Help me to remember that today with the trial I'm currently facing. Instead of running away from it and la-la-la-ing away your voice and presence, help me to press into you, to keep hearing, to keep listening, until I come to a greater picture of who you are in the midst of my suffering.

Lord, I want to have a good theology of suffering. I no longer want to live avoidant of it. Instead, teach me the power of embracing it so I will see you more and more and more. Amen.

Delight

They delight in the law of the LORD, meditating on it day and night.
They are like trees planted along the riverbank,
bearing fruit each season.
Their leaves never wither, and they prosper in all they do.

PSALM 1:2-3

Jesus, I want to take great delight in your law, but I admit sometimes I'd rather run far away from it. It's hard! I don't always want to obey, to listen to the truth of it. I confess I'd rather live life on my terms, giving in to my desires rather than yours.

But your Word reminds me that my soul will greatly prosper if I meditate on your Word, on the perfect law of liberty. The more I let it seep into my pores, the more apt I am to revere and obey it. Instead of dreading your words, I want my soul to truly take great delight in your ways. I understand if I live in the land of delight, my roots will anchor me to your heart, your truth. And with roots like that, I can't help but bear fruit.

Forgive me for wanting fruit, nonwithering leaves, and prosperity without first rooting myself in you. Forgive me for wanting instant Christianity—a simple set of rules to follow. Forgive me for preferring the shortcut to the arduous task of poking seed into the soil, growing roots, and waiting for the sun, soil, and rain to bring about its slow result.

No, I want to be different from the society I'm surrounded by. I don't want to value the sound bite of your Word, but the breadth and depth that comes from immersing myself in it.

So please grow my roots. Keep me content during the years of slow, important growth so that I can give you all the credit when I bear fruit in and out of season. I trust you to do this hidden, sweet work. Amen.

Ponder

How amazing are the deeds of the LORD! All who
delight in him should ponder them. Everything
he does reveals his glory and majesty.
His righteousness never fails. He causes us
to remember his wonderful works.
How gracious and merciful is our LORD!

PSALM 111:2-4

Jesus, when I'm mired in the day-to-day tasks of life, I tend to forget how amazing you are. Even that word, *amazing*, has lost its power. Nonetheless, you are amazing in the truest sense of the word.

You are also majestic. You radiate glory. You are holy—completely different from me. You are right, and you judge perfectly. You work on behalf of the weak, of whom I am one. You dispense grace like a steady river, flowing over its riverbanks to my broken heart. You embody mercy, and I'm so grateful.

When I concentrate solely on my problems, I forget to remind myself of your power. When I look at the waves crashing around me, I no longer lock eyes with you, and I begin to sink. I'm unmoored without you. And when I place more value on my feelings about difficult situations than on the reality of your presence in the midst of them, I falter.

So instead of miring myself in my own personal controversies today, I am choosing to major on you—my Lord, my Rock, and my sure Redeemer. You are the greatness, and I am your servant in awe of that greatness. I love you. Amen.

Blameless

Who may worship in your sanctuary, LORD?
Who may enter your presence on your holy hill?
Those who lead blameless lives and do what is right,
speaking the truth from sincere hearts.

PSALM 15:1-2

Jesus, I do want to worship in your sanctuary. Show me what that means today while I meander through my daily tasks. How can my mundane life become a cathedral of praise for you? Teach me what it means to live a lifestyle of worship, joyfully entering your presence.

I want to be considered worthy of you. Thank you that there's nothing I can do to secure my worth, no amount of wrangling or perfection seeking. You have completely provided the way toward worth and relationship by dying my death on a sinner's cross.

Because of that, and because of the perfect gift of the Holy Spirit, I can exemplify this psalm. By your power, I can lead a blameless life. By your strength, I can choose to do what is right, what makes you smile. By your wisdom, I can speak about your truth without trepidation or worry.

So I come. I enter into your presence. I climb your holy hill. Not because of my greatness, but because of yours. I'm grateful you come near to me, and in that nearness, my heart rests satisfied. Amen.

Fortress

The LORD is my rock, my fortress, and my savior;
my God is my rock, in whom I find protection.
He is my shield, the power that saves me, and my place of safety.

PSALM 18:2

Jesus, I have spent a lot of time creating fortresses around my heart. People have hurt me, have violated me, and have broken down my walls of protection. So, in response, I've built a wall. Unfortunately, in doing so I've protected myself from you—the very one who can heal me from the pain of the past.

I'm entirely fearful of giving you the key to my heart. I don't want to look at the pain from the past. I'd rather pretend it doesn't exist, blissfully unaware of what needs to be surgically removed and healed.

But this verse reminds me that you actually are my Fortress. You are the one who saves me from others, from myself, from my own bitter, unforgiving heart. You are the Rock I can run to when everything in my life feels unstable and shaky. You protect me and watch over me with diligence and extreme care. You shield me from gossip, mean words, and conspiracies. You are my safe place.

I don't want to live with a fortress around my heart—not toward others, and certainly not toward you. Take the bricks down, one by one, and heal the heart that lies beneath. I'm afraid, but I trust you today. Amen.

Safe

You hold me safe beyond the reach of my enemies; you save
me from violent opponents. For this, O LORD, I will praise
you among the nations; I will sing praises to your name.

PSALM 18:48-49

Jesus, I have no idea how many times you've rescued me from enemies or violence. Thank you for doing that, even though I don't have a
tangible list of every occurrence. What's hard about this passage is the
question: What if violence *has* happened to me? Does that mean that
you chose not to protect me? What about victims of violent crimes?
Does that mean that you don't care about them? What about people
who have been attacked by enemies, whether verbally or physically?

I choose to trust in your goodness despite these very real questions.
I know that knowing you is not a get-out-of-danger-free card—after
all, you said that in this world we would have troubles. It's that you
will be with us in the midst of them. Perhaps that's what the psalmist
meant when he penned these words. You see us, and you walk alongside us when life takes crazy turns. When we walk through the valley of
the shadow of death, we can trust that we walk hand in hand with you.

For your goodness, I will choose to praise you—and not merely in
my home or my local community. You are the God of this entire world,
and your message of hope is for this whole messy world. So show me
today how I can "praise you among the nations." What does that mean
to me? How can I love you well beyond my borders?

Remind me, too, that there are brothers and sisters around this
beautiful blue-and-green planet who are suffering tragic hardships
today—all because they follow you. I want my prayer life to be robust,
not simply for my own battles, but also for theirs. Amen.

Honesty

*Yes, what joy for those whose record the LORD has cleared of guilt,
whose lives are lived in complete honesty!*

PSALM 32:2

Jesus, this is a high bar, but oh, how I want to live up to it. Complete honesty completely terrifies me. I have secrets and internal sins aplenty, and I shudder to think that people might find out about what I hide. But before you, I am laid bare. You know everything I've done, everything I will do. You know the secret intentions of my heart. You know me. You love me anyway. That's powerful to me. And humbling.

Although I spend a lot of time re-shaming myself for my past sinful choices, that's not your highest will. Once you died on the cross for my sins, my guilt was erased, the shame obliterated by your blood. I don't need to rehash what I've done or rehearse my worthlessness. When I do that, I'm giving in to the enemy's desire to steal from, kill, and destroy me.

Instead, let me dance in light of this audacious gift: I am completely cleared of guilt. Instead of making me want to sin more so I can experience more grace, may this radical gift change my entire life so that my heart sings for you, full of praise and gratitude. I want my new actions to spring from my clean heart.

I can be honest with others about my own sin precisely because you modeled authenticity and truth when you walked this earth. I don't have to be afraid of being exposed because you were exposed before everyone, yet without sin. Amen.

Confess

When I refused to confess my sin, my body
wasted away, and I groaned all day long.
Day and night your hand of discipline was heavy on me.
My strength evaporated like water in the summer heat.
Finally, I confessed all my sins to you and
stopped trying to hide my guilt.
I said to myself, "I will confess my rebellion to the LORD."
And you forgave me! All my guilt is gone.

PSALM 32:3-5

Jesus, it's not in my best interest to hide from you or anyone else—but particularly you. You see me. You know my sin already. What you long for is relationship, and good relationships thrive in the midst of authenticity and honesty. Forgive me for trying to cover up my sin, for prettifying it in hopes of making it more palatable.

The truth is, my sin is a stench—to you and to me. It profits me nothing except maybe some fleeting pleasure. It leaves me with shame, fear, and guilt. When it hangs around my neck like a hidden albatross, I can barely walk, and my joy has left. But confession brings everything into the glorious light—your light. So I choose right now to say it all, confess my sins, and pursue you again.

It's not good for my soul to have a broken relationship with you. It's not good for my heart to constantly try to hide, pretending all is well when I know it's not. Hypocrisy curdles my soul, makes it sour. So please cleanse me and help me to walk in light of the truth today. Amen.

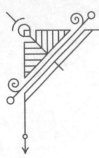

Small

The LORD looks down from heaven
and sees the whole human race.
From his throne he observes
all who live on the earth.
He made their hearts,
so he understands everything they do.

PSALM 33:13-15

Jesus, it's hard for me to understand that you see every single person on this earth—including me. Today I feel small and unnoticed—overlooked. There are times I experience the sting of neglect. But you promise that you see me. That you take note of me, no matter how insignificant I may feel.

Open my eyes so I can discern your earthward look. Raise my mind that's been more occupied with doldrums than glory. Lift my eyes heavenward where I can see you there, victorious, alive, beaming with the brightest light. And even in that place where love reigns supreme, you look on me with loving eyes.

Help me rest in knowing that you fashioned my heart. You know the worries that live there. You understand the pain that lurks and sometimes strangles. And you see what brings me deep joy. Would you please show me specifically today that you are mindful of me? A hint from nature, a string of words from a friend, a gentle peace that's eluded me?

Jesus, thank you for understanding the intricacies of my inner world and for loving me anyway. Amen.

Guide

Send out your light and your truth; let them guide me.
Let them lead me to your holy mountain, to the place where you live.

PSALM 43:3

Jesus, I live in a world opposite of your kingdom. Every day the kingdoms of this world send out darkness and lies like enticing messengers. And I'm sorry to say I am often wooed by their siren voices. My heart sometimes bends toward darkness. It loves lies because they make sense. Or maybe it's just that I want to believe lies, or I've lived in the shadow of them for so long that they've become familiar companions.

But your Word reminds me today that I cannot ever come close to you if I live in the kingdom of darkened lies. I can't feast with you in your presence on your holy hill if I constantly entertain darkness and lies as welcomed guests. Forgive me.

I truly need discernment today. Show me the darkness I've preferred over your light that sheds brightness on the darkest corners of my sins. Reveal to me the lies that have become like truth. I don't want either to become familiar any more.

Instead, make me daring enough to leave the familiar and the falsehoods. Teach me to race toward the light, shedding the sin that so easily entangles me, moving toward your truth.

I know my soul thrives when it's feasting with you. I know I'm happier, more adjusted, and more aware of my worth when I'm choosing to be near you. Replace the darkness with light today, Jesus, and the lies I've believed with truth. Amen.

Offering

The sacrifice you desire is a broken spirit.
You will not reject a broken and repentant heart, O God.

PSALM 51:17

Jesus, I love you so much, I want to give you a gourmet meal or a child's first step or the hush of dawn as my offering. But life interrupts, and I find myself beaten down and small. I'm so glad you regard my brokenness as an offering.

You, who made everything, accept the parts of me that feel unwanted. You walk in the places I'd rather hide from holy eyes. You take my embarrassment to yourself as if it were heralding praise. My awkwardness is perplexingly beautiful to you. I'm humbled by that.

No matter where I find myself, whether I'm knocking on the door of success or stumbling behind in defeat, I choose right now to offer you *me*—undecorated, freed from hiding and games. Take me, Lord. It's all I have today.

I understand that what you really need from me is intimate friendship. You don't need my religious words, my attempts at impressing you, my fear of your scorn. Like a loving daddy, your desire is presence—you and me talking freely, me sharing my day, you listening well. Help me to live in that welcoming circle of friendship.

Forgive me for forgetting how sweet your love is toward me. Thank you that I don't have to be a super Christian to woo your affection. Here I am, Jesus. Take all of me. It's all I have, and all you want. Amen.

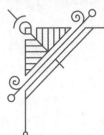

Pour

O my people, trust in him at all times.
Pour out your heart to him, for God is our refuge.

PSALM 62:8

Jesus, I am grateful today that you have called me one of your people. You chased after me, pulled me up from a pit too deep, and rescued me, calling me your child. It's overwhelming, this love you have for me.

Trust is a hard word. I tend not to trust anyone, let alone you. But because of your rescue mission toward me, I am slowly growing my trust muscle. Even when things seem like chaos and I can't see your hand, when I look back in retrospect, I can trace your handiwork in my life and see your faithfulness. So today I choose to remember all you've done and trust that you are not finished with my life. You will do good things. You have a plan for my life.

I love the word *pour*. I picture a giant pitcher with all my worries, cares, frets, and burns pouring out into your hands. I choose to pour everything out to you right now, Jesus. Please take my fear. Please take the difficult relationships in my life. Please receive my worry about provision. Please hold my wayward friends and loved ones. Please absorb my confusion and bewilderment.

Thank you that you truly are my refuge, my shelter, and my safe house. Would you hold me close as we dwell together in this space? Teach me to run to you when attack comes. Instruct me when it's right to retreat from stress and shelter myself with you. I need you, Jesus. Amen.

Near

What joy for those you choose to bring near,
those who live in your holy courts.
What festivities await us inside your holy Temple.

PSALM 65:4

Jesus, I confess that I have forsaken festivities. I've neglected to chase after you into those places where you dwell. I've been busy—too busy to hear from you, rest in you, receive from you.

I am sorry. Those three words seem small as I pray them, but I truly do feel the weight of them because I know I've missed out on being with you. Your Word says joy returns to me when you are near, but I have preferred running my own life to being still enough to hear your encouragement, experience your nearness.

I want to stop. To pause. To take this small moment and reorient my heart with yours. I want to experience your closeness in a holy moment of time. I wait. Please speak. Your servant is listening.

I love the example you gave, Jesus, of pulling away from the hustle of Galilee to experience your own jubilee with the Father. You needed guidance and presence with him, so you deliberately chose to remove yourself from the craziness of daily life to find the peace that God the Father gives. Today I choose to do the same thing. Restore to me the art of anticipation. Like a young child longing for a birthday party, may my heart long for the festivities you provide in stillness and quietness. Amen.

Answer

The Lord says, "I will rescue those who love me. I will protect
those who trust in my name. When they call on me, I will answer;
I will be with them in trouble. I will rescue and honor them. I
will reward them with a long life and give them my salvation."

PSALM 91:14-16

Jesus, I love you. As I look back on my life, I clearly see your protection and care. Thank you for your protection. Thank you for walking with me in hard times. I'm humbled that you've dignified me with honor. And, of course, all I can do is praise you for inaugurating my salvation—the greatest gift ever given.

This psalm promises that when I call upon you, you will answer me. And in your Gospels, you promise the same thing—if I knock, you will answer. Sometimes I grow weary of waiting for your response. I demand it now, or want to orchestrate exactly how and when you respond to me. I want you to meet my expectations on my timetable.

In doing this, I forget that you exist outside of time, and that everything you do is purposeful and according to your timeless plan. And I also realize that good parents sometimes make their children wait patiently for an answer so they don't grow up spoiled and enabled. So help me to have that proper perspective as I wait afresh for your answer. Instead of demanding that you answer according to my agenda, I give you permission (not that you need it) to be wildly creative and free in your response. Teach me in this waiting time to learn perseverance and trust. Amen.

Thrill

You thrill me, LORD, with all you have done for me!
I sing for joy because of what you have done.

PSALM 92:4

Jesus, when I think of the word *thrill*, I confess I don't always think of you. Roller coasters, yes. Sunsets, yes. Adventure, yes. Oh, Jesus, teach me to be thrilled by you alone, by what you have done for me.

Today I make a persistent choice to count the blessings you have brought my way. Thank you for health enough to pray. Thank you for making the vista outside my window. Thank you for restoring my life. Thank you for salvation, for peace, for settled joy. Thank you for the people with whom you've populated my life. Thank you for the trials I've endured because they made me closer to you. Thank you for removing my sin as far as the east is from the west. Thank you for friends. Thank you for the food you have provided. Thank you for the clothes I am wearing, the shelter you've given. Thank you for giving me life, even on the dark days. Thank you for your Word. Thank you for the Holy Spirit. Thank you that you've given me creativity and guts and hope.

I am thrilled by you. I choose to become hyperaware today of the ways you are good. And as I make this determination through the power of the Holy Spirit, I will look for ways to worship and praise you, even sing to you because of all you have done. Help me see your faithfulness, and in that seeing, teach me to jump to thankfulness rather than sadness and doubt. Amen.

Grumbled

The people refused to enter the pleasant land,
for they wouldn't believe his promise to care for them.
Instead, they grumbled in their tents and refused to obey the LORD.

PSALM 106:24-25

Jesus, I want to be known as a person who lets go of grumbling and embraces faith-filled trust. But I'm afraid my fallback, my automatic response, is to grumble like the Israelites—unsatisfied with living in a tent, immobilized to enter into the promised land you have for me. I'd rather look at all the reasons I'm unable to trust, listing my fears that mount by the hour, than reorient my mind to believe you care for me.

Your Word says I need to cast my cares upon you because you care for me. But instead, I rehash my cares, making them seem bigger and louder than your provision. I make doubt my common reaction. I rehearse ways you won't hear me or take care of me. I'm guilty of believing the lie that you will not pay attention to my needs. Like Eve in the Garden of Eden, I don't believe your goodness, and I plot ways to take care of myself outside of dependence on you.

And yet, you have a pleasant land beckoning me—a place whose entrance is guarded by a gate called trust. I cannot enter it until I let go of my fears, choosing to trust that you will guide me to the next place you have for me. So right now, I choose trust. Amen.

Speak

Give thanks to the Lord, for he is good!
His faithful love endures forever.
Has the Lord redeemed you? Then speak out!
Tell others he has redeemed you from your enemies.

PSALM 107:1-2

Jesus, sometimes I'm slow to speak. I'm afraid I might sound like a braggart. But you have done so much for me. Your love has swooped from heaven and rescued my insecurities. I'm praying right now because of your radical redemptive work in my life. Thank you.

It's hard to think that I might have enemies on this earth. Your Word reminds me that the real battle isn't against people who act as bullies, or whose words haunt my mind when I'm quiet or feeling small. No, the battle I fight is against the principalities of darkness, those evil spirits who love to keep people stumbling in the dark.

So thank you for delivering me from those enemies—the spirits who want to steal from me, kill my resolve, and destroy my witness.

Your love truly does endure forever. It moves beyond today's trials and yesterday's worries and even tomorrow's foibles. It extends farther than east from west, as high as the sun in the sky. Thank you for loving me so completely. Amen.

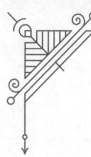

Ponder

*How amazing are the deeds of the Lord! All
who delight in him should ponder them.
Everything he does reveals his glory and majesty.
His righteousness never fails.
He causes us to remember his wonderful works.
How gracious and merciful is our Lord!*

Psalm 111:2-4

Jesus, you do amazing things. Teach me to delight in you, and in so doing, enable my mind to ponder all of them, much like Mary treasured your works and words in her heart. When life careens into crazy, hearken me back to this time of remembrance, where I listed your traits, marveled at your Word, bathed in your love. I know hard times will come, so right now, when my heart is settled, help me to truly mine the depths of your amazing love.

Like the psalmist, I declare that everything you do reflects your glory and majesty. You live in the midst of light, and you are light. You are greater than any worry I may coddle to myself. You are higher than Mount Everest. You are holier than the most holy person. You are right. You are true. You are big. You are capable. You are the smartest being in the universe. Because of who you are, I am safe because you are solidly for me, not against me. Thank you.

Today I choose to concentrate on your holiness—that righteous part of you that never does wrong, stays solidly in the light, and judges perfectly the intention of everyone's heart. Your holiness astounds and scares me. And in light of it, I'm profoundly grateful that you've chosen me to be your friend. Amen.

Delight

Your laws are my treasure; they are my heart's delight.

PSALM 119:111

Jesus, it's easy to look at you, to see what you did on this earth, how you loved people well and sacrificed your life for all of us—and delight in all that. You are easy to take delight in because you are so beautiful. But when I think of laws, I can only think in the abstract. How can I treasure stone-hewn commandments? How does holding the Sabbath as holy become a delight?

And yet, when you walked this earth, you fulfilled the law. You obeyed every moral code set forth in the Old Testament. Not one jot or tittle did you obliterate or disobey. You embodied faithful obedience. This reminds me that the laws of God are important. They are not to be disregarded because they reflect your goodness. When I call them burdensome or irrelevant, I call you the same.

Thank you for creating laws that help our society run well. Thank you that your laws protect the helpless, punish the offenders, and teach us all what it means to live out your heart on this earth. So little these days promotes your holiness or holy living. We've become a society majoring on grace while dismissing holiness.

Show me places where I haven't taken great delight in your laws, Lord. Show me where I've glossed over obedience for the sake of my own convenience. I don't want to dismiss your laws and decrees. Instead, I want to treasure them and you. Amen.

Confidence

Don't put your confidence in powerful people;
there is no help for you there.

PSALM 146:3

Jesus, please forgive me for looking to gatekeepers to open doors for me. I wrongly believe that people are bigger than you, that they dwarf your abilities to do amazing things. Teach me not to misplace my hope. Help me to run headlong into your arms for security and help and provision.

And please forgive me when I think I have to become a powerful person to do your work on earth. I love that you use the downtrodden to accomplish your great plans. You don't seek after know-it-alls or celebrities or people who have it all together. You seek out those whose hearts are completely yours, who understand their weakness and dependence. Oh, dear Jesus, would you make my heart dependent on you like that?

When my circumstances seem impossible and I want to run to others for rescue, help me to first bring my panic to you. May you be the first one I chase when I feel life is chasing me.

I want to live my life from the heart of the passions you've given me. Even when the ministries I pursue seem to fade in significance, I choose today to trust that you will open the right doors and the perfect time. After all, this whole endeavor is for you, for your fame, for your glory. Once again, I place my dreams in your hands. No one can snatch those from me when they're in that safe place. Amen.

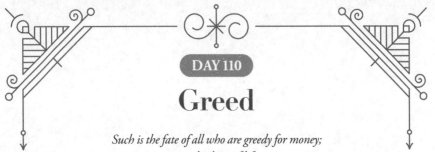

Greed

Such is the fate of all who are greedy for money;
it robs them of life.

PROVERBS 1:19

Jesus, when I run to money instead of to you, my soul shrinks a little bit more. Chasing it emaciates me. And as the Scripture says, the greedier I am, the more money robs me of joy and life. So help me to make a determination today that you are better than money. You, the Provider, are better than the provision.

Help me never to mistake the two. Help me love you for you, not simply because you provide my needs. And please help me to pepper my prayers with more than just "Give me this; give me that." I don't want to be a spoiled child who berates my parent for the next new toy, the shiniest, flashiest things the world claims will make me happy.

I want to be truly life-filled because of you and my connection to you. You are the River of Life, the Sustainer of me. You are the one who truly satisfies my soul. Forgive me for wrongly believing that money will solve all my problems.

Instead of greed that lurks deep inside, please replace it with outrageous generosity. In fact, I pray that you would place someone in my path today who needs to know you love them through something tangible I can do for them. Help me to give hilariously, with open wallet, eager and ready to let go of the money I so often grip with my fist. Amen.

Understanding

For the LORD grants wisdom!
From his mouth come knowledge and understanding.
He grants a treasure of common sense to the honest.
He is a shield to those who walk with integrity.
He guards the paths of the just and protects
those who are faithful to him.

PROVERBS 2:6-8

Jesus, oh, how I need a treasure of common sense in my life. When I rely on my own strength, I become senseless. You promise you will grant this kind of wisdom if I live honestly and with integrity, so today I wait on your voice, your wisdom. Give me clear insight in how I should live and give today.

I love that you grant wisdom. It's not something I must earn or strive for or pay homage for. Your great generosity bestows this kind of godly understanding. It's a beautiful gift, wrapped in your love.

I only need to see it, unwrap it, thank you for it, and put it to good use.

Thank you for your protection of me. I don't even realize how much you do protect me, nor do I have any idea how you will protect me today. I look forward to seeing my story from heaven's shores and realizing just how powerfully you protected me when I was wayward or unknowing. Oh, how I love your mysterious ways. Oh, how thankful I am for you, Jesus. Amen.

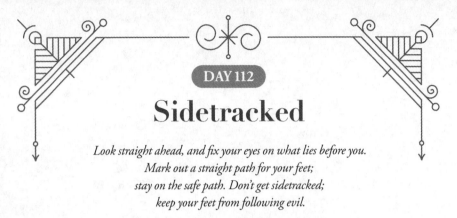

Sidetracked

Look straight ahead, and fix your eyes on what lies before you.
Mark out a straight path for your feet;
stay on the safe path. Don't get sidetracked;
keep your feet from following evil.

PROVERBS 4:25-27

Jesus, I get easily sidetracked, especially when life grows hairy and my schedule increases exponentially. It's hard to take a breath, to learn the art of focus in my unfocused world. Still, you are my center, my rallying point.

As I go throughout my day, Jesus, give me your perspective on the tasks strung out before me. Help me to say yes to the eternal and important matters and let go of the pressing ones that don't really count. Teach me what it means to have the discipline of focus. I choose right now to take my eyes off the scattered remains of my life and place them resolutely in front of me, toward you.

Would you teach me your pathway for my life? I want to have true, confident purpose. I want to know that my life counts for something. But there are so many shiny objects out there that I tend to get sidetracked.

Give me insider knowledge to discern when my impact is lessening because I'm doing too much. I give you permission to guide, direct, and reprimand me when I stray from your path, when I find the enemy's ways more enticing. And please, please send your church my way when I'm dangerously close to blowing it all. Oh, how fragile I am, Jesus. Amen.

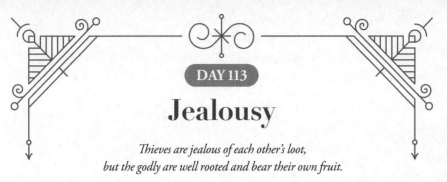

Jealousy

Thieves are jealous of each other's loot,
but the godly are well rooted and bear their own fruit.

PROVERBS 12:12

Jesus, I don't like me when I'm jealous. I'm small and petty and the worst part of myself. And yet I can't seem to help longing for what others have or resenting my friends for their abilities, cash reserves, or station in life. Please rescue me from living this way.

Replace my jealousy with zealous gratitude for what I do have. Instead of recounting the unfairness of what others possess, I will count the many things you have done in my life. Thank you for life, that I have breath. Thank you for populating my sphere with amazing people. Thank you that I am filled, that you have given me so much. In that gratitude, give me a new perspective of simplicity and giving.

I want to be so rooted in you that fruit comes naturally to me, that I'll be so preoccupied with you and your ways that I don't have time to be jealous of others. Thank you for your example in the Scriptures of the vine and the branches. You are the vine, and all of your children are branches, bearing their various kinds of fruit.

So it seems silly for me to look at the pears of one believer and be jealous while I'm bearing plums. Instead, let me rejoice in all that fruit. Amen.

Weighted

Worry weighs a person down.

PROVERBS 12:25

Jesus, I feel heavy today because of worry. The weight gain of heavy stress has not blessed my life with peace or joy or proper perspective. Instead, it's like a noose around my heart. It causes me to jump headlong into negative conclusions, even when life seems okay and sane.

Worry accomplishes nothing for me, and yet I treat it like a lover, feeding it, coddling it, wooing it. I don't want to do that anymore.

But this relinquishment of worry seems impossible to me. I'm grateful you are the God of the impossible, so I humbly ask today that you would free me of the worry beast. Today when I bend toward worries and panic, would you prompt me to choose another path? When I want to give in to my fears and let them fully vent their chaos to my mind, would you give me new perspective?

Right now I choose faith, Jesus. I choose to believe that your capable shoulders can carry my worries. I choose to believe that there is no profit in worrying. I choose to trust you for what concerns me. I choose to actively rest from rabbit trails and fears run amuck.

Bring clarity to my mind, please, and feet to my faith. I declare that you are capable of holding every worry. And because I'm so tired of holding them close to my heart, I willingly offer them up to you as sacrifice. Amen.

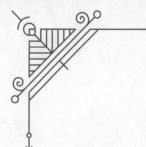

Feast

*For the happy heart,
life is a continual feast.*

PROVERBS 15:15

Jesus, I want to have a truly happy, giddy heart because of all the amazing things you have done. You lived the perfect life I could not live. You willingly headed to Golgotha, bearing the weight of my sins upon your sacred shoulders. You bled for me, for this world. You could barely pull in breath as the cross suffocated you. You uttered those forgiveness words to the people below mocking you. You set your face like flint toward your mission. And when the vultures circled the sky, when death seemed to have won a terrible victory, you defied it all by rising again, alive. So blessedly alive.

You did this so I could be redeemed, so I could experience salvation and joy and peace and honor. You endured so I could be your child. All of this is enough, Jesus. Enough to make me leap for joy at the thought of you and your upside-down ways.

But beyond all this, you bless me with little things—acts of kindness shaped in ways that make me know you understand my most intimate thoughts and dreams. You show up in the small things, and I love you all the more for it.

So please, Jesus, let me live a life of continual feasting before you. When life messes with me, and sadness threatens to throttle my voice, bring some laughter, a dose of joy, a hiccup of hilarity. Because, Jesus, you have made my life so good. Amen.

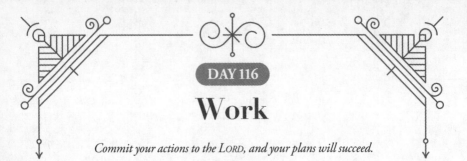

Work

Commit your actions to the LORD, and your plans will succeed.

PROVERBS 16:3

Jesus, forgive me for thinking I'm the boss of me. Because inevitably I am not. This idea of control is a false construct, something I rely on when I'm feeling scattered or insecure or afraid. I wrongly think and live as if everything is up to me.

But everything is up to you.

Jesus, today I give you my vocation, the job you've blessed me with. Help me to be grateful for these tasks today, but even more, thank you for sending my coworkers into my life. Open my eyes to their needs and desires. Give me a heart to listen rather than lecture. I truly want to be an ambassador wherever I go, reaching out to those who truly need a touch from you. So please reframe my work in light of your great kingdom.

Jesus, help me, empower me to work hard for your sake. But inevitably, I want to take my hands off the results, and I don't want to base my worth on whether or not things succeed. Help me to work hard for your sake, but leave what happens next in your hands.

My work is actually your work through me. Keep me close to this perspective today. Amen.

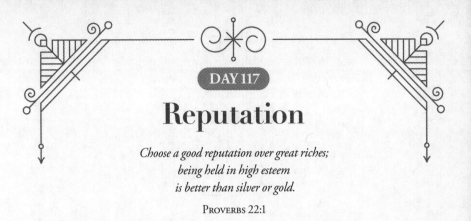

Reputation

Choose a good reputation over great riches;
being held in high esteem
is better than silver or gold.

PROVERBS 22:1

Jesus, thank you for your reputation as you walked this earth. Crowds came to see you, to experience your healing and deliverance. They sat enraptured at your words. You were kind, you lived consistently, and you walked with integrity. Thank you for the example you set.

In like manner, help me to choose to pursue the kind of life that makes for a good reputation. I want my insides to match my outside behavior. I want a good heart that produces great fruit. I want to be kind to people, even the ones who interrupt me or bother me. I want to serve the people you've placed in my life with joy, not with compulsion or resignation.

Help me process this truth when I see people with bad reputations succeeding: Your Word promises that even though they may have material wealth as a result of their schemes, ultimately they are not wealthy. True wealth is loving others and knowing you. So don't let me dwell on this kind of injustice. Instead, help me find deep satisfaction in living right, chasing after your agenda, and blessing the people you bring into my life. Amen.

Humility

True humility and fear of the LORD
lead to riches, honor, and long life.

PROVERBS 22:4

Jesus, I want to put things in proper order, just as they are according to this scripture. You come first. What you give comes a far second.

Teach me what true humility means. It is not humiliation or smallness, but an understanding of who I am in this world compared to you, who created this vast earth and the heavens above. Tonight when I look at the stars, keep me in that humble place, showing me afresh that you are the King of kings and the Lord of lords. You are the one who creates. And I sit here stunned because you call me child. *Thank you* seems very small indeed.

I want to understand what fear of the Lord means. I want to live a life of true reverence, understanding how vast, how intelligent, how understanding, how powerful, how sacrificial you are. You are bigger than my biggest worry and as intimate as the cells in my body that you knit together in my mother's womb. Oh, dear Jesus, teach me this kind of healthy fear.

And as I live in humility, as I fear you, may your blessings come in their own time. I promise to be grateful for them whether they are spectacular and miraculous or humble and needed. Thank you for being my great provider and friend. Amen.

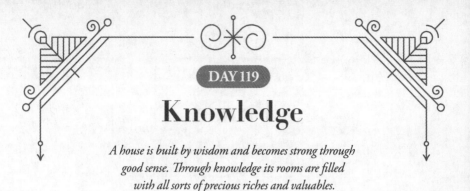

Knowledge

A house is built by wisdom and becomes strong through good sense. Through knowledge its rooms are filled with all sorts of precious riches and valuables.

PROVERBS 24:3-4

Jesus, the house of my life is sometimes crumbling, sometimes pristine, sometimes a mixture of both. But today? It needs remodeling—but not by my hand, by your carpenter hands. You are wisdom. You are the beginning of all knowledge. And you alone can rebuild my life on what counts.

I want the rooms of my heart to be filled with your wisdom—not my own catchphrases or cliché answers. Keep me close to you. Remind me again that wisdom doesn't come from me trying harder to figure out life, but it derives from my deeper connection with you. So hold me close.

You are the riches and valuables within me. My weakness, instead of something to push against, is the entry ticket for your strength and power. I'm so grateful I don't have to build this life and heart alone, unaware of the blueprints or how to create joists and support beams.

I surrender myself to your capable work. I give you control of my soul. And as my soul prospers under your kind care, remind me of those in my life today who also need reconstruction. Instead of pointing out their design flaws, I choose to pray for them, that you, the Designer of us all, would bring them closer to you. Oh, dear Jesus, don't simply rebuild me; rebuild them too. Amen.

Praise

*Let someone else praise you, not your own
mouth—a stranger, not your own lips.*

PROVERBS 27:2

Jesus, I've spent a lot of time thinking about how I can promote myself. I have run myself ragged trying to prove that I'm worthy of notice. Because of a wallflower past, I've wrongly become obsessed with praising myself—not in an arrogant way, but subtly. The tendency is there nonetheless.

It's tiring work, this seeking notice and approval. It occupies too much of my mental energy and makes me tired of performing on a treadmill that never shuts off. Settle me, Lord. Settle me into yourself, that safe place where no performance is necessary. Where I can simply be your child, loved and beloved.

And as I let out a long breath and experience that kind of welcoming grace, I'll let go of having to micromanage my reputation. Instead, let me live joyfully in anticipation of how you will move me in the future. I look forward to seeing how others might take up my cause, how friends and strangers may notice and help the causes held dear to me.

It's altogether freeing to no longer have to be my own PR manager, and I love living in anticipation of what you will do, how you will move others.

Today I pray that you would solidify this verse in my heart—not so much that I'd live hoping others would notice me (that's icing on the cake), but that I can be the kind of person who praises others. Show me folks who are doing great work, and give me creative them-shaped ways to offer praise. What joy my day will have as this prayer is answered. Amen.

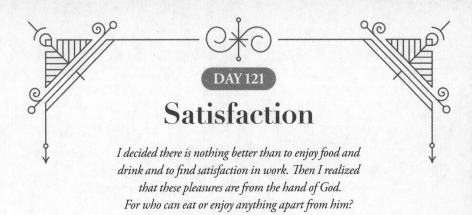

Satisfaction

*I decided there is nothing better than to enjoy food and
drink and to find satisfaction in work. Then I realized
that these pleasures are from the hand of God.
For who can eat or enjoy anything apart from him?*

ECCLESIASTES 2:24-25

Jesus, I'm grateful today for the daily bread you've provided. Thank you for clean water. You've given me both in abundance, and you've presented me with meaningful work. How can I thank you?

But there are those who struggle around this great, big world—those who don't have food or clean water. Would you show me how to be a part of the solution? Is there something I can do? Please lead me toward generosity, toward meeting the needs of my brothers and sisters around the world.

Forgive me for thinking that my daily life is my doing. I didn't create food. I didn't provide water from deep within the earth or from the clouds in the sky. All of this is from you. My work and the wealth that comes from it are yours too.

This is all an illusion of control that I like to maintain—that I provide for myself, that it's all up to me. And yet, you feed the sparrows. You orchestrate this world and bring provision my way without me even knowing about it.

I want to live openhandedly—grateful for the provision you've given, and full of acute awareness that you are the one who blesses us all. I love you, Jesus. Amen.

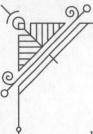

Scope

Yet God has made everything beautiful for its own time.
He has planted eternity in the human heart, but even so, people
cannot see the whole scope of God's work from beginning to end.

ECCLESIASTES 3:11

Jesus, I don't always see the ends of stories. And some of my own stories are untied threads with no knots ending them nicely. But you are the great storyteller and story weaver. You are always at work, even when I sleep or sickness overtakes my productivity. Your surprising task is to make every story beautiful in its own time.

Help me to be patient with your story crafting, not demanding a premature ending before the story has played itself out. And forgive me for asking to know everything up front. A good story has conflict, and I don't always know the ending, which makes turning the page all the more exciting. Instead, I want to trust what you're doing despite what I see.

I understand that I won't see everything tied up in a bow on this side of eternity. I cannot know all the stories, all the endings, all the conflicts, all the climaxes and denouements. But I can know you. I can choose to trust when things feel chaotic. Why? Because you are the one constant in my life, and you are a good God.

I end this by praying for those in my life who are wandering around lost. You say you planted eternity in their hearts. Would you gently remind them today that you love them, and you have a good story for them to live? Amen.

Final

I know that whatever God does is final. Nothing can be added to it or taken from it. God's purpose is that people should fear him.

ECCLESIASTES 3:14

Jesus, you have the final word in my life—and in the lives of everyone in this world. Forgive me for thinking I have the final word, that outcomes are my sole responsibility. And when you act, that's it; it's finished.

That reminds me of your words on the cross—the holy exclamation point to your time here on earth. As you forgave those who put you up there, grew thirsty, forgave the thief on the cross, you also said, "It is finished." All that separation of sinful man from your family in that moment was erased. Because of that, I am now your friend, which is a beautiful term.

But don't let me take that friendship for granted by living laxly or by minimizing sin. Sin is a big deal, and if I walk in it, I will live far away from you, away from your sweet, encouraging presence. My purpose isn't to live as if your death was no big deal. It's to live on this earth revering you, having a healthy fear of your holiness, a strong respect and fear for who you are and what you did.

I rest in your purpose for me today. I am grateful that when you're in the midst of a plan, it cannot be thwarted. I'm grateful that even I can't change or re-channel your plan. Thank you that your purposes on this earth do prevail. Help me to live in light of this truth today. Amen.

Accept

Even so, I have noticed one thing, at least, that is good. It is
good for people to eat, drink, and enjoy their work under the
sun during the short life God has given them, and to accept
their lot in life. And it is a good thing to receive wealth from
God and the good health to enjoy it. To enjoy your work and
accept your lot in life—this is indeed a gift from God.

ECCLESIASTES 5:18-19

Jesus, help me to find satisfaction in a job well done. Instead of dreading the tasks of the day, help me to truly enjoy the work you've set before me, seeing it as a privilege, a way to tangibly honor you. I choose today to work hard because I want to honor you. And as I work, I rely on your Spirit within me to carry out whatever you have for me. I want my work here to make you smile.

In my finances today, Lord, I ask for help. Would you remind me again that you see me? That you know my financial wants and needs? I choose to reorient my thinking—I am not my provider; you are. So I look to you today. I give you all my money anxieties and ask for peace as a better replacement.

I lift up my body today—particularly my health. You are the Great Physician, and you know what's right and what's wrong. I entrust my health to you. Show me where I need to be disciplined in my eating and exercise. Help me not to be discouraged about my appearance, but to entrust all that I am to you. Any health I have today I acknowledge is a gift from you. Amen.

Better

But even though a person sins a hundred times and still lives a long time, I know that those who fear God will be better off.

ECCLESIASTES 8:12

Jesus, it's the age-old question: Why do people who continually sin, spending their lives mocking you, seem to live as if it doesn't matter? And why do bad things seem to happen to good people? It doesn't seem to make sense. The wicked prosper. The righteous suffer. And the world feels topsy-turvy in the aftermath of it all.

So help me reconcile what I see in my daily life with scripture like this. It's hard for me to see your goodness when those I love suffer. It's difficult to understand your love, when I try to do the right thing, but it's either not recognized, or I suffer because of it.

I need to remember your perfect justice, and that it will all make sense someday—maybe not today, maybe not tomorrow, but in eternity. You will set right those who have been wronged. You will mete out justice in the most perfect way because you know every single angle of every single story. Help me to rest in that. I don't want to live with a vengeful heart, trying to bring justice when I don't have the whole story.

You are holy and righteous. You will judge fairly. I am thankful that my pain and the injustices I've suffered are held today in your hands. When I try to grab my pain back and fix my problems, remind me that you will take care of me. I simply need to trust. Amen.

Conclusion

That's the whole story. Here now is my final conclusion:
Fear God and obey his commands, for this is everyone's duty.
God will judge us for everything we do,
including every secret thing, whether good or bad.

ECCLESIASTES 12:13-14

Jesus, I'm grateful you've made life so clear in this passage. For so long I've complicated my relationship with you, crowding it with lists and tasks and confusing agendas. But really all you require is to fear and obey you. That's the conclusion you come to, the bottom line of what I'm to do.

Show me areas of my life where I'm not holding you in reverence. Do I need to adopt new holy habits? Stop doing something that hurts my soul? Spend time away in a quiet place? Have better Sabbath rest?

Uncover places where I'm not obeying you. Is there someone I need to forgive? Where am I embittered, and why? Have I held back my resources in how I worship you? Is there something further I need to give for your kingdom? Is there some task you've set out for me that I've been reluctant to do? Do I need to apologize to someone? Please search my heart and help me have a clear conscience before you and others.

Although it's scary, I'm also thankful you know everything about me, even the secrets I try to hide. Thank you for loving me through them. Give me the power and ability to live an authentic life, admitting my sin to you and to others. Amen.

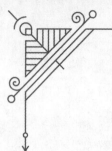

Banquet

He escorts me to the banquet hall;
it's obvious how much he loves me.

SONG OF SONGS 2:4

Jesus, I love this picture of you being my escort, my welcoming committee to a grand banquet hall. I want to feast on your goodness alongside those who love you. I need both those kinds of fellowship—intimate connection with you and easy communication with friends and family.

This invitation reminds me that you love me. The host of a feast doesn't often invite those he hates to his party. No, he invites those he wants to celebrate with—friends who are cherished and valued. Jesus, you call me your friend. You love me well. You give me new perspective over my situation. You open my eyes to the needs of those around me, demonstrating what love really looks like.

Because you've welcomed me, would you please make me into a person who welcomes others? Teach me the power of hospitality, where I invite new friends, and sometimes even strangers, to share a meal. May your banquet of love inform the way I reach out to others.

Would you bring to mind three people who need to know they're invited to the banquet? I'll write them down and pray for each one this week. And if I can swing it, I'll invite them over the threshold of my front door, into my home and life. All because I love you. Amen.

Love

Place me like a seal over your heart, like a seal on your arm. For love is as strong as death, its jealousy as enduring as the grave. Love flashes like fire, the brightest kind of flame. Many waters cannot quench love, nor can rivers drown it. If a man tried to buy love with all his wealth, his offer would be utterly scorned.

SONG OF SONGS 8:6-7

Jesus, thank you for placing me like a seal over your heart, on your arm. Your love is actually stronger than death and the grave; your love conquered both on the cross. You endured beyond the grave in order to show me the kind of love that brings pardon and forgiveness.

Your love is brighter than fire. No amount of water aimed at its flames will stop it. No one can stop your relentless burn. The rich young ruler couldn't buy this precious commodity, nor did he really want to. But oh, how I need it today.

Sometimes love seems so abstract, so unreal. But you demonstrated love. You embodied it, lived it. You stooped to dignify the broken. You found the outcasts and welcomed them home. You sought out the unsought, giving them a place in your kingdom. You died for all of us. Love nailed you to the cross, and love kept you there.

I want to love like that. Teach me what it means to sacrifice for those I love. Help me to forgive my enemies and pray for them today. Give me your vision for this world. Open my eyes to the needs of those around me, particularly the overlooked ones. I know that this dying world will know I follow you by the way I demonstrate love. Amen.

Rest

This is what the Sovereign LORD, the Holy One of Israel, says:
"Only in returning to me and resting in me will you be saved.
In quietness and confidence is your strength.
But you would have none of it. You said,
'No, we will get our help from Egypt.
They will give us swift horses for riding into battle.'
But the only swiftness you are going to see is the
swiftness of your enemies chasing you!"

ISAIAH 30:15-16

Jesus, forgive me for my restlessness. Oh, how I need your strength today, but like the Israelites, I often "have none of it." I'd rather help myself or rely on others than run to you for help. I wrongly think that swift horses (money, power, status, personal strength) will deliver me and bring victory.

But that is not your highest for me. It's substantially less. Anything I rely on other than you is shifting and unsteady. My strength comes in quietness, in those unseen places where I refuel with you. Help me be like you, Jesus, who broke away from the hustle and bustle of Palestine to find refuge in the mountains alone with your Father. Oh, how I need that. But I keep running on and on in my own strength.

Because of that, I don't have confidence. The things I trust in fail, and my strength fails along with them. But you are the Rock. You are my rest. You alone provide confidence—not in my own grit, but yours.

In my weariness, thank you for showing me again that every other avenue of help is lifeless. Only you bring genuine rest and life. Amen.

Claim

*I will say to the north and south, "Bring my sons and
daughters back to Israel from the distant corners of the
earth. Bring all who claim me as their God, for I have
made them for my glory. It was I who created them."*

ISAIAH 43:6-7

Jesus, you gathered the outcasts, the exiled, and the broken. You
did it during the deportation of Babylon, when the Israelites were without a country, a Temple, a livelihood. But inevitably, even though they
came back to Jerusalem joyfully weeping, they were still enslaved—by
their sin.

Your rescue mission meant you left heaven and came to earth, an
ambassador of your Father, in order to rescue all of humanity from sin.
Because of you, I am unshackled, set gloriously free.

Remind me today as I see people in my life that you also went to
the ends of the earth to bring all of us back to you. Everyone I see today
is made in your image, for your glory. You desperately and beautifully
love them, and your desire is to woo them back to yourself, away from
slavery and exile into sweet relationship.

May that view of others influence the way I pray today. I confess
I've often grown faint in my intercession for those who seem exiled
beyond reach. But you love them more than I can ever love them. So I
entrust them to you. Amen.

Alone

*This is what the L*ORD *says— your Redeemer and Creator:*
*"I am the L*ORD*, who made all things.*
I alone stretched out the heavens.
Who was with me when I made the earth?"

ISAIAH 44:24

Jesus, why do I sometimes live as if I made everything, or that every task is up to me? I go minutes, hours, and days without acknowledging you—caught up in my own little world. But I didn't make my world, my relationships, and my sphere. You did.

And if I lift my eyes above the reach of my own life, I realize again that you made every single thing I see. The butterfly outside my window. The smile that crosses a friend's face. The ocean, wild and endless. The stars ambling across the night sky. All of it can be traced back to your creation.

No one was with you when you spun this universe into existence. No one helped you form the earth from formlessness. No one gave you the formula for oxygen. The air you breathed into Adam's virgin lungs was yours alone, wholly created by you. The plants, the sky, the mountains—all fashioned by you and your wildly creative mind.

Help me pause today and revel in the truth of your creation. It astounds me. I cannot fathom your mind. And yet? You still love me. You still love this crazy world. Help me live in gratitude because of that, Lord. Amen.

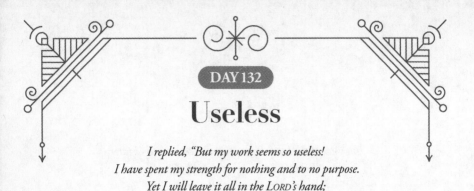

Useless

I replied, "But my work seems so useless!
I have spent my strength for nothing and to no purpose.
Yet I will leave it all in the LORD's hand;
I will trust God for my reward."

ISAIAH 49:4

Jesus, I will choose to trust you for my reward. Thank you that you see me, and you know how hard I've worked. Even when it seems like all my busy rushing ends in nothing, you take my small efforts and make them count in your kingdom. Nothing is ever wasted, that which is wrought in faith and prayer and dependence.

Remind me of the purpose you have for me so I don't lose heart. When the road seems long and I have blisters and I'm short of breath from the climb, strengthen me. Bring me to a higher place so I can look back with perspective and discern the why of it all. I do want to fulfill the purpose you have for me.

When I can't see the fruit of my labors and I'm teetering toward despair, please elevate my gaze to the heavens. Give me an eternal perspective. This life is not all there is, Jesus. And my works will follow me to the other realm. So please help me to live in light of eternity, for the praise of heaven, not the accolades of earth. Give me the gumption I need to persevere, and in the midst of it, would you provide a cup of joy?

I choose right now to trust you for the perfect reward you have for me. Amen.

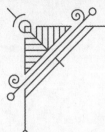

Say

I will say to the prisoners, "Come out in freedom,"
and to those in darkness, "Come into the light."

Isaiah 49:9

Jesus, sometimes I'm so enmeshed in my own life that I forget the freedom path you've wrought in me. I don't recall your faithfulness to me, or that you rescued me from great, great darkness. And yet, both these things are true: faithfulness and rescue. I pause today to count the ways you have been good to me.

In this forgetfulness, my eyes also dim to the needs around me. Forgive my dull vision to the hurts of this world. Open my eyes afresh to the pain around me, not to make me sad or overwhelmed, but for the sake of prayer and possible action.

When you walked the earth, you walked toward those who needed freedom and light. The world was and remains full of enslavement and darkness. So as your ambassador today, awaken me, enlighten me, hearken to me, and alert me to those who may need a touch of liberation and light.

Teach me the art of intercession. Give me boldness to approach the downtrodden. Make me a person of prayer in the moment, not just a disciple who casually utters, "I will pray for you." Please use my life to be a conduit of your goodness and blessing, so others can experience emancipation and rescue from the dark. Please reveal the needs of those around me, Jesus. I choose to obey your promptings as you send them my way. Amen.

Warm

Who among you fears the LORD and obeys his servant? If you are
walking in darkness, without a ray of light, trust in the LORD and
rely on your God. But watch out, you who live in your own light
and warm yourselves by your own fires. This is the reward you
will receive from me: You will soon fall down in great torment.

ISAIAH 50:10-11

Jesus, I have done this, and I am sorry. I've orchestrated my life around building dazzling fires of my own making, standing above them satisfied with a job well done, while the sparks fly heavenward. In that frenetic stick gathering and ignition, I happily forget you. And then I realize that the fire I built is achingly cold. It cannot warm my hands, let alone my heart. And I shiver.

But you, Lord, are the greatest fire I need. Deep within my bones, I need your life, your spark, your warmth. I cannot walk life's pathway without it. Oh, I try. I try like crazy. But it ends in rush and huffing and burnout.

Like Isaiah, I will run to your light. Help me to see it in this world of artificial light that mimics your warm radiance. I've satisfied myself with lesser light. The two words I want to typify me are Isaiah's: *trust, rely.*

Would you show me today where I'm not trusting in you? How I am relying on myself rather than you? It hurts to know the truth, Lord, but I open myself up for your inspection. And in the closing of this prayer, I choose again to trust and rely. Amen.

Remain

"For the mountains may move and the hills disappear,
but even then my faithful love for you will remain.
My covenant of blessing will never be broken,"
says the LORD, who has mercy on you.

ISAIAH 54:10

Jesus, these words were penned before you stepped your foot on the earth. Your eyes watched the mountains form. You've witnessed earthquakes and tumult. And even in that splendor and knowledge, you care for me. I don't know what to say except thank you. Thank you that you choose to love me, that your covenant ways are sure and assured.

Even though I fear. Even though I wander. Even though I shake. Even though I question. Even though I grieve.

Even though.

Your Word promises me that you will remain. And I am grateful. Help me become the kind of follower who remains—true to others, close to you, near to your heart. I want to be the remaining type, even when I'm faced with betrayal or indifference.

Thank you for the example you set throughout the ages. You remained true to Israel, even as they wandered and chased after other gods. You remained true to your Word when you rescued all of us from the shackles and weight of sin. You are faithful and kind and full of mercy. Thank you. Amen.

Womb

I knew you before I formed you in your mother's womb.
Before you were born I set you apart and appointed
you as my prophet to the nations.

JEREMIAH 1:5

Jesus, I know you said this about Jeremiah, and you had a very specific (and often painful) plan for him to step into. The life of a prophet was certainly not easy or profitable. And yet he kept prophesying, even while the nation around him hollered wrath and anger and closed their ears to his pleading words. So he needed to know that you set him apart for such a difficult task.

But it's also equally true that you have known all of humankind before we yelped our way into this world. Before I pulled in my first breath and heaved out a raucous cry, you knew me. You formed me in my mother's womb, safe and sound. Before I had a thought, you were thinking of me. It's too much. I cannot take it all in.

I pray two things because of this truth.

First: When life gets frustrating and I question the calling you have on my life, remind me that you set me apart in my mother's womb to do great things, to obey you, to follow you wherever you go.

Second: When people frustrate me, help me remember that you fashioned them in the womb. You love them too. Give me new vision for the people in my life. Amen.

Idols

I will be merciful only if you stop your evil thoughts and deeds and start treating each other with justice; only if you stop exploiting foreigners, orphans, and widows; only if you stop your murdering; and only if you stop harming yourselves by worshiping idols. Then I will let you stay in this land that I gave to your ancestors to keep forever.

JEREMIAH 7:5-7

Jesus, it's hard in today's culture to understand what idols are. Most of the people around me don't have shrines set up in their homes, nor do they venture to high places to sacrifice to pieces of metal or wood. Open my eyes to modern-day idols—chasing money, serving image, pursuing acclaim, or purchasing stuff.

I understand that serving an idol instead of serving you grieves your heart. You deserve all my affection and reverence. You deserve all my life. You deserve energetic worship all because you are the worthy one.

Yet I settle for other things that bring me comfort. I wrongly believe that more money will solve all my problems. I live in that land of "if only." If only that person would like me. If only I would finally reach that goal I've been pursuing. If only I could look a certain way or have certain things...then I would be happy.

My happiness should be solely tied in knowing you love me, you rescued me, and you bring me worth. Forgive me for the rabbit trails I run on to discover my worth in empty, fleeting ways.

So, Jesus, would you show me the idols in my life? The things I chase that are lesser than you? I want to chase you instead. I want to find value and peace in you alone. You are worth all my life, my affection, my allegiance. Amen.

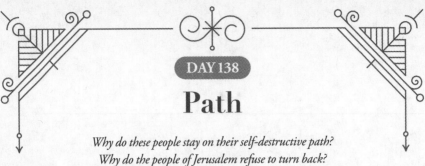

Path

Why do these people stay on their self-destructive path?
Why do the people of Jerusalem refuse to turn back?
They cling to their lies and will not turn around.

<small>JEREMIAH 8:5</small>

Jesus, first of all, I don't want this scripture to be about me today. As I look over yesterday and last week, I see how there have been times I've walked the wrong path through my choices. I haven't taken care of myself. I've battled self-centeredness. I've preferred my comfort to your will. Please forgive me for following that kind of path, preferring destruction to life.

Today I want to seek out the path of life where you walk. I want to hold your sacred and pierced hand, hear your voice, and experience your presence. Your Word promises that in your presence is fullness of joy, so I covet it, long for it, welcome it.

I want to be the follower who clings to truth, not lies. I want to be reversible, a person with the kind of heart that notices destruction and turns the other way, fleeing from temptation and sin.

As I pray this, I can't help but pray for those people in my life who seem to love the path of destruction. They are blind to your ways and truth, and they chase after things that break my heart and yours. Jesus, would you please take hold of them? Please don't let them tarry on the death path for too long. Rescue them. I know you love them far more than I do, so I entrust them to you. Amen.

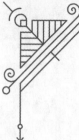

Boast

This is what the LORD says:
"Don't let the wise boast in their wisdom,
or the powerful boast in their power, or the rich boast in their riches.
But those who wish to boast should boast in this alone:
that they truly know me and understand that I am the LORD
who demonstrates unfailing love and who brings justice and
righteousness to the earth,
and that I delight in these things. I, the LORD, have spoken!"

JEREMIAH 9:23-24

Jesus, what does it mean to truly know you and understand that you are the Lord? Remind me what the word *lord* means—someone who rules and reigns and deserves utmost respect and allegiance. Instead of ruling and reigning in my own life, help me relinquish my control to you, the apt Lord of lords.

In light of who you are, it's strange that I would even think to boast about my wisdom because any wisdom I have is derived from you. Any riches I could boast about come from your generous hand. Everything I have overflows from your abundant gifts.

You demonstrate love. Your love is not simply word, but action. So please help me follow in your footsteps. I don't want to merely tell the people in my life that I love them; I want to demonstrate it. Show me tangible ways I can do that today.

You are a God of justice. You are utterly fair and judge correctly all day long. Because of that, help me to give you the slights and pains others have thrown my way today. Instead of acting as the judge and jury, I give it all to you. Amen.

Everywhere

"Am I a God who is only close at hand?" says the LORD.
"No, I am far away at the same time.
Can anyone hide from me in a secret place?
Am I not everywhere in all the heavens and earth?" says the LORD.

JEREMIAH 23:23-24

Jesus, this is a terrifying truth for those who are living secret, sinful lives. But it's the best news of all for those who long for your nearness. As I look back on my own life, I see my misery when I was trying desperately to cover everything, look like an acceptable citizen, while deceiving everyone—sometimes even myself. I'm grateful you chased me down and found me and offered me grace and truth.

You are everywhere, Lord. You are in every country of this earth. You see prejudice. You are aware of every act of terrorism. You understand the cries of the hungry. You feel the weight of the martyrs' cries. You sit on your throne, even as evil dictators steal their thrones and oppress thousands and millions of people.

Because you are everywhere, and because you have an unfathomable plan, remind me to look beyond my zip code to the cries of the oppressed everywhere. I confess that this completely overwhelms me, and there are days I want to turn off every piece of media I own and crawl into a quiet hole.

I want my heart to break, though, with the things that break your heart. Keep me aware without letting me dive into despair. Amen.

Covenant

*"This is the new covenant I will make with the people of Israel
after those days," says the L*ORD*. "I will put my instructions deep
within them, and I will write them on their hearts. I will be their
God, and they will be my people. And they will not need to teach
their neighbors, nor will they need to teach their relatives, saying,
'You should know the L*ORD*.' For everyone, from the least to the
greatest, will know me already," says the L*ORD*. "And I will forgive
their wickedness, and I will never again remember their sins."*

JEREMIAH 31:33-34

Jesus, you are the covenant-keeping God. All through the Old
Testament, you rescued your people, promising much and delivering
every bit of promise—even when your followers were fickle and ran
the other way. Thank you for your ardent faithfulness. I cannot fathom
that kind of loyal love.

You didn't leave humanity without hope. You promised in this verse
to do something entirely new—to give people new hearts that actually
want to obey you. I am the recipient of that amazing grace today, as the
Holy Spirit informs and enlivens my life. He is the answer to everyone's
prayer—a constant companion, a source of strength, and the unction
we all need to obey you.

Thank you for not leaving me here on this earth as an orphan, abandoned and unable to follow you. Thank you for sending your Spirit to
convict and comfort me.

Today, I want to respond to the Spirit. I want to pray for those
whom you prompt me to pray for. I want to do risky things where I'm
led. I want to see this life as an adventure in following you. Amen.

Ask

Ask me and I will tell you remarkable secrets
you do not know about things to come.

JEREMIAH 33:3

Jesus, throughout your time on earth, you reminded your followers to simply ask things of you. If I ask, I will receive. If I seek, I will find. But so many times, I give in to lethargy, wrongly believing that this is my lot in life and that I just need to slog my way through. I forget to ask. I forget your availability.

In the quiet place, you love to reveal your secrets. You show me what you love, what makes you smile, what brings you joy. You uncover darkness where I've conveniently tried to lock it behind big, heavy doors. You show me places where I can grow, and you encourage me where I've made progress. All this comes in the circle of relationship we experience together, and it hinges on the simple word *ask*.

So I ask you for help today.

Show me how to love that difficult person. Give me the guts to forgive. Reveal to me any hidden sin, and help me as I confess it. Help me to extend grace to someone who needs it. I need wisdom with my banking account, how to handle my finances. Please help me think wisely about my future, but not so much that I'm hindered by one pathway of thought. Give me the perspective I need today to live with open hands, willing to give, able to give up, hopeful through it all. Amen.

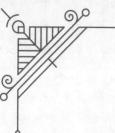

Afresh

Yet I still dare to hope when I remember this:
The faithful love of the LORD never ends!
His mercies never cease. Great is his faithfulness;
his mercies begin afresh each morning.

LAMENTATIONS 3:21-23

Jesus, why is it that I wrongly believe your love ends? That it runs out with my four-hundred-ninety-first sin? I somehow think I can exhaust your love, or that when you see me pleading for help, you think, *Oh no, not that person again.*

That's not who you are. You have an unending well of mercy and faithfulness, a supply that never runs out. Mine does run dry—often—which is why I do much better when I am connected to you, asking for your help in every area of my life.

Thank you for the gift of mourning and morning. My mourning and grief may happen for a night, but joy will return when the dawn comes. The sun reminds me of your constant faithfulness, even when I'm down or nursing faithlessness.

Teach me to remember this. Every day this week when I rise from sleep, don't let me stand up without declaring, "Your mercies begin afresh each morning." I want to live joyfully in light of that truth, carrying it around in my heart so I can give it to others. I want to live lightheartedly because of your love, and only you can perform that miracle. I trust you for it. Amen.

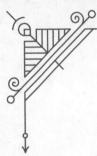

Inheritance

I say to myself, "The LORD is my inheritance;
therefore, I will hope in him!" The LORD is good
to those who depend on him,
to those who search for him. So it is good to wait
quietly for salvation from the LORD.

LAMENTATIONS 3:24-26

Jesus, teach me what it means to live in such a way that you're my inheritance. You have purchased my life with your blood. You have secured my eternal home. With you, I am the richest of followers, beautifully loved and wholly secure. I do not trust in things, but I wholeheartedly rely on your name and nature.

Reveal to me where I've misplaced my hope. Have I relied more on health, or have I given in to fear about my health? Have I taken stock of all my assets without first realizing all of it came via your sovereign hand? Have I connected all my joy to my personal success? Have I decided I'll hope if and when all my relationships are in order?

Or have I truly hoped in you? (I hope so.)

Teach me patience today. Teach me to wait quietly (not complainingly) for your rescue and salvation. Instead of rehearsing my fear, let me practice trusting in you. Instead of depending on myself, let me practice the art of depending on you. Amen.

Grief

*Though he brings grief, he also shows compassion
because of the greatness of his unfailing love.
For he does not enjoy hurting people
or causing them sorrow.*

LAMENTATIONS 3:32-33

Jesus, when grief knocks on my door, I confess I don't want to answer it. I would rather not welcome in heartache and pain from loss. Sometimes I feel like all my losses added up are too much of a mountain to climb. Help me remember that this life is not all there is, that I will experience ultimate joy after I've endured the grief on this earth.

But in the meantime, right now where I'm settled into grief, show me your compassion. Reveal how close you are. Remind me that you love me. Although it may feel like you enjoy inflicting pain on me (oh, how it feels like too much), your Word promises that you don't. In fact, my pain agonizes you.

Help me move a little bit beyond my own grief today by opening up my eyes to my neighbors, friends, and relatives who are battling this beast as well. Instead of solely lamenting my own pain, remind me of others' pain. Who can I pray for today? Who needs flowers or a card or a home-cooked meal? Who needs a reminder of your grace? I want to exchange my own pain for empathy for others.

You are a compassionate God. You do demonstrate unfailing love. Help me to represent your heart to others today. Amen.

Lawyer

Yes, you came when I called; you told me,
"Do not fear."
Lord, you have come to my defense; you have redeemed my life.

LAMENTATIONS 3:57-58

Jesus, you are my advocate, my lawyer. You have pled my case before the Father, and you have interceded where I could not. You became the sinless sacrifice on my behalf, satisfying the judgment.

It's too much; I cannot bear the thought of it—you hanging on the cross with my sin keeping you there. You carried the weight of every angry word, every sinful act done in secret, every regret, every broken relationship, every idolatrous chasing, all my fickle ways. Oh, how it must've heavied you.

It's hard for me to believe you love me that much, to suffer my consequences though you deserved none of them.

Let it be that I live loved today. That I believe in your continual and sacrificial love. That I remember what it cost you to bring me into right relationship with the Father. May I never count it cheap, but spend my life praising you for the cost.

I live redeemed right now. Bought back with the price of your blood and body. Set free by the stripes and the thorny crown. Oh dear, dear Jesus, thank you. Amen.

Responsive

I will give them singleness of heart
and put a new spirit within them.
I will take away their stony, stubborn heart
and give them a tender, responsive heart,
so they will obey my decrees and regulations.
Then they will truly be my people, and I will be their God.

EZEKIEL 11:19-20

Jesus, I'm so grateful for you, how beautifully you fulfilled your Word through Ezekiel. Because of you, because of your life, death, and resurrection, I now have a new spirit, the Holy Spirit, who enables me to live powerfully and with purpose. I am no longer alone, trying to fend for myself, desperate to make right choices but powerless to do so.

Would your Spirit quicken me to be responsive today? Show me relationships in which I need to repent or apologize. Reveal times where I've made myself the center of everything. Help me let go of all that control I so think I need. What commandments have I shied away from? When have I neglected to do something good? Are there people I've been unkind to?

Search me. Refresh my heart again. Give me a new vision for life, not only for today, but also for the rest of my days. I know I am your child, and you are my God. Help me live in light of that profound truth.

When I forget your goodness, Jesus, remind me again that you took my stony heart and gave me a brand-new one. Show me how far I've come—not to shame me, but to show me how you've worked in my life over the years. Amen.

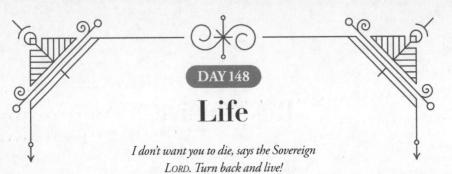

Life

I don't want you to die, says the Sovereign
LORD. Turn back and live!

EZEKIEL 18:32

Jesus, words from you bring life, but sometimes I've preferred to do my own thing, my own way. As I look back on my life, I see some pretty awful choices that didn't bode well carried to their logical conclusion. Thank you for rescuing me from myself, for showing me that a life lived solely for myself is a small one indeed.

Today I'm burdened by the people I know who are walking down a destructive path. Their choices have blinded them to you, Jesus, and they're running blindly toward pain and more bad choices. Their minds are darkened.

Jesus, I know you love my loved ones more than I can even imagine. Would you intervene in their lives today? Make the deepest pit seem deeper, so that they will finally reach heavenward toward your rescue. Make the sin they indulge in repulse them and make them sick. Make them deeply weary of their selfishness. Break through their pathway with light and hope. Please protect them from making permanent decisions that will alter the course of their lives—and not in good ways.

You've been so good to me. You've shown me the path of life. Please, please show it to those people I love who have wandered from your pathway too. Rescue the wayward. Bring hope to the hopeless, light to the darkened. I cannot intervene, though I've tried. But you can woo. You can powerfully intersect their lives. I entrust them to you. Amen.

Give

I will give you a new heart, and I will put a new spirit in you. I will take out your stony, stubborn heart and give you a tender, responsive heart. And I will put my Spirit in you so that you will follow my decrees and be careful to obey my regulations. And you will live in Israel, the land I gave your ancestors long ago. You will be my people, and I will be your God.

EZEKIEL 36:26-28

Jesus, you exemplify giving. Not only did you demonstrate a lifestyle of giving on this earth, but also you ultimately sacrificed everything for the sake of all of us. You have personally given me so much; let me count the ways.

You forgave my sins, and you continue to do so—past, present, and future sins. You made me clean from all the muck and mire sin soaked me in. You set my feet on a rock, making my footsteps firm. You rescued me from those who were too strong for me. You readied me for battle. You called me by name. You gave me a new heart, without blemish. You sought me like I was a lost lamb, and you welcomed me home. You healed my past. You set me free from the sin that so easily entangled me. You gave me a new vision for this world, and my heart now beats with your love. You restored relationships. You made a way so I could be in relationship with the Father who created me. You made sure I was never alone by giving me the indescribable gift of the Holy Spirit. I could go on and on and on, Jesus. Settle my soul today into this kind of gratitude. May it sustain me throughout the day and night. Amen.

Pour

I will never again turn my face from them,
for I will pour out my Spirit upon the people of Israel.
I, the Sovereign LORD, have spoken!

EZEKIEL 39:29

Jesus, as I pour my morning beverage or open up the tap to wash a dish, help me meditate on the word *pour*. To pour is to douse, to overwhelm, to fill to capacity and to overflowing. When I'm showering, water pours from the showerhead, completely drenching me, washing me and making me clean. This act of pouring cannot be undone. Once something is poured, you can't un-pour it.

This is how I want to view my life with your Spirit. Pour it all out. Drench me with your presence, your power, and the ability to discern the workings of this world. I need to be doused with you, surrounded by your goodness, enmeshed in your love. Your pouring will enable me to pour out to others. Because you have been so generous with me, I will be able to be wholly generous with the people in my life.

Teach me the lesson of pouring out—that as I do, others receive perspective and love. But I cannot pour what I don't yet have. Instead of burning out on the needs of others, pouring my finite self out constantly, bring me back to you so I can receive all I need first.

You are a wellspring of life. You give rest to the weary. You are grace and truth. I position myself under your spigot today. And drink deeply. Amen.

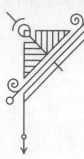

Praise

He said, "Praise the name of God forever and ever,
for he has all wisdom and power.
He controls the course of world events;
he removes kings and sets up other kings.
He gives wisdom to the wise
and knowledge to the scholars.
He reveals deep and mysterious things and
knows what lies hidden in darkness,
though he is surrounded by light."

DANIEL 2:20-22

Jesus, my view of you is too small. Please forgive me. You deserve all praise for who you are, what you know, how you've behaved in and toward this world. When I grow weary and frightened of the politics of this world, remind me of your sovereign hand. No one escapes your notice. Political systems rise and fall. Rulers rule with wrath. And yet you are above it all, in control.

You are wiser than the smartest guru, more loving than any spiritual guide, stronger than the mightiest army, more intelligent than all the geniuses put together, brighter than the most astounding light. You are greater than my worries, fears, and heartaches. You know all mysteries.

And yet, you open your arms to me, a child. It's like you're the president of an important country plus the greatest rock star, combined with the most selfless humanitarian—the famous one—and yet you welcome me to your table. I'm stunned. And I praise you. Amen.

Rules

This has been decreed by the messengers;
it is commanded by the holy ones,
so that everyone may know that the Most High
rules over the kingdoms of the world.
He gives them to anyone he chooses—even to the lowliest of people.

DANIEL 4:17

Jesus, you are not capricious, ruling willy-nilly. But neither are you predictable, aligning with the strong and mighty. When you were on this earth, you demonstrated that you gravitated toward the marginalized, the downtrodden, the overlooked. I'm so grateful for that because it gives me hope.

Give me that kind of lens for the world. Remind me today of your upside-down, topsy-turvy kingdom that honors the unseen, notices the broken, empowers the sidelined, and helps the helpless. I don't want to be a person who gravitates toward the popular. When I walk into a room of folks, Jesus, please keep me close to you—able to discern who needs to know your love.

In the same way, help me not to show favoritism to the popular ones, preferring them to the folks in the background. Help me be aware when I'm fawning over someone—it's not good for them anyway, and it puts way too much pressure on them. Instead, let me be fair-minded—able to get along with all different people. May it be that when I'm faced with a crowd, they see your face in my behavior.

Jesus, would you show me one person to encourage today who may feel downtrodden and unnoticed? Give me creative ways to love that person, ways that show them they're loved and valued. Amen.

Miraculous

I decree that everyone throughout my kingdom
should tremble with fear before the God of Daniel.
For he is the living God, and he will endure forever.
His kingdom will never be destroyed, and his rule will never end.
He rescues and saves his people;
he performs miraculous signs and wonders
in the heavens and on earth. He has rescued
Daniel from the power of the lions.

DANIEL 6:26-27

Jesus, remind me in this sometimes humdrum life that you are a God of miracles. When I read about you in the New Testament, I see healings, exorcisms, and demonstrations of power. You did none of that for your glory, but for your Father who sent you.

I confess that my heart has grown cold when I think of miracles. I forget that you are great, and you supersede even the laws of nature. In light of this, teach me to pray gutsy prayers, full of faith. You promise that you will hear and respond to my prayers, and that the effective prayer of a righteous person accomplishes much. You've modeled prayer by asking that the Father's will would be done on earth as it is in heaven (and in heaven everything is righted).

So today I bring you my most complicated, miracle-needing prayer request. Hold it in your hand. Remind me to believe in your bigness as I pray it. Please, if it be your will, inaugurate a miracle in my midst—in your timing and for your glory. Amen.

Confessed

I prayed to the LORD my God and confessed:
"O Lord, you are a great and awesome God!
You always fulfill your covenant and keep your promises of
unfailing love to those who love you and obey your commands."

DANIEL 9:4

Jesus, sometimes I believe confession is all about my downfalls, the ways I've failed throughout the day, and how much I need to learn as I move forward. It's like the saddest to-do list of my failure. But Daniel did something entirely different when he confessed. He didn't rehearse his shortcomings—he lauded your power!

So today I confess your greatness over my life. You are strong. You are a covenant-keeping God, never failing me, and always keeping your promises. You love me well—so much so that I can turn around and love the people in my world. You empower me, through the Holy Spirit, to obey you and follow you closely.

You have created everything I see. You are greater than my deepest worries, stronger than the heaviness of all my sin, deeper than my well of insecurities. You create beauty out of nothing, hope from hopelessness, courage from fear. Everyone is laid bare before you. No man can stop your ways. No act of war can thwart your purposes. No government can ruin your sovereign plan.

I confess all your traits to you, Lord. Amen.

Deeply

*"Don't be afraid," he said, "for you are very precious to God.
Peace! Be encouraged! Be strong!"*

DANIEL 10:19

Jesus, I want to understand what it means to be deeply loved by you. I have a hard time wrapping my heart around that truth. Why? Because my own experience and understanding of love is shallow compared to your long-suffering love. I cannot perceive a love like yours that pursues me even when I run the other way.

As I look back on my life, I see a consistent thread running through my narrative, and it's your deep love. When others have hurt me, sent me in a tailspin, you were there, picking up the pieces of my heart, empathizing with me. When I hurt myself through self-critical thoughts and sinning for a season, it was your kindness and love that wooed me back to your side. When I despaired, you pointed out hope.

Your Word via Daniel resonates with me today. I can be loved. I am your beloved. Because of that, I don't have to fear. The future will always be brightened by your presence in this life and the next. All my worries come when I forget that your love is deep (and wide and long and high). So today would you settle me into my new and accurate identity?

I need not give in to fear because I am deeply loved. Because of your deep love, I can be peaceful, strong, and courageous. Oh, let it be so, Lord Jesus. Amen.

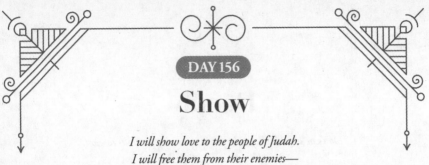

Show

I will show love to the people of Judah.
I will free them from their enemies—
not with weapons and armies or horses and charioteers,
but by my power as the LORD their God.

HOSEA 1:7

Jesus, you play holy show-and-tell every day I walk this earth (and every day before and after me). You show love to your people, your dearly loved children. You tell us, through your words and actions, that we are set free from enemies. You show and tell because you're powerful and strong, even when I'm small and weak, because you want me to know you're real and available. Thank you.

Would you show me where I've relied on other things in my life to get me through the days and weeks? Where have I trusted people more than I've trusted you? When have I wrongly believed that the solution to my problems is money? How have I trusted in my own stealth and ability without first going to you? What kind of wisdom have I harbored that is the opposite of your kingdom wisdom?

Lay me bare, Jesus. Expose those parts of me that show my lack of trust. I know that without faith it's impossible to please you, and that if I'm not rightly connected to you, I can do nothing significant in the kingdom of God. Root out my self-righteous and self-centered ways.

You are my God. I want to live my life in such a way that others would see this as clearly evident. Amen.

Wife

I will make you my wife forever,
showing you righteousness and justice,
unfailing love and compassion.
I will be faithful to you and make you mine, and
you will finally know me as the LORD.

HOSEA 2:19-20

Jesus, marriage is a profound mystery, and your words here to Hosea and the nation of Israel reflect that. You are the most faithful spouse, true to your Word, full of open-armed welcoming and forgiveness. I want to be like that. But so often I'm the opposite.

Instead of righteousness, I satisfy myself with what I want when I want it, setting aside holiness. Instead of letting you be the purveyor of justice, I hold grudges and secretly plot ways to get even, forsaking forgiveness and embracing bitterness to myself. Instead of unfailing love, my love fails to go the distance with difficult people. I lack compassion. Honestly, I can be fairly compassionate with myself (unless I'm yelling at myself), but it's hard for me to muster up compassion for those in my life who make the same mistakes over and over again. In terms of faithfulness, I fail in that arena too.

I am not like you. But I have your Spirit within me, hearkening me to be more like you as I love the friends and family in my life. I'm grateful for that. Thank you for demonstrating your very real love. Quicken me to share that kind of love with those who desperately need it today. Amen.

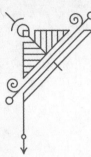

Raise

*At that time I will plant a crop of Israelites
and raise them for myself.
I will show love to those I called "Not loved."
And to those I called "Not my people,"
I will say, "Now you are my people."
And they will reply, "You are our God!"*

HOSEA 2:23

Jesus, for all those times I felt unloved, I rest in knowing you love me well. For all those times I felt like an outcast, I praise you, for you have called me to be your child. You are my God. You are the only one who has stuck by me all these years. I love tracing your faithfulness over my life.

Would you bring healing closure to some of the hauntings of the past? I have some stories that are yet unfinished, and I'm longing for new perspective. I know that on this side of eternity I won't understand everything about what happened, but would you open my eyes to your perspective today? Help me to view my past through the lens of your kingdom instead of viewing everything from a position of pain.

You are good. And you do good things. And you bring good out of bad, beauty from ashes, perfection from chaos. Please help me rest my past in your hands. Let me let you shoulder my story, no matter how heavy, because it weighs on my soul and shifts me toward bitterness.

I surrender me—the past me, the today me, the me I want to become—to you, the one who chose me and loves me. Amen.

More

I want you to show love, not offer sacrifices.
I want you to know me more than I want burnt offerings.

HOSEA 6:6

Jesus, I admit it is easier for me to ask you for a list of things to do to be a "good Christian" than it is to really press in to know you and your heart. Just give me the list, and I'll happily complete it independently of you. I want to offer my simple sacrifices without getting my heart involved.

And for a time, that kind of superficial living works. I can playact my way on this earth, fooling others, and feeling a wee bit proud of myself. But you are not fooled. You remind me that it's me you want, not my rote actions meant to check off a spiritual list. You couldn't care less about my religious activity, particularly when it's devoid of meaning.

Of course there's a place for devotion, but it must spring from my heart. So, Jesus, would you remake my heart today? Would you stir up my desire to know you? Remove the lethargy of my heart and replace it with a holy desire to know you, to press into discerning who you are apart from my vague interpretation of you.

I want to know you—the real you. Not the one preachers have told me about. Not the one my culture defines. Not the one who can be understood easily. Not even the one I've convinced myself is really you. I want to shed all that pretense and, instead, be in a place where you can dazzle me with who you really, really are. I wait in anticipation right now, dear Jesus. Amen.

Plant

I said, "Plant the good seeds of righteousness,
and you will harvest a crop of love.
Plow up the hard ground of your hearts,
for now is the time to seek the LORD,
that he may come and shower righteousness upon you."

HOSEA 10:12

Jesus, I don't want my heart to be hard. But I fear there are areas of it that are nearly rocklike. Please forgive me for settling for a relationship with you that's one-sided—me listing all my needs and wants like a Christmas list you need to fulfill. I tell you things, but I don't bother to listen. I shy away from anything that will make me examine what's really going on inside me. To be honest, I'm terrified of what I'll find in me if I stop long enough to look.

Remind me that my time on this earth is short. I don't have time to play these games of hide-and-seek (I hide; you seek.). Instead, I come out of hiding, unclothed and ashamed, longing for your covering and love. I want to seek you. And I desperately need you to cleanse me with the shower of your love.

No more pretense, Jesus. No more faking. No more hiding. I am done with all of that nonsense. I choose today to follow you wherever you will lead. I choose to be like the good farmer who plants seeds along the open, plowed soil. I now understand that I can't forge fruit or plants on my own initiative. You bring the increase. You show up. I'll simply ask that you be near. Amen.

Pity

Should I ransom them from the grave?
Should I redeem them from death?
O death, bring on your terrors! O grave, bring on your plagues!
For I will not take pity on them.

HOSEA 13:14

Jesus, I like un-messy devotional thoughts. I like scriptures that speak of your love and compassion, but I shy away from your justice. Oh, I want it for those who have exploited others, but I certainly don't want it for me. I know how sinful I can be. Forgive me for worshipping an incomplete you. Forgive me for wanting you to only be grace, but not hard-hitting truth. I know grace and truth were both realized in you, but I'm sorry to say, I rather prefer grace.

You are a God who judges rightly. You are holy. You are entirely different from me, from my nature. You always have the correct thought. Every action you take is righteous. You know all things. You can do all things. You are magnificently beautifully, stunningly breathtaking. You are light. In you there is no darkness or shifting shadow. You never change. You keep your promises. You are truth.

I pray today I would worship you as you are, not as I think you are or how the world wants you to be. You are holy. I am not. You are good. I struggle to be good consistently. You are creative and wild and the author of freedom. I sometimes chase things that enslave me. You are big. I am human. And I love you. Amen.

Shout

The Lord is at the head of the column. He leads them with a shout.
This is his mighty army, and they follow his orders.
The day of the Lord is an awesome, terrible thing.
Who can possibly survive?

Joel 2:11

Jesus, when I look around this world and absorb the difficult news of wars and rumors of wars, I retreat into myself and try not to think about it all. The end of the world seems like a topic I don't want to pursue or explore. But there will be an end of days. There will be a Day of the Lord. And because of that, I want to live in such a way that I'm ready.

Instead of burying my head in the sand, help me live alert. I want to be like a faithful farmhand who stewards the farm well in anticipation of the farmer's imminent arrival. I want to be like the virgin whose lamp is lit, full of oil, waiting for the bridegroom to pass. I want to be found faithful until I breathe my last or you come back, Jesus.

Jesus, help me to not give into fatalistic thinking—that since everything will end, I may as well hunker down and wait it out. Instead, let me be enmeshed in your kingdom, wholly aware of your desire that no one would perish, but many would come to know you. Ignite my missionary heart. Help me to see each day as a holy opportunity to spread your amazingly good news to a dying world.

I'm grateful you lead this world with intelligence and diligence. I'm also aware that there's a spiritual battle going on, and I need to stay close to you to embrace victory. Hold me close, Jesus. Amen.

Turn

That is why the LORD says, "Turn to me now, while there is time.
Give me your hearts. Come with fasting, weeping, and mourning.
Don't tear your clothing in your grief, but tear your hearts instead.
Return to the LORD your God, for he is merciful and compassionate,
slow to get angry and filled with unfailing love.
He is eager to relent and not punish."

JOEL 2:12-13

Jesus, in this world of "it's all about me," this message is a hard one to internalize and practice. Folks don't want to know about sacrifice and surrender. They want to hear about love and lives that work well. They want to hear about success stories and financial gains. They prefer pragmatic advice to calls to repent.

I don't want to live that way, lulled to sleep by my own desires. Instead I want to turn. In this moment, I realize time is flying by, speeding past me. It takes away opportunities to repent, if I let it. So I stop. I turn your way. I give you my heart.

Teach me what it means in my context to fast, weep, and mourn. What does fasting look like in the land of plenty? How does weeping accomplish your will? How can I have a godly sorrow that leads to my own repentance? So many want to arrange their lives to avoid having to admit they're wrong. I don't want to do that.

I want my heart to be honest and pliable in your hands. I repent of trying to run my life on my terms, for my glory, for my comfort. I want to return to you because your Word promises you are loving and kindhearted. Please forgive me for hurting your heart, and thank you for greeting me with mercy, not punishment. Amen.

All

I will pour out my Spirit upon all people.
Your sons and daughters will prophesy.
Your old men will dream dreams,
and your young men will see visions.
In those days I will pour out my Spirit
even on servants—men and women alike.

JOEL 2:28-29

Jesus, I love that you don't show favoritism. You pour your Spirit on all people—young, old, men, women, slave, free. Help me remember that today as I go about my work, as I encounter people. All of them are recipients of your grace, and all have the potential to experience your Spirit. May that inform the way I interact with your image bearers, Lord.

Jesus, I also need your pouring today. I cannot love the unlovely, forgive the frustrating, heal the broken, without your Spirit poured in and through me. You are my best thought, my best intention, and my best act of love. Keep me so close to you that I can't help but pour your love out to others.

I need power. I need a prophetic vision for my life and the lives of those around me. That we're not on this earth to punch a time clock or tick off to-do lists. We're not here to live, then die. We're here to make an impact for your kingdom, and you are the only one who gives us the ability to do that. Enlarge the way I dream about my own life, Jesus. Give me a refreshed vision today. Amen.

Shaped

For the LORD is the one who shaped the
mountains, stirs up the winds,
and reveals his thoughts to mankind.
He turns the light of dawn into darkness
and treads on the heights of the earth.
The LORD God of Heaven's Armies is his name!

AMOS 4:13

Jesus, wow.

I cannot fathom how you shaped the world I walk on. How you gathered mountains in your hands and formed them like cathedrals to the sky. When the wind whips around me, I am stunned because you created the forces that make it. When the sun sets, I'm reminded of how you set the earth in the perfect place to be habitable, and its orbit keeps us alive.

Right now, it feels like the sun won't rise. Yet my feelings of helplessness can never overpower the truth that you hold this universe in check. You are on the throne. You are the Lord God of Heaven's Armies. Like a benevolent ruler, you reveal your thoughts to your creation. You don't leave us helpless or in the dark. You communicate with us because of your great love.

Love and power—these are yours in abundance. Help me to rely on both. Your love because without it I'm insecure and lost. Your power because my strength often wanes because this world is a difficult place to live.

Jesus, I need you today. My family needs you. My circle of friends needs you. This crazy world needs you—you who spun it all into being and know best how to help us in times of bewilderment and need. Amen.

Turns

It is the LORD who created the stars,
the Pleiades and Orion.
He turns darkness into morning and day into night.
He draws up water from the oceans
and pours it down as rain on the land.
The LORD is his name!

AMOS 5:8

Jesus, you are a God who turns. You exchange my darkness for your light. You make sure the night sky has light in it so we don't despair or lose hope. You turn bodies of water into rain that refreshes a thirsty land. This is your name. This is your heritage. This is the way you interact with the world you created.

I need to remember this today. I need to remind myself that you are capable even when I feel incapable in my own life. You can turn my heart away from chasing what is shiny toward chasing after you. You can turn my affliction into praise and worship. You can alter my perspective, lifting my face, reminding me that I am not alone in my worries or sorrow.

I'm so grateful, Jesus, that you tabernacled on earth. You understand my frailty, my bent toward worry. You know what it's like to be betrayed and hunted and out of place. You know keenly that the human heart is fickle, turning this way and that.

And yet you never change. You empathize with my frailty, but your strength remains constant through it all. I cannot rely on myself. I certainly cannot trust my emotions to be the truth. But I can trust you, the one who turns hearts but doesn't change. Amen.

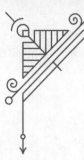

Pretense

*I hate all your show and pretense—the
hypocrisy of your religious festivals
and solemn assemblies.
I will not accept your burnt offerings and grain offerings.
I won't even notice all your choice peace offerings.
Away with your noisy hymns of praise!
I will not listen to the music of your harps.
Instead, I want to see a mighty flood of justice,
an endless river of righteous living.*

Amos 5:21-24

Jesus, I don't like pretense in others. And I certainly don't cherish it in myself. Please show me where I'm acting my way through life, pretending to follow you when it suits me, but secretly engineering my choices in my own strength. These verses remind me how distasteful acting and pretending are to you. Lip service does not satisfy you; instead, it hurts your heart because it's insincere, and it's lying.

I don't want to hurt you that way. I love you. Help me look realistically today at the way I micromanage my life without you. Show me where I'm being a functional atheist by my choices and my attitudes. I know that choices stem from what's already in my heart, so please root out those self-sufficient parts. Purify my heart so that my actions will make you smile.

Help me become an agent of your justice in this world. Show me where people need rescue or a listening ear. Rile me up at the things that make you cringe. Reveal corners of my everyday life where oppression reigns. By your strength, I will dirty my hands and trust in you. Amen.

Done

The day is near when I, the LORD, will judge all godless nations!
As you have done to Israel, so it will be done to you.
All your evil deeds will fall back on your own heads.

OBADIAH 15

Jesus, I know you've said that in the same way I've judged others, I will also be judged. What a cautionary tale! I've been a person of unclean lips, sometimes doling out judgmental statements without considering that there's a person on the other end of my judgment.

Open my eyes to the ways I have hurt and harmed others. I don't want to be like the Israelites, reaping what I've sown by my own sin. I don't want my evil deeds to come back to haunt me.

I rest right now in your saving grace, Jesus. Because of you, because you died on the cross for all my sin and evil deeds, I can stand here today completely clean, set free from the sin that so quickly ensnared me. While the Israelites had yet to experience this kind of substitutionary grace, I have the privilege of living and moving and breathing in the atmosphere of grace.

May your surprising, sweet grace inform the way I live my life—not in bitterness, caustic interactions, or finger-pointing, but in humility, kindness, patience, and grace. Your Spirit inside me enables me to live this way, full of joy and anticipation of what's next. I trust you to help me love well today. Amen.

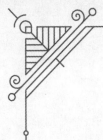

Rescued

*Those who have been rescued will go up
to Mount Zion in Jerusalem
to rule over the mountains of Edom.
And the LORD himself will be king!*

OBADIAH 21

Jesus, when I'm tempted to believe that a human being will solve my problems through political maneuvering and cleverness or power, remind me again that you are the King. Today I lift up my leaders—in my city, my geographic region, and my country. I pray they will become agents of justice and love. Bring great people into their lives who will enable them to lead with diligence and truth. Don't let deceivers whisper foul ideas into their ears. May integrity mark my leaders, and may they turn to you when they need wisdom and guidance.

This land is your land. Where I hang my hat is your space. You are concerned about what concerns me. And you are intimately connected in every area of my life, including the nation I live in. I trust you. I rely on you. I believe you are the genuine answer to every human problem.

Forgive me for thinking a political system or leader is my salvation. Forgive me for putting ultimate trust in people. Instead, Lord, I choose to believe that you run this universe beautifully. I may not always understand why there are corrupt political leaders, or why the oppressed continue to be oppressed, or why money seems to be at the root of all national sin, but I do understand that you love this world you made, and you are King of kings and Lord of lords. Amen.

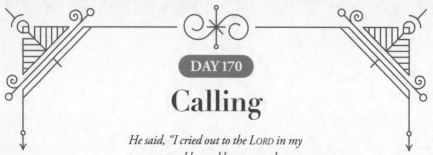

Calling

*He said, "I cried out to the L*ORD *in my*
great trouble, and he answered me.
*I called to you from the land of the dead, and L*ORD, *you heard me!"*

JONAH 2:2

Jesus, I relate to Jonah, how he heard your clear call to do what was right and ran (literally!) in the opposite direction. I do that too. Sometimes often. Yet you are so good to me. You hear me when I call out from bad situations—some of which I've ventured into willingly.

While I might not be in that place of great trouble today, I know people who are. So would you be gracious to my friends and family and loved ones who are scattering from you, who are closing their ears to your voice, who wrongly think they can pursue life without your help? Rescue them, Lord.

For those whose choices carry the ring of death, go after them. Lift them from pits too deep, wanderings too far, places too enticing. Remind them that you are not so far away that you can't rescue them. You hear their cries, however faint. You love them, no matter how far they've meandered. You love to come to the help of those who call upon you.

Bring life where there's been decay. Bring hope when hopelessness has threatened to overcome. Bring grace to rebellion, cleanness to shame. I trust you, Jesus, to interact beautifully with those I love today. Amen.

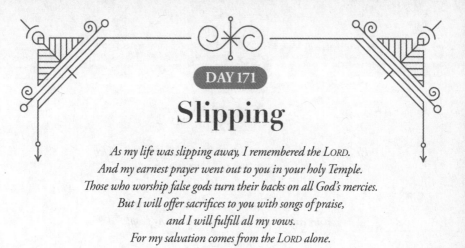

Slipping

As my life was slipping away, I remembered the LORD.
And my earnest prayer went out to you in your holy Temple.
Those who worship false gods turn their backs on all God's mercies.
But I will offer sacrifices to you with songs of praise,
and I will fulfill all my vows.
For my salvation comes from the LORD alone.

JONAH 2:7-9

Jesus, I give you my health. There are days I can see myself aging, and it scares me. I realize every day that I'm growing older, and my mind and body follow suit. I cannot control whether I get cancer or a bad knee or if I develop a sudden allergy that threatens my life. My health is in your hands. Help me to age gracefully, fully dependent on you for perspective and strength.

For those in my life who are facing health crises, I act like the friends of the paralyzed man who lowered him through a roof so you could heal him. Lord, I present them to you. Please hear their cries for help and healing. May your will be done on earth as it is in heaven in relation to their help. Give them eyes to see how they can glorify you beautifully through their suffering.

Whether it's them or me suffering, may we all learn the art of stepping aside, pulling away in order to praise you. Regardless of our situations, empower us to rejoice in you, thank you for all your work, and follow you wholeheartedly. You are the source of joy and health and life. And someday, when my body fades into eternity, and I see you face-to-face and gaze into your eyes, all will be well. I am grateful that you will one day wipe away every tear from our eyes. Amen.

Anger

*He complained to the LORD about it: "Didn't I say before I left
home that you would do this, LORD? That is why I ran away
to Tarshish! I knew that you are a merciful and compassionate
God, slow to get angry and filled with unfailing love.
You are eager to turn back from destroying people."*

JONAH 4:2

Jesus, if justice were up to me, I'm afraid it'd be a bloodbath. I would want revenge, not kindness. Justice, not mercy. I am prone to see people who don't agree with me as enemies, not friends. I don't pray for their welfare because I don't want to, even though you instructed me to pray for my enemies and those who persecute me. After all, you're the one who offered forgiveness for the very people who crucified you.

But you are a merciful God. You send rain on the just and the unjust. You spin this world on its axis for dictators and the downtrodden. I don't understand it all. I only see dimly. But I know you're good, and you love your children. Instead of seeing people as folks meant for wrath, instead let me view them through your lens of love. Next time I'm tempted to say or think something unbecoming, remind me that you absolutely love and created that person.

I am where I am today because you didn't give up on my story or me. You were not eager to let me be destroyed. Please help me return the favor by granting the same kind of grace to others today. Amen.

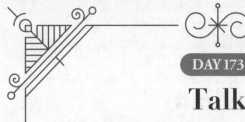

Talk

Should you talk that way, O family of Israel?
Will the LORD's Spirit have patience with such behavior?
If you would do what is right, you would find my words comforting.

MICAH 2:7

Jesus, today I give you my words. Would you remind me to be slow to speak, quick to listen? I want my speech to make you smile, build others up, and open doors to your love. But I fear there have been times when my mouth has not only gotten me into trouble, but has hurt others and your cause. Forgive me.

Help me be gentle in my words today. Remind me to talk to others in the way I'd prefer to be talked to. Let me give the benefit of the doubt. Instead of always assuming the worst, help me assume positive intent. Maybe I'm overreacting to others because there are still parts of my heart that need healing. If that's the case, would you please do more healing? Would you show me that you've got the tender places of my heart held in your care?

I've heard that hurt people hurt people. So uncover the raw places. Let me do the work needed so I don't continually hurt others by my words and my actions. I want to be soothed by you so I can be an agent of calm for others.

Comfort me today, Lord—especially in the places where I'm hurting from the sting of others' words. Renew my mind, and keep me close to you. Amen.

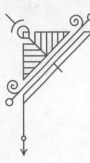

Mediate

The LORD will mediate between peoples and will
settle disputes between strong nations far away.
They will hammer their swords into plowshares
and their spears into pruning hooks.
Nation will no longer fight against
nation, nor train for war anymore.

MICAH 4:3

Jesus, I'm so grateful you are the great mediator between my Father and me. You stood in the gap between my sin and a holy God, enabling me to draw near because of your sacrifice on the cross. Eventually this world will wholly reflect that reign and rule, but for now, help me become a person of peace in this world.

I'd love to become a voice of reason amid all the shouting of opinions. So little negotiation and mediation happen because we'd rather vent our opinion than sit quietly and dignify someone else's opinion. Oh, let me become more diplomatic.

I'm grateful that wars will eventually cease. They plague this world right now, and I scarcely know how to deal with the atrocities that arise in the aftermath. In my home, my neighborhood, my community, I'd love to become a person of peace. And remind me to stay on my knees for the welfare of nations and the people they represent. Forgive me for forgetting to pray about these huge issues. Thank you that you're bigger than these conflicts, and you know them more intricately than I do.

To bring this down to my level, Lord—because that's where I live—teach me to love those who you send my way. Grant me a quickness to listen rather than explain. Help me to serve rather than demand my rights. Amen.

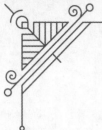

Behalf

But you, O Bethlehem Ephrathah,
are only a small village among all the people of Judah.
Yet a ruler of Israel, whose origins are in the distant past,
will come from you on my behalf.

MICAH 5:2

Jesus, "O Little Town of Bethlehem" is true: It's small. Unnoticed. Overlooked. And yet from that little village you changed the world! It reminds me that little is much in your big hands, and that I don't need to fret about feeling small. In fact, my smallness is a great place to rest because it opens the door to your bigness.

I love that you came on behalf of God your Father, sent like a pristine and joyful messenger to bring good news and glad tidings. On his behalf, you showed us what was in his great heart—compassion, mercy, beauty unmeasured. Because of what you did on his "behalf," God is no longer abstract and distant—he is gloriously near.

Jesus, I don't want my own obscurity to obscure your majesty. I'm grateful that it can't. But sometimes that feeling of being unnoticed shortchanges my faith as well as my dreams. I think small. I don't dream big dreams because my own limitations limit my vision.

Remind me today that you can enlarge my influence (not for my sake, but for yours) regardless of how I feel. You do great work, beautiful work, through those who are surrendered to you. Amen.

Confidently

*As for me, I look to the L*ORD *for help.*
I wait confidently for God to save me, and
my God will certainly hear me.

MICAH 7:7

Jesus, when I look around at my heart and actions, my confidence sometimes tanks. I consider myself as less than, and I shake in my boots, afraid to take the next step of faith you beckon me to. Like Micah, I want to confidently approach you. And as I do, I know you will imbue a new level of strong confidence in me. For that, I'm grateful.

There are so many shiny things that distract me when I'm hurting, so you tend to take the backseat when I need help. Forgive me for looking to money for help. I'm sorry I've first turned to friends before I consulted with you. There have been several times I've chased security instead of following you.

No more.

I need help, Jesus. I need esteem. I need to know I'm worthy, and that I'm endowed with worth. I need your guidance and wisdom every single day. Forgive me for living as if you're a tiny appendage. In actuality, you're my heart, my reason, my Savior. As I live and move and have my being today, show me where you are. Keep my ears tuned toward your voice. Open my eyes to your activity in my life. Help me slow down enough to experience you in the mundane.

I love that when I crane my neck toward you, you are certain to hear me. It may not be because of my ability that confidence comes. No, it erupts from my times of fellowship with you. Amen.

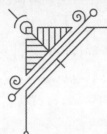

Close

The LORD is good, a strong refuge when trouble comes.
He is close to those who trust in him.

NAHUM 1:7

Jesus, you are good. Goodness is how you conducted yourself on earth, and this unusual quality informs the way you've loved me—in so many ways. Thank you. I could spend hours recounting your goodness to me. Right now I'll simply thank you for a body that can dance and sing (however limited and off tune that might be), and I'll thank you for all the relationships you've sent my way over the past few years.

Trouble often knocks at the door of my life. Instead of fleeing in frustration or hollering in fear, teach me to acknowledge it without freaking out. Instead, I want my first reaction to be to hasten to you the moment trouble interrupts me.

And when I look back on my life, it's during these tumultuous times of trouble that I experienced your goodness and your very real presence. Thank you for that. Thank you that you are the kind of friend who sticks by when I laugh like crazy or cry like crazy. You are steadfast and honest and so very available.

I run into your arms today, my dear, dear Shelter. And even when I'm the troublemaker and I cry out to you in repentance, you sit with me and set me back on my feet. Amen.

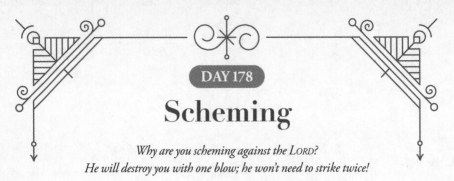

Scheming

Why are you scheming against the LORD?
He will destroy you with one blow; he won't need to strike twice!

NAHUM 1:9

Jesus, oh that word *scheming*. I'm guilty of it. I have tried to create my own heaven on earth by masterminding the best ways to live, orchestrating relationships (it didn't work out so well), and determining that I would only be happy if my shortsighted expectations were met. When I take the reins of my life, I steer away from you. And you're left on the outside of me, watching me make a mess of things.

I'm tired of all the effort it takes to fashion my life a certain way. It's worn me clear out. My soul is tired, my heart too. I've spent so much time on self-improvement that I've lost my connection to you—the only one who can improve my heart. I miss you, Lord. I miss our times together, dreaming. I miss connecting with you about every care, sharing my heart, releasing my burdens. Scheming has stolen my joy.

Restore that joy to me today. I don't want to work against you. I don't want to live independently. Instead, I long for dependence. Trust. Faith. I want to be someone who follows close to you, anticipating your direction and care.

As I look back over my life, I've seen many crashes, and most have come by my own hand, by relying on scheming rather than your sweet sovereignty and help. Today is a new day. I give up my schemes for your story, Jesus. Amen.

Chains

This is what the LORD says: "Though the Assyrians have many allies,
they will be destroyed and disappear.
O my people, I have punished you before,
but I will not punish you again.
Now I will break the yoke of bondage from your neck
and tear off the chains of Assyrian oppression."

NAHUM 1:12-13

Jesus, I need this. I'm sure there are still chain remnants holding me back from genuine freedom. I'm sure I'm carrying around yokes of bondage that hinder my joy. Would you show me them? Would you deliver me?

The thing is, the chains and yokes have become terribly familiar to me, like companions I nurture instead of anomalies I should shun. They are my normal. And so without even knowing it, I walk around shackled, and I can't even see where they're cutting into my soul anymore.

Would you send a good friend, a wise person who sees chains more easily than I do, who can reveal where I need new freedom? Someone who can gently guide me toward health and a new way of living? Because living tethered to the past, haunted by it, is not a victorious way to live. I need emancipation.

But honestly? That scares me. I like my normal. It's how I've navigated life for so long; it's like a comfortable blanket. Help me to see it for what it is: a hindrance to growth. Please set me free today, Jesus. Amen.

Crooked

Look at the proud! They trust in themselves, and their lives are crooked. But the righteous will live by their faithfulness to God.

Habakkuk 2:4

Jesus, the road is narrow that leads to you. And few are those who find it. I know that without you, I will default to trusting in my own means. Left to my own devices, I would lead a crooked life, with misplaced faith in myself instead of in you. I cannot be right with you on my own. I desperately need you.

Teach me today what it means to be faithful to you. I'm worn thin from fickle living, dashing here and there, wanting to be filled by the latest and greatest thing. In this gold-plated world, I run to shiny but neglect you, the Creator of all things.

What does it mean to live by my faithfulness to you? Give me faith like Abraham, who believed you could make a nation from a barren womb. Help me trust you as Gideon did, who by your strength delivered the nation of Israel. May I become like Esther, faithful to you in crooked times. I'm often like Peter, making ardent declarations of my love for you one minute, then forgetting you altogether the next.

But your Spirit lives within me. I'm so grateful. He will show me the un-crooked path. He will lead me beside still, quiet waters when I'm overwhelmed. He will comfort me, and more than that, he will enable me to faithfully pursue you today. Amen.

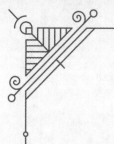

Silent

The LORD is in his holy Temple.
Let all the earth be silent before him.

HABAKKUK 2:20

Jesus, before you came to earth, your presence manifested itself in the Temple. You visited your people via an edifice. And in that holy place, the people of God trembled, silent and still. Because you were and are utterly holy, deserving of respect, honor, and glory. Forgive me when I forget how amazing you are, when I treat you like a good buddy or a distant deity. Neither is true. You are far more than both.

But now, I am the temple of God. I house you. You no longer dwell in stone, wood, and gold structures—I am the structure. It's humbling and entirely unexpected. How can I host God? And yet your Spirit dwells magnificently within me. Just as the Israelites fell silent in your presence, may I not forget a similar reverence.

I know my interaction with you has been quite vocal on my part. I've listed sins I've cherished, asking for forgiveness—quite a necessary penitence. I've let you know about all the relationships I fret about. In case you might forget, I remind you of my money worries, my career stress, and my worries over how I look. You've heard it all—this jabbering on my part.

Today? Teach me the discipline of silence. After I pray this prayer, seal my lips, and open my ears. I want to think about your power and majesty in utter silence. Fill me with awe and an upturned face and heart. Amen.

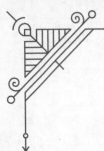

Need

I have heard all about you, LORD.
I am filled with awe by your amazing works.
In this time of our deep need,
help us again as you did in years gone by.
And in your anger, remember your mercy.

HABAKKUK 3:2

Jesus, you are famous. Your Word reveals that renown by your mighty acts, benevolence, and holiness. As I look back over my journey, I see all those traits traced through my story. You have acted on my behalf. You have given me more than I could think of asking for. You have taught me how to live.

I come to you as Habakkuk did, with deep need. Something's meandering around in my heart—an unsettledness I can't seem to shake. I'm not sure why, but you who created my heart know exactly the reason for this unease. Would you work in and through me to help me heal? Help me to see my current situation and needs from the perspective of your kingdom and not my own?

Sometimes my need grows teeth, and I feel its bite so keenly I can't concentrate on other things. I am distracted by pain, Jesus. Overwhelmed by it. I need your mercy to intersect my depressive thoughts. I need your hand to settle upon my heart, bringing calm to the fear that lurks there. I'm choosing to believe today that my deep pain cannot compare to your deep love. Overcome the doubts and despair I am carrying, and set me free to experience your mercy in new ways. Amen.

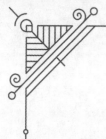

Lowly

Those who are left will be the lowly and humble,
for it is they who trust in the name of the LORD.

ZEPHANIAH 3:12

Jesus, you are not looking for the put-together, splashy folks whose social networking sites display a pristine, hip life. You're not seeking the trendy, the popular, or the rich. Your Word says that you know the proud from far away. No, as evidenced by your life on earth, you seek out the lowly and humble—those who know their lot and desperately need you.

Even though I know the world doesn't praise lowly and humble, oh, dear Jesus, I want to live that way. Lowly enough to realize I'm no better than anyone else, and that I'm often captured by sin and selfishness. Humble enough to admit I have needs, realizing that I don't have it all together anymore.

You are God. I am not.

Teach me what it means to trust in your name and character. I want to live fully present with you, asking for your strength especially when I feel lowly and humble. I trust that you see me. I trust that you are good. I trust that you will come near to me when I cry out for you. I trust you will bring new, joyful outcomes from my weeping. I trust your hand, your direction, and your guidance.

I humble myself under your mighty hand that I might be exalted in your perfect timing. I choose to stay in the smallest, lowest place, taking the last seat at the table all for your glory. In that place, pour your love into me. Amen.

Gladness

The LORD your God is living among you. He is a mighty savior.
He will take delight in you with gladness. With his love,
he will calm all your fears.
He will rejoice over you with joyful songs.

ZEPHANIAH 3:17

Jesus, it's on days like today that it's hard for me to believe you delight in me. I'm broken. I am hurting. I worry far too much. And yet your Word says you take delight in me—and not only that, but it tells the manner in which you delight: with gladness. You want to delight in me. You are glad to. It brings you pleasure. That's overwhelming in the best possible way. Thank you for loving me that way. I scarce can take it in.

I give you my fears today—money fears, worries about family members, health scares, broken relationships, work difficulties, hurting friends. Please take all of it and bring calm to my peace-less heart. As a lake eventually calms after a storm, reintroduce peace to my soul. Oh, how I need it.

I love that you sing. Help me to strain to hear your voice from heaven, singing songs of great joy over me. Just as good parents sing songs over their children, you croon melodies over me. Why? Why do you do this? You are so good to me. I pray your goodness will overwhelm me today—so much so that I can turn around and begin to sing my worries away.

You truly are a mighty Savior. You are full of love and truth. You come to the aid of those who call on you. As your child, I settle into your kindness today. Amen.

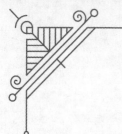

Afraid

My Spirit remains among you, just as I
promised when you came out of Egypt.
So do not be afraid.

HAGGAI 2:5

Jesus, I love that you keep your promises. When you comforted the disciples before your death, you promised them you'd be with them always, and you hinted at your Spirit that would fill them to overflowing. More than simply remaining with us, you, through the Spirit, indwell us.

Therefore, I am never alone. While there are times when I feel abandoned or give in to my fear and worry, the truth is you will never leave me, and you'll never forsake me. You are with me always, closer than my breath, bigger than my doubts. Infuse my life today with your presence. Remind me of your very real promises and your constant companionship. I need both.

It's amazing to me how many times your Word talks about fear being the opposite of trust and faith. I know that without faith, it's impossible to please you. I know fear means I'm not trusting you with everything. So right now, I am grabbing a piece of paper and a pen, and I'm writing down all my fears today. As I write them, may my heart lighten because you are taking them away from me. I am safe in your presence, and I rest in your care. Amen.

Shake

For this is what the LORD of Heaven's Armies says: In just a little while I will again shake the heavens and the earth, the oceans and the dry land. I will shake all the nations, and the treasures of all the nations will be brought to this Temple. I will fill this place with glory, says the LORD of Heaven's Armies. The silver is mine, and the gold is mine, says the LORD of Heaven's Armies. The future glory of this Temple will be greater than its past glory, says the LORD of Heaven's Armies. And in this place I will bring peace. I, the LORD of Heaven's Armies, have spoken!

HAGGAI 2:6-9

Jesus, my world feels off-kilter and shaking today. Stress has earth-quaked me, leaving me unsteady and needy. But you are greater than the shaking, and although the world will hold tribulations aplenty for me, you are able to hold me tight through it all.

Thank you that in you there is no variation or shifting shadow. You can be trusted. You are reliable. You are available. And for all those things and many other reasons, I cling to you.

Help me rest in knowing everything is all within your control. The earth and all it contains—you made it all. You own the cattle on a thousand hills, and you are able to feed, clothe, and house me. Help me remember the birds of the air and the flowers of the field when financial instability threatens to steal my joy.

Replace my turmoil with peace. Substitute my worry for a warrior's heart. Replenish my faith, giving me the guts to trust you through lean times. Amen.

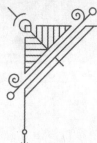

Armies

Therefore, say to the people, "This is what the LORD
of Heaven's Armies says: Return to me, and I will
return to you, says the LORD of Heaven's Armies."

ZECHARIAH 1:3

Jesus, I confess that I forget you are the commander of a vast army. No one is equal to your strength—not even the enemy of my soul, Satan. You are stronger than the evil that pervades this world. And you are victorious even now.

I know my own personal battle today isn't against people who hurt me; it's against the principalities and powers of darkness that rule this world. I know Satan is not your equal, but he still exists and loves to steal, kill, and destroy this world.

Encamp around me, Lord Jesus. Fight on my behalf. Stir your angels to protect my family—and me particularly as I face a battle I can't seem to see or understand. Open my eyes to the battle all around. May I not be frightened into inactivity, but may the very real presence of evil compel me to get on my knees and pray for deliverance.

I choose to speak truth where lies prevail. I choose to love my enemies and pray for those who persecute me. I choose to forgive those who have wronged me. I choose to turn my back on my sinful bent. I repent of my sins. These are all things I can do.

But you, O Lord, are a shield about me. You're my glory, the lifter of my head, just as the psalmist prayed. You protect me. You battle on my behalf. You are my defender, my strength, and my very real help in times of trouble. Oh, Lord of Heaven's Armies, I need your presence today in the midst of the battle I face. Amen.

Rebuilt

*This is what the LORD says: "I have returned to show
mercy to Jerusalem. My Temple will be rebuilt, says
the LORD of Heaven's Armies, and measurements will
be taken for the reconstruction of Jerusalem."*

ZECHARIAH 1:16

Jesus, the devastation of leaving their homeland, then returning to a Jerusalem in utter ruins must've been painful for the exiled Israelites. But you enabled them to rebuild. You sent leaders to help them, and you brought peace on every side. You empowered them to rebuild their lives.

That's what I pray for myself today. I need rebuilding. There are places in my heart that have grown cold toward you. I've been lukewarm in my fervor in serving you. I've let my soul fall into disrepair. And as I survey the damage of my own neglect, I am ashamed.

Thank you for not scolding me about where I am. You are like the father who welcomes the prodigal back, arms open, robe given, signet ring offered. I'm so grateful you don't let me wallow in what I deserve. You don't allow me to live saddened amid the ruins. Like the carpenter that you are, you help me rebuild.

I marvel over your mercy, Jesus. Because of your great rebuilding of my life, help me become someone like you—a merciful person who doesn't scorn people for walking away, but welcomes, then rebuilds them. Fixing folks is hard, but you do so with joy. Amen.

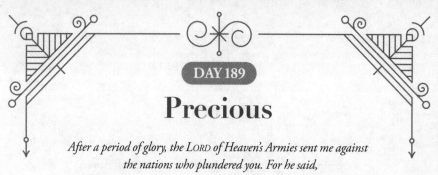

Precious

After a period of glory, the LORD of Heaven's Armies sent me against the nations who plundered you. For he said, "Anyone who harms you harms my most precious possession."

ZECHARIAH 2:8

Jesus, it's hard for me to understand the word *precious* when it comes to me. I live in my mind. I'm completely aware of my shortcomings. In fact, I rehearse my sin over and over again at day's end, berating myself for continuing to fall short. How can I be precious to you? How can I be valuable in your kingdom?

I feel insignificant and useless. And yet, you feel hurt when others hurt me. Why? Because I am loved by you, and I'm important to you. This baffles my mind.

I want to live in light of being precious. Tear down the half-truths and outright lies I've believed about my worth. Silence the words spoken over me in childhood, as a teen, and even into my adult years. Help me sift through what is true and what to discard. I have failed in believing your love for me. Instead, I have nurtured my own words of hatred toward myself.

I want to learn how to treat myself like I treat my closest friend. How do I do that? How can I learn compassion for myself? I know there's something to loving others as I love myself, but I have a hard time putting into practice the second part. Jesus, teach me today that I am precious to you. Amen.

Force

This is what the LORD says to Zerubbabel: It is not by force nor by strength, but by my Spirit, says the LORD of Heaven's Armies.

ZECHARIAH 4:6

Jesus, I forget this truth often. I think it's all up to me to live this life of love. But life for you is all about relying on the Spirit for all things. This means I need to learn to take my hands off my messes and instead hand them over to you for safekeeping.

For my relationships that are hurting today, may your Spirit infuse my responses and my prayers on their behalf. For my health, I ask your Spirit to give me strength when I'm worn out. For my job situation that has its ups and downs, I pray your Spirit would enable me to work hard, for your glory. For my financial worries, would your Spirit bring deep peace—a peace that's less dependent on the sum in my wallet and wholly dependent on your supernatural provision?

For my dreams and hopes, may your Spirit show me clearly what the next steps are. Where should I step out in faith, and when should I hold back and be patient? Teach me to rely on the unction of your Spirit. I want to obey even when it seems silly or counterintuitive. I want to follow you wherever you lead. Please lead with peace. I need your wisdom and counsel today, and I trust that you won't leave me resource-less.

Intercede for those I love today. Show me where I can be part of the solution for the trouble in their lives. How can I tangibly help them? Empower me to love well, listen attentively, and serve with power. Amen.

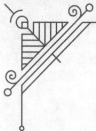

Mercy

This is what the LORD of Heaven's Armies says:
Judge fairly, and show mercy and kindness to one another.
Do not oppress widows, orphans, foreigners, and the poor.
And do not scheme against each other.

ZECHARIAH 7:9-10

Jesus, I am amazed when I ponder you as the Lord of Heaven's Armies. All those angels under your powerful authority! I want to picture that, and, as I do, rest from worrying about all the battles in my life. Thank you for fighting for me. Help me to see my enemies as miniscule compared to your vast greatness.

In light of all you do, I want to be like you in this world. Give me the ability to judge fairly, as the scripture says, and not jump to conclusions. I want to give others the benefit of the doubt before rushing to judgment.

Teach me what it really means to have mercy on others, even those who I perceive as enemies. Thank you for showing mercy to so many when you walked this earth, and please give me your eyes to see those who desperately need kindness. I choose to recall other acts of kindness toward me as an example to be outrageously kind and generous, particularly to those who suffer.

Enlarge my view of the world. Expand it to include widows, orphans, and the poor. Sometimes it's overwhelming to think of how I can help because I'm just one small person and the needs loom like skyscrapers, but I trust you will lead me to the ministries you want me to pray for and support. Amen.

Render

But this is what you must do: Tell the truth to each other. Render
verdicts in your courts that are just and that lead to peace. Don't
scheme against each other. Stop your love of telling lies that you
swear are the truth. I hate all these things, says the LORD.

ZECHARIAH 8:16-17

Jesus, to be honest, it's easier for me to live passive aggressively than
to tell the truth. I'd rather avoid conflict than produce it. Fear has held
me back. I so want to be liked and applauded, but you would rather I
be truthful no matter what the outcome. Teach me what it means to
live a life of integrity, where my insides match my outsides. (This means
I am living in truth.)

I also want to learn how to speak the truth with love, not disdain.
When I have to render an opinion in the midst of a complicated situation, enable me to see the other person as affectionately loved by you.
It'll help me temper my words. And in the midst of truth telling, keep
me close to you, willing to listen, able to ask clarifying questions. I
don't want to merely hand out my wisdom, but I want to participate
in helping others find your wisdom. I can't do that when I'm completely one-sided.

Instead of fretting about someone and sharing my worry with
someone else, I want to be honest and forthright instead. Give me the
guts I need to speak the truth directly with the person I'm involved
with, keeping it to a circle of two. When gossip comes my way, help
me redirect the conversation in an edifying way.

Please, too, show me where I'm telling or living lies. I want to be a
person of truth. Amen.

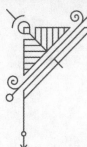

Nations

*"But my name is honored by people of other
nations from morning till night.
All around the world they offer sweet incense and pure
offerings in honor of my name. For my name is great
among the nations," says the LORD of Heaven's Armies.*

MALACHI 1:11

Jesus, in the midst of my own culture and the bustle of my daily life, I forget that you're the God of the whole world. You are loved in every culture. At the end of the age, your Word promises that every knee will bow and every tongue confess that you are Lord—all for God's glory. People from every tribe and tongue will praise you.

Open my mind to your greatness throughout the whole world. Help me remember to pray for my persecuted brothers and sisters who are losing their lives and livelihoods because they follow you. Open my eyes to the needs directly around me, yet expand my concern to the four corners of the earth.

Show me if I'm supposed to travel to new places and share you with others. Broaden my horizons. Help me see the Internet as a place to expand your message and interact with other believers in different locales. Keep me humble and teachable as I learn about other cultures.

Your body expands beyond my borders. Your praise is currently being sung in nearly every language. Oh, how you love your church. Teach me to see beyond the four walls of my congregation to embrace the global body of Christ. Amen.

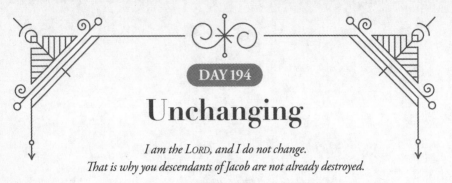

Unchanging

I am the LORD, and I do not change.
That is why you descendants of Jacob are not already destroyed.

MALACHI 3:6

Jesus, in a world of chaos and constant change, where progress marches forward at breakneck speed, you are my unchanging Lord. You are also compassionate, and even while I was a sinner, you chose to die for me and for your church. Instead of destroying us, you delivered us. And for that I'm grateful.

Life has gotten too hectic. I feel harassed by tasks, overwhelmed by the pace of my life. Every time I turn around, there's something else I need to do or learn or relearn. It's exhausting. I don't value rest; instead, I forge ahead, neglecting my health and burning out. I know this can't be your will for me, but I can't seem to jump off this treadmill. Help me.

When everything whirls around me, you are my changeless one—the anchor who holds me in the tempest that rages. You are honest and true. You speak words of life over me amid my chaos. And still, I tend to prefer the noise of my breakneck life to the quiet of your counsel. Settle me down, Lord. Help me slow my pace enough to really hear from you. I need your perspective.

There is more to life than running ragged. Reorient my heart. May my choices reflect the fact that you are in control, not me. Amen.

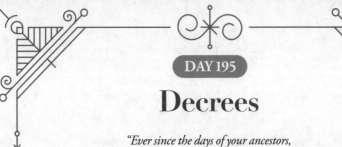

Decrees

"Ever since the days of your ancestors,
you have scorned my decrees and failed to obey them.
Now return to me, and I will return to you,"
says the LORD of Heaven's Armies.

MALACHI 3:7

Jesus, I don't want to scorn your decrees. Remind me, through Psalm 119, just how beautiful your laws are. They are meant for my good. Like a strong and faithful parent, you created parameters for us all, so we would live with wisdom and intention. You did not create laws to stifle my creativity. You enacted decrees for my own good.

But my heart likes to rebel against your highest will. I'd rather slip into sin than wholeheartedly pursue you. I'm grateful you haven't left me alone in my battle to obey you. Your Spirit, alive in me, reminds me when I'm veering off the straight and narrow path and gives me the power to obey you. I'm so grateful.

I understand that when I obey you, I'm showing you how much I love you. That's what I long for you to know, Jesus—that I love you and want to honor you with the way I live my life. Thank you for loving me enough to show me the path of life. As I walk it, I have peace and joy.

Make the way of destruction a stressful, peace-less pathway. Lead me by your Spirit. Oh, how I love you. Amen.

Leaping

*For you who fear my name, the Sun of Righteousness
will rise with healing in his wings. And you will go
free, leaping with joy like calves let out to pasture.*

MALACHI 4:2

Jesus, when I read about fearing your name, I wonder if I really know what that means. I fear what others think of my name. I'm often dedicated to how other people see me. So fearing your name must be similar. If I fear your name, I become jealous for your fame, dedicated to revealing the real you in my life so others can accurately see who you are. I become consumed by your glory and reputation in this world.

Oh, let it be so! May I take my eyes off myself today long enough to long for your presence. May I tremble at the thought of your power. May I actively pursue a life that exemplifies your heart.

Your promise in this verse makes my heart leap. Because the sweet reward to living deeply connected to you is freedom. You are like the sun upon rising, dousing the darkness I coddle with rays of shimmering, life-giving light. You are the author of my healing, and I'm grateful.

I want to walk in freedom, Lord. And I know you're the avenue to bring that about. I wait on you, trusting that your healing hand will heal the broken parts of my heart in your perfectly timed way. Instead of fretting about how much healing needs to happen in my life, I pray I would take this moment to thank you for the ways you've already healed me. Amen.

Syria

*News about him spread as far as Syria, and people soon
began bringing to him all who were sick. And whatever
their sickness or disease, or if they were demon possessed
or epileptic or paralyzed—he healed them all.*

MATTHEW 4:24

Jesus, you are real. Your life happened on a world stage not unlike today's. News about you hastened to the borders of ancient Syria, and today your fame reaches the coastlines of the world. How real and how great you are!

Thank you that I don't have to do all sort of gymnastics to bring people your way. Instead, I need to let you be you, and your winsome ways will draw people from all the corners of the world. You are the famous one. You are the healing one. You are the Deliverer this world needed and needs.

In this passage, it says you healed them all. You didn't heal the important people, leaving the outcasts behind. Nor did you favor the broken over the "important." You are no respecter of persons—which is why your fame bounced from person to person until it reached the outer areas of the empire. All this without modern technology! Bring me back to that place, Jesus. That place where we first met, where I was deeply astounded by your miraculous ways and infectious love. I want to return to you as my first love, reveling in how beautifully unpredictable and loving you are. Settle me into that place of dedicated trust, and open my eyes so they're like yours—attentive to the needs of this dying world. And after resting deeply in your love and power, make me your ambassador, sharing who you really are with a world in need of freedom. Amen.

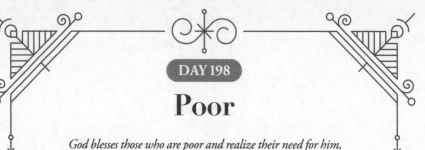

Poor

God blesses those who are poor and realize their need for him,
for the Kingdom of Heaven is theirs.

MATTHEW 5:3

Jesus, when I look around at this world's economy—the way the world works—I don't necessarily see this couplet lived out. Our world tells us the wealthy and strong rule it—that they are the blessed ones. But you spin an entirely different story. Your ways are upside down, counterintuitive principles that play out on another stage.

I'm grateful, but sometimes I'm perplexed because the world shouts louder, Jesus. It megaphones its logical truths, while your ways seem eclipsed by all the noise. Still my heart to hear your whispers, to not only understand your kingdom ways, but to exemplify them.

The kingdoms of this earth are flashy; the kingdom of heaven is simple. The kingdoms of this earth make sense; the kingdom of heaven isn't intuitive. The kingdoms of this earth deal in power and might; the kingdom of heaven deals in your power for my lack. I choose to rely on your wisdom today.

I am poor. Anything I have is from your hand anyway, and you own this entire universe. My abilities, health, and breath—all these come from you. I am helpless without you sustaining me. Because of this, I acknowledge my gaping need for you. Open my eyes to your beautiful kingdom today, as I choose again to surrender to you. Amen.

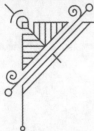

Salt

You are the salt of the earth.
But what good is salt if it has lost its flavor?
Can you make it salty again?
It will be thrown out and trampled underfoot as worthless.

MATTHEW 5:13

Jesus, when I've had food without salt, I cringe. It's not that it's horrible; it's simply not enhanced. It's palatable, but not amazing. Flavorless food is hard to eat. And it doesn't entice.

I want to be flavorful in your kingdom, Jesus. When people see me today, may they see a seasoned follower of you, fully alive, infectious, vibrant. May they walk away from meeting with me with a yearning to know who it is I follow. Because you are who makes me truly alive, Jesus. You give texture and joy to my life.

Show me where I've become bland in my connection to you and others. You've said that I'm to follow two basic commands—to love you and to bring that same love to others. Where have I lost my vital connection to you? In what areas have I turned away from you? How has my love grown cold toward others? Do I need to forgive someone? Apologize?

Salt by itself is not amazing. It's when it's added to other things where its properties of flavoring and preserving come to bear. So intersect my life with those who need it. And keep my eyes open to those who desperately need you. Amen.

Misunderstand

Don't misunderstand why I have come.
I did not come to abolish the law of Moses
or the writings of the prophets.
No, I came to accomplish their purpose.
I tell you the truth, until heaven and earth disappear,
not even the smallest detail of God's law will
disappear until its purpose is achieved.

MATTHEW 5:17-18

Jesus, I hear a lot these days about "my truth," all the while disregarding your truth. It seems like more and more folks are making you into their image, only a slightly better version of themselves, ignoring the laws of God that they don't like. Oh, dear Jesus, keep me grounded in your ways.

Thank you that you didn't come to abolish holiness, but to fulfill it. You accomplished what none of us could, and now you've sent your Spirit to enable us to do the same. I don't want to be guilty of misunderstanding the magnitude of what you've done. You lived a sinless life, keeping every jot and tittle of the law, in order to become the perfect atoning sacrifice for the sin of humanity. What a beautiful, sacrificial gift.

Because of that great truth, I don't want to lessen the cross by minimizing sin or dismissing it altogether. You paid a life debt because of sin. Your purpose was to come here to earth to show us a better way.

Show me, please, where I've cherished "my truth" about the law of God over the actual truth of it. Where have I dismissed your mandates? Give me a healthy fear and respect for the law and sin, not so I'll cower under the weight of it, but so I'll fully worship you for all you've done to accomplish your purposes on earth. Amen.

Enemies

But I say, love your enemies! Pray for those who persecute
you! In that way, you will be acting as true children of your
Father in heaven. For he gives his sunlight to both the evil
and the good, and he sends rain on the just and the unjust
alike. If you love only those who love you, what reward is
there for that? Even corrupt tax collectors do that much.

MATTHEW 5:44-46

Jesus, I'd rather not pray for the people who hurt me. To be honest, my heart is petty, not pretty. I want revenge sometimes. I want the people who hurt me to experience hurt themselves.

But I can't stay in that place, Jesus, because I know you ask more from me. This passage of Scripture makes it utterly clear that you want me to bless those who cause me pain. You want me to be like you, who when you were betrayed, still called Judas "friend."

How do you do that, Jesus? How do you love so well? How did you forgive the people who put you up on the cross?

And even as I pray these words, I realize I put you up on that cross. My sin held you down as you bled for my caustic words, my unrighteous anger, and the things I've done that I deeply regret.

You've forgiven a mountain of sin between us. And I have a hard time forgiving the molehill between my friend and me. To love them well, I must let go. Help me remember I'm more like you when I'm offering grace than when I'm spewing judgment.

I choose right now to give you my pain in this situation, and I ask for your help. Please give me love for my enemy. I recognize that I don't have it in me to do that. But you do. You're good at it. So I trust you right now. Amen.

Give

When you give to someone in need,
don't do as the hypocrites do—
blowing trumpets in the synagogues and streets
to call attention to their acts of charity!
I tell you the truth, they have received all
the reward they will ever get.

MATTHEW 6:2

Jesus, I love your example when you made earth your home. You did so many seemingly unnoticed acts of kindness. You didn't blow the trumpet. So often you asked the folks you healed to quietly report their healing to the synagogue, and you often instructed them to be quiet about what you did.

I don't want to be a hypocrite, shouting my good deeds for the sake of getting attention or filling a need deep within myself for recognition. I want to learn the power of secret acts, things no one knows about except you and me.

Keep me mindful today about these silent acts. Point out people who need random (anonymous) acts of kindness. Thank you ahead of time for leading me to give in unnoticed ways.

In my family today, I pray I would be motivated to serve them— not to be praised or recognized for my sacrifice, but simply because it's the right thing to do, and it will communicate love in an important way. Grow my soul. Expand it so I long for unnoticed service like this. Amen.

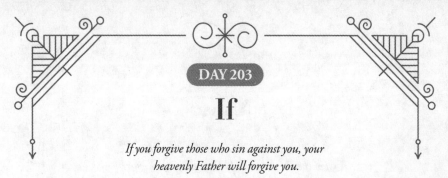

If

If you forgive those who sin against you, your heavenly Father will forgive you.

MATTHEW 6:14

Jesus, help me understand this powerful verse today. I'm reminded of the parable you told about the man who owed a great debt, begged for forgiveness, then strangled a man who owed him little. It was obvious his heart had not been changed by that wild act of forgiveness. He still lived for himself, demeaning the outrageous gift that the landowner gave him.

I don't want to be like that, Jesus. I want to rest in the word *if,* even though it causes me tension. If I forgive, then you will forgive. But maybe it's better understood in light of that parable. A forgiven person naturally will forgive. One who hasn't taken in forgiveness is prone to be stingy with forgiveness.

As I look back on all my sin (there is so much), and I think about you on the cross, Jesus, paying the ultimate price for my rebellion, may it compel me to see the world in the same way—as helpless and needy and broken, in need of a Savior. Instead of rehearsing that person's egregious sin, may I remember my own, and the price you paid to set me free.

I do want your gift to inform my actions from now on. So please show me folks I have yet to forgive. Bring me to a new mountain of understanding when it comes to my own sin's forgiveness so I can walk in forgiveness. Freely I have received forgiveness from you—so freely I want to grant it. Amen.

New

No one puts new wine into old wineskins.
For the old skins would burst from the pressure,
spilling the wine and ruining the skins.
New wine is stored in new wineskins so that both are preserved.

MATTHEW 9:17

Jesus, I want the new wine of your presence, your way of doing unexpected things in my life, but oh, do I have boxes. These boxes contain all the ways I think you should act in my life, ways you must accomplish my specific prayers, patterns I assume you'll follow, trails I believe you'll take to rescue me.

Forgive me for not allowing you to be wildly creative in my life.

Forgive me for assuming things of you that aren't true.

Forgive me for box-ifying you.

I need new wineskins, a freedom-based way of looking at the way you work in my life and in the lives of others. I love that when you walked this earth, you often confounded others by how differently you acted. I love that you are not safe, that you don't always do what's expected.

So Jesus, today I want to live expectantly. I want my life to be a new wineskin to hold you and your sometimes crazy ways. I want to experience your presence without me trying to control what that may look like. Bring freedom and joy as I learn to let you be you. Amen.

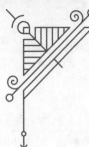

Entrusted

My Father has entrusted everything to me.
No one truly knows the Son except the Father,
and no one truly knows the Father except the Son
and those to whom the Son chooses to reveal him.

MATTHEW 11:27

Jesus, I'm utterly grateful that the Father has entrusted everything to you, including me. And I'm amazed that you both are an example of deep, genuine relationships. Your trinity reminds me that ultimately we are all made for community and communion. When I'm tempted today to isolate, withdraw, or nurse a bitter heart, remind me of the intimate dance of the trinity.

I want to know the Father. I need a dad who will never leave me nor forsake me. Please reveal the father heart of God to me. I need to settle myself into his arms, and you are the sweet avenue to his embrace.

Thank you that in you all things hold together, even my heart. When I feel scattered or torn or betrayed or humiliated, remind me that you can shoulder everything.

And as I nestle into your presence, I would love to follow your example and be entrusted with greater responsibility in the kingdom of God. Grow me deep and wide. Make my foundation a fortress so greater works come my way. I trust you. Amen.

Tree

A tree is identified by its fruit. If a tree is good, its fruit will be good.
If a tree is bad, its fruit will be bad.

MATTHEW 12:33

Jesus, I have to confess it's confusing to see others who, with elaborate words and proclamations, say they follow you, yet their lives don't measure up. In perplexing moments like that, remind me of this verse. It's really quite simple—I will know a person's heart by how they act out what's in their heart.

But folks can live in denial. They can even be hypocrites. And I can't figure it all out. So here's how I'll pray today: Teach me discernment. Show me those who are pretending, not so I can expose them per se, but so I'll be aware. I don't want to align myself with people who say they love you but don't act like it—particularly when those people are leaders in your church.

But instead of fretting about who is fruitful and who isn't, help me rest all my relationships in your hands today. Please sort it all out. I know I can't change them, but I can open my heart to be changed by you.

I want to be fruitful for your kingdom. I understand this might mean death on my part—dying to my dreams, my pet sins, and my way of doing things. It means picking up the cross and carrying it. It means humbling myself before you, entrusting my life to you. You will bring the growth. You will move in my heart so it can birth new fruit. You can do all things as long as I abide in your trunk, deeply connected and rooted in you. Amen.

Cross

Jesus said to his disciples, "If any of you wants to be my
follower, you must give up your own way, take up your cross,
and follow me. If you try to hang on to your life, you will lose
it. But if you give up your life for my sake, you will save it."

MATTHEW 16:24-26

Jesus, you hung on that cross for me, for all. And yet I try to hang on to my life, terrified I will lose my way. Forgive me.

There are crosses aplenty facing me, and in my flesh I'd rather take the easy route around them. I don't much like Golgotha, the place of the skull. I don't like suffering outside the camp, embarrassed, naked, broken, dying. I would rather chase after prosperity and my own pet view of truth.

But this is not the way of the kingdom. The way up is down. The way to life involves death. The way of truth means forsaking all lies.

I want to willingly bear the things you want me to bear. If it means suffering, give me a new theology of suffering. If it is sacrifice, remind me that you walked before me, and your Holy Spirit will truly enable me to act rightly. If it is serving unseen, bring joy while I perform for an audience of one. If it is choosing to forgive an enemy, remind me that you forgave me.

Your cross speaks death, but it is the avenue to life. With upturned face, full of joyful surrender, I take up my cross today. Amen.

Important

Do not neglect the more important things.

MATTHEW 23:23

Jesus, there are many unimportant things that clog my mind and inform my actions. But I want to be like Mary, who sat at your feet, choosing the truly important one: you. And in that choosing, I trust that you will reveal to me throughout the day just what your agenda is, who to pray for, who to offer encouragement, who to love. Because the most important things in this life aren't things. They are people.

Help me to bless my community today, no matter what that looks like. Do you want me to write a letter? Do you want me to make a phone call? Should I text someone? Should I buy a gift or serve in a sacrificial way?

Help me to be mindful of my neighbors, whether they be living in my neighborhood, attending my church, or working alongside me. Lead me clearly toward good deeds that truly impact people for eternity.

And as I seek you for the people you want to bless through me, don't let me forget you. I want to praise you in the midst of stress, fear, tasks, drudgery, and the mundane parts of life. I want to lift my eyes heavenward, reminding myself that you made the beautiful sky I see today. I want to sing songs to you through joy and sorrow and the typicality of today. Why? Because you are important to me, Jesus, and I love you dearly. Amen.

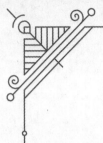

Understanding

To those who listen to my teaching,
more understanding will be given.
But for those who are not listening,
even what little understanding they have
will be taken away from them.

MARK 4:25

Jesus, there is so much I don't understand in my life right now. Why do my friends suffer? Why aren't prayers seemingly answered in a timely manner? Why do evil people seem to gloat and win? Why do scoundrels get away with things? Why do I work so hard and see so little gain? When will my loved one bow the knee to you, even after years and years of prayers?

But you promise understanding. I need this! Understanding your ways comes from spending time with you, listening to your heart, being willing to hear the hard things as well as the kind words you bring. Give me a listening ear. I want to welcome your feedback instead of running a thousand miles away from your scrutiny.

Remind me that your love compels you to love me. You can't help but love me, your precious child. And because you so beautifully love me, you want what is best for me. So your advice and wisdom will ultimately benefit my soul. I may not understand in this moment, but you will give me holy perspective to endure when my questions crowd out my intentions. Teach me to listen for your heartbeat today, and then to trust that you are managing my world just fine. All is well. All will be well. Someday I will have perfect understanding. In the waiting time, keep me near you. Amen.

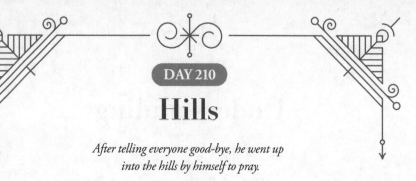

Hills

After telling everyone good-bye, he went up
into the hills by himself to pray.

MARK 6:46

Jesus, there are times I think you're a wild extrovert, hanging out with the crowds who pressed in on you, daring to heal them all. Demons roiled. Sickness fled. Limbs grew. Hearing came back in surround sound. Darkness became light. All in the midst of a teeming humanity that you both loved and lamented over. You certainly rubbed shoulders with us all, and for that I am grateful.

But you also had introverted ways. You refueled in a circle of two—in the wilderness alone with your Father. You pulled away to pray, to become refreshed, and to hear what your Father had for you next. He showed you what he was doing so you could follow obediently in the aftermath of such beautiful revelation.

Help me heed this example today, Jesus. I definitely interact with the world, brushing against people with needs that exceed my ability to help them. (I am unlike you in this, Lord Jesus. You could fill them up.) After a long exposure to needs, my own need blares, and I need to pull away.

Show me what my wilderness looks like. What is my circle of two, and where is that? I desperately need to know what you are doing in this earth so I can do what I see you doing. I need rejuvenation on a cellular level. My heart needs courage. My resolve has melted, and my emotions are raw.

Replenish me. Give me quiet and peace. I choose today to pray only to you, silencing all the clamor around me that shouts for my attention. Oh, how I need you, Jesus. Amen.

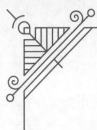

Child

He put a little child among them. Taking the child in his
arms, he said to them, "Anyone who welcomes a little child like
this on my behalf welcomes me, and anyone who welcomes
me welcomes not only me but also my Father who sent me."

MARK 9:36-37

Jesus, you welcomed children. In your arms. When you walked this world, you showed us just how important they were—not to be exploited or marginalized or harmed, but dignified and loved. It's easy for me to see this beautiful word picture of you with children laughing with you, but sometimes difficult to see myself that way.

I was once a child. And you loved me then as I looked at the world with wide-eyed wonder. When I couldn't tie my shoes or spell my name, you loved me still. When there was nothing I could do to evangelize the world, you simply had affection for me. I'm humbled and so grateful.

This picture of you with the vulnerable reminds me to live life tenderly today, to seek out those who may be overlooked or seen as unimportant in this great, big world of productivity, fame, and money. Open my eyes to the "children" in my midst, and may I become a person with arms open wide, welcoming many through the power and love of your Spirit within me.

Because of your great love for me, whether I was toddling or solving algebraic equations or paying my mortgage, I can love those who seem to have little to offer society, but so much to offer you and me. Amen.

Servant

Jesus called them together and said,
"You know that the rulers in this world lord it over their people,
and officials flaunt their authority over those under them.
But among you it will be different.
Whoever wants to be a leader among you must be your servant,
and whoever wants to be first among you
must be the slave of everyone else.
For even the Son of Man came not to be served but to serve others
and to give his life as a ransom for many."

MARK 10:42-45

Jesus, in this world of leaders and leadership and gurus and authorities, I think we may have it all wrong. It's not the cool or the prestigious or the famous who mean anything in the kingdom. You could care less about pedigree or number of followers.

No, you are most concerned with people who take the lowest place on purpose, who humbly serve without tooting their horns or shouting for all the world to hear or see.

I confess I don't know much about what it means to be a slave to someone. But I do want to serve others. It's tiring and boring to only serve myself. Besides that, it's empty, and those actions won't count in light of eternity.

So teach me the value of service, of quiet love, of making a gift for a friend, or of praying in the moment or sacrificing my time for someone who desperately needs to know love. You provided the most amazing example of this when you came to earth, leaving the splendor of heaven for the muddy mess that is us. Thank you.

You willingly gave your life. In gratitude, I want to give mine. Amen.

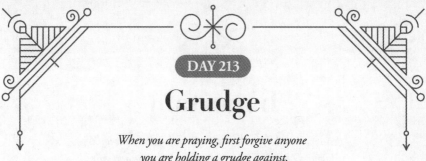

Grudge

When you are praying, first forgive anyone
you are holding a grudge against,
so that your Father in heaven will forgive your sins, too.

MARK 11:25

Jesus, I don't want to grudge my way through life, but there are some broken relationships that still haunt me, and I battle bitterness when they come to mind. This discourages me because I thought I'd forgiven them. And yet they re-offend, and I sulk back into grudging.

Instead of viewing new reminders of old offenses as indictments against my lack of forgiveness, help me see these reminders gently, as ways to grow a little bit more toward healing and grace.

You have done so much in my life. You have delivered me from many offenses. You have taught me to let go of pain, to hold people loosely, to create good boundaries, and to freely forgive. You will continue to do that good work in me, even when I'm hurt afresh. I trust you to shepherd me toward new levels of freedom.

Right now, I give you all those parts of me that want to grab onto a grudge, those parts that want others to pay for their offenses against me. Instead, I open my hands, place my difficult relationships there, and ask you to take them. Help me to see them as you do, as dearly loved children of yours. Help me to revel in your amazing grace enough to internalize it so I can extend it to those who have hurt me. Because you forgave me of so much, I can turn around and do the same. Besides, I don't much like bitter me. I like free, grudgeless me. Amen.

Important

Jesus replied, "The most important commandment is this:
*'Listen, O Israel! The L*ORD *our God is the one and only*
L*ORD. And you must love the L*ORD *your God with all your*
heart, all your soul, all your mind, and all your strength.'
The second is equally important: 'Love your neighbor as
yourself.' No other commandment is greater than these."

MARK 12:29-31

Jesus, when I look at the Ten Commandments, my heart gets over-whelmed. I see myself in them, the ways I've fallen short. I'm grateful that you've provided a simplification to those lofty commands, a way for me to filter them as I go throughout my day—to simply love you and love others. All the commandments weave in and through those two sentences.

Today as I go about the tasks set before me, I want to know what it means to love you supremely. Instead of mindlessly performing my day, let me invite you into the deepest parts of me as I pray all day long, longing to interact with you, hear your voice, and experience your presence. I want to see this day as you do, and I want you to know I love you as I live.

And for those you bring near, help me to hold my tongue when I'd rather say a harsh word. Give me glimpses into people's hearts so I know better how to bless them tangibly. Show me gifts I can give, prayers I can pray, words I can say that will not only give them joy, but also point them to you.

In this quiet moment, I want you to know how ardently I love you. You are good. You are strong. You are the greatest part of me, the one who cheerleads me when I'm feeling small and unnoticed. You rescued me. Oh, how I love you. Amen.

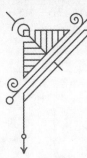

Signs

When the Lord Jesus had finished talking with
them, he was taken up into heaven and sat down
in the place of honor at God's right hand.
And the disciples went everywhere and preached,
and the Lord worked through them,
confirming what they said by many miraculous signs.

MARK 16:19-20

Jesus, I can't imagine what it must have been like to see you die, then resurrect. But as I read these verses, I'm struck with the miracle it must've been to see someone fly into the air, far before hot-air balloons, blimps, or airplanes. And how would they know you sat at God's right hand unless they actually saw it? Miraculous. Humbling. Even a little scary.

I'm grateful that you are seated at God's right hand. It means you've finished the work he gave you to do, and now you are constantly interceding for your children. I'm humbled by that thought and oh, so thankful. When life spins out of center, help me fix my mind on this beautiful picture—my Savior pleading on my behalf to my Father.

The disciples were utterly changed by your life, death, resurrection, and ascension, Jesus. So much so that they couldn't help but spread the news about you everywhere they went. And you confirmed your Word through signs. In a skeptical world surrounded by proofs and scientific rationalism, help me remember that you still perform miracles today. I want to be open to whatever it is you want to do on this earth. Keep me close to you so that I can continue to pray for big things, not putting you in a carefully constructed box of ways I'm comfortable with you working, but letting you be gloriously you in the midst of my life. Amen.

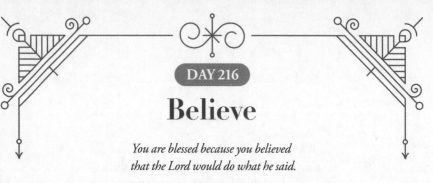

Believe

*You are blessed because you believed
that the Lord would do what he said.*

Luke 1:45

Jesus, I struggle with faith, with believing the things that I can't see will actually happen. I have small faith and big stress. Forgive me for making my worries bigger than your abilities. Teach me to be like Mary, who heard of a miracle through the angel's voice and believed that you could accomplish it.

Remind me to take a moment today to remember all the ways you have been faithful to me over the past week, month, year, and decades. I could not list how many ways you have rescued, healed, wooed, repaired, reinstated, and blessed me. They are too numerous to count. And yet, I still struggle to recall them.

Help me get to the place where it becomes second nature to me to count the blessings you have sent my way. I want my fallback to be gratitude, not fear. And in that gratitude, please sow in me the kernel of belief. I realize it's as small as a mustard seed, but I also know you make little things big.

So please water my seed. Bring your light to my wavering faith. And plant me down deep so I'll grow and learn to follow you more joyfully. That word, *believer,* slips off my tongue so easily, but I truly, truly want to learn what it means to live as one who believes. Amen.

Good

But to you who are willing to listen, I say, love your enemies!
Do good to those who hate you.
Bless those who curse you. Pray for those who hurt you.

LUKE 6:27-28

Jesus, this is a hard command—not one I follow naturally. I'd much rather marginalize my enemies, point out their flaws, untangle their arguments, eviscerate them, and curry favor for people to join my side against them. For those who hate me, I don't instinctively want to do good. I'd rather do "bad." For those who have cursed me, I'd like to return the favor. And for those relationships that represent deep wounds, I confess my first reaction is to pout or retaliate or nurse grudges, not to pray for them.

Today I pray for a reversal in my heart. When I see the face of an enemy, instead of jumping to negative conclusions, may I fall on my knees. Why? Because I am most like you when I work toward reconciliation. I am most like you when I pray, "Father, forgive them, for they don't know what they are doing." I am most like you when I intercede for those who want my demise.

But you have called me to do more than pray. Your death on the cross was an action, followed by your prayer in the Garden of Gethsemane. May I follow your pattern today—to pray, then act. What does it mean today to do good toward those who differ from me, who act like enemies in my life? Teach me.

Instead of cursing the enemies in my life, show me what it means to bless, to encourage, to listen, to take the last seat and humble myself—not to be a doormat, but to show your irresistible love to those who need to experience it as I have. I absolutely cannot do this without you. Empower me to love. Amen.

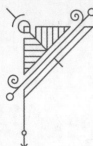

Much

*"I tell you, her sins—and they are many—have been
forgiven, so she has shown me much love. But a person
who is forgiven little shows only little love."
Then Jesus said to the woman, "Your sins are forgiven."*

LUKE 7:47-48

Jesus, I want to live with a grateful posture, fully aware of the magnitude of my sins, so much so that I love you much. And I wonder if those who think they have little need of forgiveness understand gratitude. My hunch is that they're weighed down by the sin of pride that blocks out large sections of their own sin, so much so that they treat your forgiveness casually. May that never be me!

I want my love to be much. I want my life to be one long testimony of your goodness, provision, and empowerment. Teach me today what it means to live in gratitude instead of indentured servitude. I don't grit my way through life, lovelessly obeying your commandments, hoping to curry favor. No, you have changed me from the inside out, and my natural response is to live a life of love in response. It's all a matter of perspective.

Jesus, thank you for forgiving me—of all I've done that I regret, of the pet sins I nurse today, and the sin I will embrace (sadly) in the future. You are full of forgiveness, even when I've been full of myself. I'm humbled and grateful. Amen.

Registered

Don't rejoice because evil spirits obey you;
rejoice because your names are registered in heaven.

LUKE 10:20

Jesus, my security doesn't come from being powerful—so powerful that spirits obey me. It's about where my registration is—in my secure home in heaven. Yes, I'm grateful that the enemy of my soul, Satan, has to cower beneath your name. I'm thankful that evil spirits must flee when confronted with your name and power. I'm utterly befuddled by how beautifully powerful you are when it comes to conquering and vanquishing evil.

But that astonishment cannot compare to the joy I have in knowing your ultimate conquering was your long walk to Golgotha, step by painful step, toward the place where you'd be crucified for my sin. That is the true miracle. And my heart is alive and peaceful because of that revolutionary, obedient act.

You have made a way for me to be right with the Father. You are the way, the truth, and the life I now lead. You gave me the Holy Spirit as a down payment—a guarantee that there's a place created in heaven for me. My name is now written in the Book of Life, and no one can snatch me from your hand. My eternity is secured—all because of you, all because you dared to love.

Jesus, today let me rest in that deep knowing. It's not power that attracts me to you; it's your love. I sit here completely loved by you, when I should have been shunned and separated. It's too much. Far too much. And you are too much—too much goodness for me to comprehend. Amen.

Need

Don't be concerned about what to eat and what to drink.
Don't worry about such things.
These things dominate the thoughts of unbelievers all over the world,
but your Father already knows your needs.
Seek the Kingdom of God above all else,
and he will give you everything you need.

LUKE 12:29-31

Jesus, this is hard for me, this idea of trust. And it's hard to read that being stressed is what consumes and dominates the thoughts of those who don't love you because I'm very guilty of the same thing.

That word *dominate* haunts me. Teach me what it means to relinquish control, Jesus, to let go of the things that dominate my heart and mind and to trust you instead. Please replace my fretting with faith, my worry with proactive belief, and my stress with strength in your presence. Oh, how I need you in this world.

Forgive me for thinking only on superficial things. Forgive me for playing worries over and over and over again in my head. I spend so much energy feeling sick about what hasn't happened or what might happen that I can't find joy in the moment.

Deliver me, Jesus, from believing it's all up to me. Reframe the way I see today—not as a series of stressful worries, but as a venue to see you work and move and help. Because of your work on my behalf, I choose to trust you first today, to seek you first.

Forgive me for reversing the order—chasing provision first rather than the Provider. You have given me everything I need, Jesus, because you have given me the outrageously beautiful gift of yourself. Help me to find true contentment there. Amen.

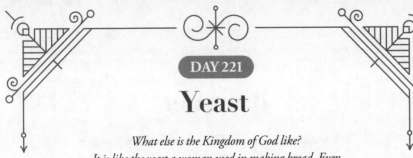

Yeast

What else is the Kingdom of God like?
It is like the yeast a woman used in making bread. Even
though she put only a little yeast in three measures
of flour, it permeated every part of the dough.

LUKE 13:20-21

Jesus, I want to understand your kingdom more, especially as it relates to yeast and dough. I know that dough without yeast, left in a warm room, will do nothing but sit there and eventually grow moldy. I certainly don't want to be like that. Instead, I want my life to gloriously expand, open to new ways of thinking in your kingdom.

I don't want my life to shrink, and it often does when I give in to fear. I worry what other people think, so I become safe and smaller. I stress about the state of the world, so I shrink inside myself or lash out. I fret about where our society is headed, so I become immobilized. Fear shrinks me. But faith expands me.

As I grow older, remind me of this. Teach me what it means to believe that you hold the whole world in your hands, that you are truly in control, and that you are utterly trustworthy to carry out your good plans on this earth. Like yeast in dough, your kingdom is expanding, and the gates of hell will not prevail against it. Your will is being accomplished on this earth, despite what the news media over-report.

I pray that I will become yeasty—infiltrating the enemy's territory and gloriously expanding through the power of the Holy Spirit to woo people and transform lives. Open my eyes to new possibilities in your kingdom, Lord, and expand my ministry influence for your glory. Amen.

Banquet

> *Then he turned to his host. "When you put on a luncheon or a banquet," he said, "don't invite your friends, brothers, relatives, and rich neighbors. For they will invite you back, and that will be your only reward. Instead, invite the poor, the crippled, the lame, and the blind. Then at the resurrection of the righteous, God will reward you for inviting those who could not repay you."*
>
> LUKE 14:12-14

Jesus, teach me what this story means to me in my everyday life. What does it mean for me to invite people into my life who absolutely cannot repay me or offer an invitation in return? I'm reminded of passages where hospitality might involve entertaining angels without realizing it. But more than angels, remind me that I will find you on the face of the broken, marginalized, and forgotten.

I've become insulated in my cozy world, so much so that I'm hard-pressed to see those who are hurting. Would you open my eyes to the needs of those around me, and show me tangible ways I can feed and love folks in the margins? Help me go out of my way to find people who need to know you have not forgotten them, who are mired in depressing circumstances.

I'm reminded, too, that you invited me to your banquet. You invited everyone, but only a few stragglers came. The way to heaven is narrow, and few are those who find it. I'm so grateful for the daily invitation you send my way. Help me live out that gratitude by generous living today. Amen.

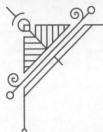

Dearly

The Pharisees, who dearly loved their money, heard all this and scoffed at him. Then he said to them, "You like to appear righteous in public, but God knows your hearts. What this world honors is detestable in the sight of God."

LUKE 16:14-15

Jesus, when I've thought of the Pharisees, I've considered their religious fervor, their staunch adherence to regulations, and their proud outlook on life. But this passage? It stuns me. They dearly (dearly!) loved their money. Their affection for "their" money influenced the way they treated you, so much so that they scoffed at you.

I don't want to be a Pharisee, Jesus. I don't want you to correct me about appearing to be holy, but my heart being far, far away. I don't want to honor what this world honors. Instead, I want to honor you.

So elevate my perspective today. Show me where I've veered into dearly loving money more than I love you. Rejuvenate my heart so that the outside of me matches a heart fully changed by you. Keep me close to you so I know to honor what you honor. Help me grow in your wisdom so I don't slip into thinking my culture must dictate my morality. Free me from the confines of this world so I can live freely for you in this moment.

Ultimately, I choose to trust almighty you over financial provision. You are my sustenance, my hero, the one who knows what I need before I even ask. It's you I depend on today. You are my dearly beloved, and I choose to trust you again. Amen.

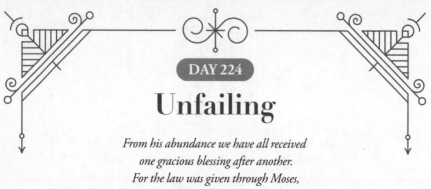

Unfailing

*From his abundance we have all received
one gracious blessing after another.
For the law was given through Moses,
but God's unfailing love and faithfulness came through Jesus Christ.*

JOHN 1:16-17

Jesus, you gave the law through Moses, and that law became the tutor that taught us all about our need for you. Because of the law, I realized I could not fulfill its requirements in my own strength. In fact, it became a megaphone, shouting my inadequacy. I could not, in my own strength, make peace with you.

But you demonstrated your love for me by coming to earth. Even though humanity was dead in sin, you chose to go to the cross for us, making a way for peace and relationship. It's a beautiful thing, the cross, even though it also symbolized the most brutal death.

Because of what you've done, I can live with peace. I no longer need to rehearse my shame or remind myself of my constant shortcomings. Instead, I can rely on the unfailing nature of your love. Unfailing means your love never, ever fails. It is not a well that runs dry. It is a spring of abundance, constantly flowing, cleansing me.

Let today be a day of profound gratitude, where I remember what you have done, Jesus. I want to sing about your faithfulness to me, even when I've been faithless. Your faithful love continues, and it's not dependent on my nature, but yours.

Keep my eyes open to each gracious blessing you have for me. Let me count them one after the other. Instead of concentrating on all the bad things that happen to me, may today be different. I want to be alert to your activity in my life. Amen.

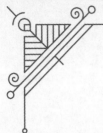

Drink

Jesus replied, "Anyone who drinks this water
will soon become thirsty again.
But those who drink the water I give will never be thirsty again.
It becomes a fresh, bubbling spring within them,
giving them eternal life."

JOHN 4:13-14

Jesus, I'm thirsty. My soul is parched. My eyes are weary of seeing horrible things in the media. My tongue sticks to the roof of my mouth, unable to speak because of the stress in my life. Oh, how I need a deep drink from your fountain.

You promised the Samaritan woman at the well that your spring brings fresh water—the kind of thirst-quenching drink that truly satisfies. So I choose to stop in this hesitant moment and drink thoroughly. Forgive me for drinking that which does not satisfy: reputation, renown, and recognition.

Thank you that when we drink of the water you bring, it transforms into an ever-giving well, emerging from within us. What a beautiful picture of the Holy Spirit, present always, spilling over into the lives of those I love.

May I live in true connection to the Spirit today, hearing his voice, obeying his promptings, giving away the love he provides. Oh, please spill over into the lives of those I love today. I want to be a cool, refreshing drink to my loved ones. Amen.

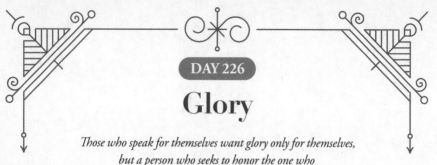

Glory

Those who speak for themselves want glory only for themselves,
but a person who seeks to honor the one who
sent him speaks truth, not lies.

JOHN 7:18

Jesus, you have sent me into this very dark world as an ambassador for your unusual kingdom. I want to honor you. I want to speak truth, even when it hurts. I want to live my life in such a way that you get the glory.

But Jesus, it's hard. I confess that I really like my own personal glory. I love having people see or recognize or praise me. I work very hard to accomplish things so I'll be noticed. I spend a lot of my life worrying about what others think, and sometimes I adjust my personality in order to fit in.

Please forgive me for forgetting you, the famous one. Today I pray that you would help me to see just how big and beautiful and surprising and lovely you are. Open my eyes to your fame, to your glory, to your ways. Steep me in it like a tea bag in very hot water. Permeate me with your otherness, your surprising power.

Because when I live with the discipline of astonishment rather than ferreting after my own personal glory, I have so much more joy and purpose. Elevate my eyes and my heart to the bigger picture of your kingdom today. I'm so tired of building my own empire. Amen.

Darkness

Jesus spoke to the people once more and said,
"I am the light of the world.
If you follow me, you won't have to walk in darkness,
because you will have the light that leads to life."

JOHN 8:12

Jesus, I don't want to give in to darkness, but it's hard. There are many around me suffering, others who have walked away from you, and still some who seem to prefer darkness to light. People making bad choices surround me, and I feel alone. But you promise that your light leads to life, and that's where I want to live today.

I don't want to let other people darken my view of you. In that sense, they become idols in my life because their actions affect me more than your actions on my behalf. Open my eyes, Lord, to what you are doing in this world. Show me where your light is penetrating the darkness. Remind me that faithfulness to you matters. Steep me in the truth that your church is being built, and hell's gates cannot overcome it.

This is a dark world, sin stained and scary. But you have promised an abundant life. You have already lightened the world, and if I'm surrounded by dark thoughts, I need to reorient my thoughts toward you. Lift my head. Shine in and through me. Rescue me from circular thoughts that spiral downward. I trust you.

I want to learn what it means to be disciplined in the way I follow you—to wholeheartedly pursue you, especially when things get hard. Show me your path that leads to light and life today. Amen.

Slave

*Jesus replied, "I tell you the truth, everyone who sins is a slave of sin.
A slave is not a permanent member of the family, but a son is part
of the family forever. So if the Son sets you free, you are truly free."*

JOHN 8:34-36

Jesus, thank you for telling me the truth. I'm grateful that throughout the Gospels, you remind the disciples that you are telling them (and all of us) the truth about our situation, who you are, and how we can be set gloriously free. Remind me what my life was like apart from you. Sometimes I forget just how enslaved I was to sin, how I couldn't help but continually disobey your laws. I had no rest for my soul, and I feared death.

But you changed all that. You called me your child. You secured my release from sin's prison. You purchased me with your blood—a costly sacrifice I'll never be able to repay except by my life lived in worshipful reverence to you. You have welcomed me to a new family—of brothers and sisters who are broken but free. And, oh yes, you have unlocked complete freedom.

Show me where I've opted back into sin, when I've let it entice me back to slavery. I know your Spirit within me will check me if I stray, and I'm so grateful for that. I am also thankful that the Spirit will empower me to live as a freely loved child, no longer enslaved to fear and regret and shame. What a glorious inheritance I have! How great a love you have given me. I scarce can take it in. Amen.

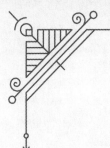

Praise

For they loved human praise
more than the praise of God.

JOHN 12:43

Jesus, my prayer is that these words are not true of me. Bring me to a place of such dependence on you that I only long to hear your voice praising me. Enable me to keep an eternal perspective, looking forward to the day you say, "Well done, good and faithful servant."

But I confess my need for human praise, my desire to see my work and life praised by others. While it's not wrong to be praised, I realize how misplaced it can be when I search for it rabidly, clamoring after it like it's all I need for life. The truth is that only you can fill the deepest parts of my soul. Even if all the human praise in the world came my way and piled on top of itself into a mountain bigger than Everest, it still would not satiate me.

Free me from chasing after it, Jesus.

Free me to follow you, to live in such a way that people see me but praise your good works. And when praise comes my way today, give me the gumption to quietly turn it heavenward, where all praise belongs. Because someday every knee will bow and every tongue confess that you indeed are Lord.

I want to practice that kind of praise today. I want to prepare myself for my eternal occupation of praising you. Amen.

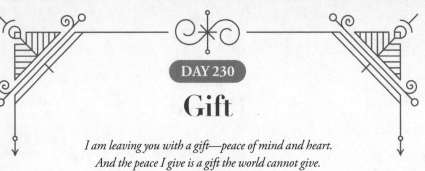

Gift

I am leaving you with a gift—peace of mind and heart.
And the peace I give is a gift the world cannot give.
So don't be troubled or afraid.

JOHN 14:27

Jesus, I am so sorry that I haven't received your gift of peace as often as you have offered it. I've shunned it, loved my own control-centered peace, or I've simply turned the other way. Your peace, I know, is what my soul needs today. Please help me figure out why I don't always welcome it like a friend.

I pray for peace of heart, where my relationships live. There are some people I'm having a hard time forgiving. Help. There are people whom I'm embittered against. Help. There are people who have walked away from me. Help. There are people I have hurt. Help. There are people who I need to pursue. Help. In the great, big melting pot of my relationships, Jesus, help me to find your peace.

I pray for peace of mind, where my thoughts live. I have bullying thoughts that taunt me and tell me I'm unlovely or unlovable. Free me. I have obsessive thoughts that threaten my joy. Release me. I have angry thoughts toward others that I can't seem to work through. Help me. I have scattered thoughts that mess with my purpose and concentration. Center me.

I love your peace, Jesus. Help me to live life in such a way that I truly embrace it wholeheartedly. Amen.

Overflow

I have told you these things so that you will be filled with my joy.
Yes, your joy will overflow!
This is my commandment: Love each other
in the same way I have loved you.
There is no greater love than to lay down one's life for one's friends.
You are my friends if you do what I command.
I no longer call you slaves,
because a master doesn't confide in his slaves.
Now you are my friends, since I have told
you everything the Father told me.

JOHN 15:11-15

Jesus, overflow doesn't always define my life these days, but oh, how I want it to. I pray that your extension of friendship to me would wow my heart today, that you would cause the overflow of joy I so desperately desire. I want to represent you well. I want my life to be irresistible, just as yours was when you busied yourself on earth. I know my joy comes in direct proportion to my closeness to you, so please draw near.

I do want to be your friend, Jesus. As I survey today, help me prepare my heart to meet it with gusto, fueled by the strength of the Holy Spirit. Help me to rest in knowing that you have already called me your friend, and that my appropriate response is to interact as a friend would—listening and sharing my day.

But our friendship is more than that because you are God and I am not. You have things you want me to do: tasks to perform, people to love, a life to live wholeheartedly. I show you my friendship by my obedience to you, the holy one. Amen.

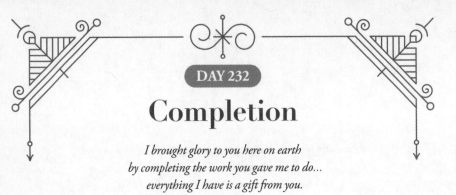

Completion

I brought glory to you here on earth
by completing the work you gave me to do...
everything I have is a gift from you.

JOHN 17:4,7

Jesus, you are my example today of accomplishment and completion. I'm grateful you showed us how to go about the work of your kingdom—listening to your Father, hearing his direction and guidance, and then obeying him, no matter how strange the outcome might be. Put mud in someone's eyes? Call out the guy in the tree and have dinner at his house? Turn around when the bleeding woman touched you in a crowd? You knew the Father's heart in each situation.

Similarly, I want to be so connected to my Father that I truly hear his voice. I want to be ready to listen, then obey. Bring me to a new level of listening and obedience.

So many things in my life are undone. So many loose ends are unraveled and confusing. All this mess makes it hard for me to complete the simple things in front of me. Help me to choose love over obligation. Give me the power to say yes to you even if that yes makes it look like I'm not productive. Jesus, I want to be interruptible.

I acknowledge right now that everything that happens today is sheer gift. You have gifted me with so much—a family, lungs that breathe, a mind that can think, hands that can embrace. You have fed and clothed me. Help me live in radical joy because of these simple, sometimes-overlooked things. Oh, how I love you, Jesus. Amen.

Believe

Then he said to Thomas, "Put your finger here, and look at my
hands. Put your hand into the wound in my side.
Don't be faithless any longer. Believe!"
"My Lord and my God!" Thomas exclaimed.

JOHN 20:27-28

Jesus, I love that you knew everything about Thomas. You knew
his thoughts, the doubts he nursed, the hesitant can-it-be-true he pon-
dered. And yet you didn't scorn him or point him out in shame. No,
you simply invited him to participate in the miracle. I'm sure the other
disciples wanted to put their fingers in your wounds to test their verac-
ity. But you fulfilled Thomas's curiosity by welcoming his touch.

I'm like Thomas too. There are times I wonder if I've made up
this whole Christianity thing, or if I'm living a fantasy. But as I look
back over my life and see your intersection with it, I know you're real.
Though I haven't touched you, I know your story is the most real story
arc in the universe.

Still, I need you to come near. Show me your wounds again. Welcome my touch. Teach me to ground myself in your narrative—that
you came to earth to profoundly deal with our sin problem, mess with
the devil's plans, and shine a great light into the darkness of this world.
These were all acts of a loving Savior to his people—proof of your love
for all to see. And then? The resurrection proved everything about
you—something Thomas did not yet know in this story.

I choose to believe in the power of the gospel today. Would you
bring others into my circle who doubt? I would love to share with them
about your faithfulness and how you've constantly proved to me that
you're real, and that your love is for all of us. Amen.

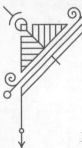

Power

You will receive power when the Holy Spirit comes upon you.
And you will be my witnesses, telling people about
me everywhere—in Jerusalem, throughout Judea,
in Samaria, and to the ends of the earth.

ACTS 1:8

Jesus, I love that the evidence of the Spirit in my life isn't manifestations, but it's power—power to live life for you. I also love that the word *witnesses* is the same word for martyrs, which means your Spirit within me gives the power I need to love you even if I face death for believing in you. That is power!

But so often I live powerless because, instead of relying on you, I tap into my own small strength. I burn myself out trying to prove my worth instead of first resting in the unchanging truth that you are for me, and you have accomplished everything I need on the cross. I cannot add to your work. I cannot make myself more or less acceptable.

No, my outworking of the salvation you've given isn't something I need to tackle in my own power, but instead my work should result from a completely transformed heart. I take a moment right now to rest in that truth. You are God. I am not. You are strong. I am weak. You are good. I strain to understand goodness. Change my heart, Jesus, so my heart will naturally live for you.

Today help me to see the circles of influence you have placed me in. Help me to love my family with joy. Show me ways to bless my community. Remind me to pray for the leaders of my country. And widen my perspective of serving you to the whole world. Amen.

Raised

God raised Jesus from the dead, and we are all witnesses of this.
Now he is exalted to the place of highest honor
in heaven, at God's right hand.
And the Father, as he had promised, gave him
the Holy Spirit to pour out upon us,
just as you see and hear today.

Acts 2:32-33

Jesus, wow. Raised from the dead. I cannot comprehend it. I know it's true because history records it, and the lives of your followers were profoundly changed by the resurrection. I want to live in light of it as well—a believer who doesn't forget to share about this amazing feat.

There's even more to your story of life, death, and resurrection. After that, you gave instructions, then ascended into heaven. You are now in the place of complete power at God's right hand. Thankfully, you didn't leave your followers to work out all that miraculous intervention on their own.

Thank you for sending the Spirit to live within the first members of your church, and continuing to do that through the ages up until now. It's a deep mystery to me that God the Spirit actually lives inside me, giving me comfort, enabling me to live joyfully and empowered throughout my days.

I don't want to quench or grieve the Spirit within me. Show me if I've done that, and keep me close to you. I want my life to be a testimony—not to my ability to live it, but to point to your ability to work within me. Amen.

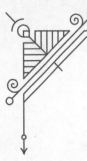

Goodwill

*They worshiped together at the Temple each day, met
in homes for the Lord's Supper, and shared their meals
with great joy and generosity—all the while
praising God and enjoying the goodwill of all the people.
And each day the Lord added to their
fellowship those who were being saved.*

ACTS 2:46-47

Jesus, I love the story of the early church because it shows the power of your people loving others—that kind of fellowship turned the world upside down. Help me live with others in a like manner—opening up my home to people who love you, being generous in ways that make no economic sense to the world, taking the bread and wine with followers of you (and remembering your sacrifice).

Yours is a table spirituality, but so often I eat cocooned in my safe home, insulated from the needs of others. Or I saturate myself with media and immediately become overwhelmed by the needs of this world. Oh Lord, give me balance in my perspective. Help me to love the people you've put in my path without getting overwhelmed by all the needs in the world.

I want my life to be typified by joy and generosity. Joy because you've rescued me from myself. You've healed my heart of so much. You've set me amazingly free. You've given me a new identity as a child wildly loved by you. Generosity because I have all things in you, and since I have all these spiritual blessings, I should freely give them away. Teach me today to live openhandedly, willing to give away what you've already blessed me with. Amen.

Through

And now, O Lord, hear their threats, and give us, your servants,
great boldness in preaching your word. Stretch
out your hand with healing power;
may miraculous signs and wonders be done
through the name of your holy servant Jesus.

ACTS 4:29-30

Jesus, this is such a powerful prayer. I pray it today. It's not popular to share your truth in a world in love with lies. It's not fun to be threatened by people who would rather wallow in their sin (and promote it as good) than bend the knee to you. Still, help me view those who don't yet know you as potential friends, not enemies. And I certainly don't want to see them as projects. They're people who desperately need your love.

So I ask for boldness. Teach me what it means to preach your gospel in a sin-scarred land. Make my words winsome, intelligent, yet firm. I don't want to shrink back. I don't want to exchange your truth for a lie so I'll be palatable to others. I know that adhering to a biblical worldview will not be popular, so strengthen my resolve and keep me close to you.

Remind me that you're a big God, full of power and miracles. I don't want to quench what you intend to do. Help me welcome your supernatural intersections with this world. I want to pray bigger prayers—to see healing, deliverance, and provision in the midst of your people. Instead of shrinking back, expand my view of you and your capabilities, Jesus. You are bigger than my expectations, Jesus, and for that I am so grateful. Amen.

Steadily

But Stephen, full of the Holy Spirit, gazed steadily into
heaven and saw the glory of God, and he saw Jesus
standing in the place of honor at God's right hand.
And he told them, "Look, I see the heavens opened and the Son
of Man standing in the place of honor at God's right hand!"

ACTS 7:55-56

Jesus, I'm amazed by Stephen's faith in this passage, and I confess that when I read it, I wonder if my faith is way too small. Would I be able to die for you? Would I have the confidence Stephen possessed? Would I be steady in the midst of torture and pain? All I know is that you are best able to come to my aid when I face any sort of trial, and that gives me confidence. Stephen was not alone, and I won't be either.

It's beautifully curious to me that you're standing in this passage, Jesus. When you ascended into heaven, you sat at the Father's right hand, having completed the work he wanted you to do. But as Stephen is welcomed into heaven, you stood. Just as a dignitary receives the honor of a standing room, you stood as a sign of honor to him. What a beautiful act. It brings me comfort that you saw Stephen and his plight and sought to dignify him. You, who do not change, will do the same for me. Thank you.

By his obedience, Stephen saw your glory. Let that be an important lesson to me today. I'm grateful that you see every obedience, even the small ways I follow you. Thank you that nothing escapes your notice, and that you reward those who faithfully follow you. Lord, as I end this prayer, I ask that you would open the heavens in reference to a prayer I've prayed a very long time. Help me know that you will answer it, and that you are working behind the scenes. Amen.

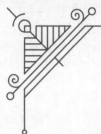

Fell

Even as Peter was saying these things, the Holy Spirit fell upon all who were listening to the message. The Jewish believers who came with Peter were amazed that the gift of the Holy Spirit had been poured out on the Gentiles, too.

ACTS 10:44-45

Jesus, I am grateful that throughout history, it's been your aim to bring all humanity to you. Your people were to be lights for Jew and Gentile alike, showing the world how amazing you are. And when the fullness of time came, you came and gladly demonstrated in the flesh what God is like. When you walked the earth, your arms opened to broken people, and you didn't shy away from Gentiles who were seeking you.

As I sit here praying, I'm astounded that I live and breathe because of you. Your Spirit is gloriously alive in me! I am set free by this outrageous gift. Instead of focusing on how my life isn't turning out the way I want it to, instead help me concentrate more on how crazy it is that your Spirit lives within me. It's a miracle I should never get used to, nor should it be a ho-hum truth.

May your love for the entire world infuse my day, Jesus. I lift up those I know who desperately need you, but are running a thousand miles in the other direction. Intersect their fleeing, Lord. Show up in dreams. Do something surprising and them-shaped, utterly unique so that they, too, can receive the promised gift of the Spirit. May my downtime be consumed with interceding for lost people today, Jesus. Amen.

Kingdom

For the next two years, Paul lived in Rome at his own expense.
He welcomed all who visited him, boldly proclaiming
the Kingdom of God and teaching about the Lord
Jesus Christ. And no one tried to stop him.

ACTS 28:30-31

Jesus, I confess I often look at my limitations and let them stop me from doing the work you have called me to do. But here we see Paul imprisoned in Rome, and yet he continued to teach about you with everything that was within him. Help me identify my "prisons" that I use as an excuse not to share you. May your Spirit help me overcome my fear and shyness so I can freely share about your kingdom unhindered.

I pray for the place I live, that your kingdom would come. Show me where you are working to set people free. Reveal the people who are open to you. Reveal people of peace to partner with in good work for your glory and advancing your kingdom. If there are volunteer opportunities that fit me well, show me. And give me the guts to say *yes* when I would rather shrink back and stay safe with my *no*.

Instead of occupying my mind with what bad things might happen when I step out in faith, remind me of these verses. No one opposed Paul, though I'm sure he could have used that excuse to stop talking about you. So instead, he plowed forward, and the church grew relationship by relationship.

Like Paul, let me see my limitations not as barriers but as opportunities to share you with others. Open my eyes to new ways of seeing my world. Deliver me from pessimism, and empower me to take that next step of faith. Amen.

Sky

For ever since the world was created,
people have seen the earth and sky.
Through everything God made,
they can clearly see his invisible qualities—
his eternal power and divine nature.
So they have no excuse for not knowing God.

ROMANS 1:20

Jesus, no matter what the weather today, give me a glimpse of the earth and sky, and as I gaze in both directions, I want to hear your heartbeat for this world. I choose to marvel in your creation because it points to your creativity, Word, and power. You fashioned everything I see today—every cherry blossom, June bug, nasturtium, nature trail, and local pond. They shout your abilities.

Thank you that you have revealed yourself to people who haven't even heard your name—through the earth and sky. I pray for them specifically today that you would enlighten them to understand your eternal power and divine nature through the created world. It seems like an impossible prayer, but you are the God of impossibilities.

In light of that, help me not to take for granted this great salvation. You've taught me so much about what it means to live for you. I don't want to hoard this wisdom for myself, but instead I want to share it freely. Whatever my circle of influence is, enlarge it so that I can take every opportunity today to confirm to those who don't yet know you that you are powerful and interested in relationship with everyone. Would you give me a bigger heart for those who are far from you? Replace my judgment with compassion, my fear with joy, and my reticence with a desire to engage. My heart is to see many find the freedom I have found in you. Amen.

Made

We are made right with God by placing our faith in Jesus Christ.
And this is true for everyone who believes, no matter who we are.

ROMANS 3:22

Jesus, I could not make myself right with you. Nothing I could do or make would reconcile me to a holy God. Without you, I am lost in my sins, forever separated, lacking peace and joy. Teach me what it means to truly have faith in you. I realize that faith isn't a magic formula where I pull the right levers and out pops all my selfish desires fulfilled. No, you tell me clearly that to follow you means I need to take up a cross, to die to myself. That is my perfect response to you making me right.

Teach me afresh that anything I do outside of faith is useless. When I think about all the work I've done for your kingdom in my own strength, I grow weary and afraid. I think about the final day when all my works will be revealed, the fire will consume, and only what's done for you (and in your power) will last like gold.

Keep me so close to you that I don't dare to live faithlessly. I don't want to live as if I'm agnostic, fully relying on my small wisdom to tackle today's big problems. Forgive me for thinking Christianity is me doing a bunch of good acts on my own. No, Lord, instead would you enlarge my heart's capacity to experience your love? Only then will I grow in faith, and naturally outpour my love for you through my service and in the power of the Spirit.

Faith means I believe the truth about who you are—the Savior of the world. And I also confirm the truth about myself—that the Savior of the world loves me and will give me the strength I need to live today with abundance. Amen.

Help

We can rejoice, too, when we run into problems and trials, for we know that they help us develop endurance. And endurance develops strength of character, and character strengthens our confident hope of salvation. And this hope will not lead to disappointment. For we know how dearly God loves us, because he has given us the Holy Spirit to fill our hearts with his love.

ROMANS 5:3-5

Jesus, I would rather have joyful things happen to me than trials. But your Word reminds me over and over again that I don't grow through having an easy life. I grow when trials and problems shout their way into my life. Help me to embrace the trials and problems I experience today. I want to bear up under them, milk them for all their worth, so that I will grow deeper and wider in my understanding of who you are.

Would you rebuild me? I want to be a person of character, not shrinking back when difficulties knock on my door. To be honest, it seems masochistic to want to welcome them, but I welcome a heart that can endure better, that can see the gift in the midst of the trial. Elevate my perspective from this world to heaven's where everything matters for eternity. My small obedience during a difficult time may seem insignificant in today's economy, but it is chronicled for eternity in heaven's shores.

Instead of trials shrinking my heart, making me suspicious and stingy, would you amplify my love? Empower me to surrender more, to take the last seat, to dare to forgive what seems unforgivable. Oh, how I need you today as I face more stress! Amen.

Choose

*Don't you realize that you become the slave of whatever
you choose to obey? You can be a slave to sin, which leads to
death, or you can choose to obey God, which leads to righteous
living. Thank God! Once you were slaves to sin, but now
you wholeheartedly obey this teaching we have given you.*

ROMANS 6:16-17

Jesus, thanks to your work on the cross, I don't have to be enslaved to sin. You have made a pathway for me that is full of richness and joy—no more shame, no more guilt, no more accusations. Help me live in light of all you've done. I don't want to become like a dog who returns to his vomit. I don't want my heart to be fickle, chasing after sin when I've experienced wild deliverance. Remind me that's like being an Israelite who looked back longingly on the slavery experienced in Egypt. Why would I want to return? It makes no sense.

But sin entices. It looks fun. It appeals to my desire to live my life on my own for the sake of my pleasure. Open my eyes to the reality of sin in the long run. In the short term, it appears tantalizing. But as it plays out, chains wrap around me, and I'm no longer free.

I would rather be an obedient servant than a slave to sin. I would rather spend my days in your presence than fretting over my guilt and shame. I would rather live in truth, gloriously set free, than live in darkness, wallowing in my addiction to wrongdoing.

I love that word, *wholeheartedly*. Would you show me today where I'm not obeying you wholeheartedly? I want my whole heart to live for you, to surrender to what you have for me, to obey you with abandon. Amen.

Miserable

Oh what a miserable person I am! Who will free me
from this life that is dominated by sin and death?
Thank God! The answer is in Jesus Christ our Lord.
So you see how it is: In my mind I really want to obey God's law,
but because of my sinful nature I am a slave to sin.

ROMANS 7:24-25

Jesus, without you I am utterly miserable. When I was lost in my sin, I couldn't help but do the things I determined I would never do. I repeated the sins my parents committed against me, though I swore I never would. I filtered my life through the lens of selfishness and narcissism, and my heart was both broken and cold—utterly lifeless and without hope.

But you, Jesus, changed all that. Help me to live in joyful response to your deliverance today. I choose to sing praises to you, even if I look awkward or crazy. I choose to say, "You are good," out loud. You have set me free, and I am grateful.

You are always the answer, Jesus. You give me the power to obey you in small ways and large. Today I give you the way I handle money. May I exercise faith in the way I give and manage what you've provided. Instead of spending money however I want, I choose to lay my resources at your feet and ask for your help in doling them out. In my anxious places, I pray you would remind me that you are rich and see my need.

Would you set me free in the way I see my finances? Would you show me the ways I've lived for myself in the way I spend my money? Thank you again for delivering me from sin. Teach me what it means to respond to your power by the way I live my life—right down to my wallet. Amen.

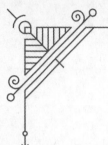

Condemnation

*So now there is no condemnation for those
who belong to Christ Jesus.
And because you belong to him, the power of
the life-giving Spirit has freed you
from the power of sin that leads to death.*

ROMANS 8:1-2

Jesus, I confess I have taken up the mantle of condemnation, even though you have set me free from it. What Satan has reminded me of (my sin), I have amplified in my mind, calling myself all sorts of names. It seems condemning myself has become my daily pastime, and I'm nearly helpless to stop it. Oh, please set me free from my erroneous thoughts!

My emotions don't determine how you see me, but often I live as if that were true. Help me reverse that, to so ground myself in the truth of your Word that I can easily recognize the voice of the enemy when he spews hatred in my ears. The truth? I am your child, gloriously loved, completely set free, utterly forgiven. I am no longer shackled to sin, nor does it define me. What defines me is my identity as a child of God.

While it's easy for me to tell others this important truth, for some reason it's harder for me to internalize it for myself. I am well aware of my own tendency to sin, to live in judgment, to curse, rail against, and harm others. And instead of confessing those sins and receiving your forgiveness, I agree with them, tell myself I'm beyond hope, and then continue to do them. Please set me free! Give me a right understanding of who I am in you. I am not condemned. You have not condemned me. I am perfectly aligned with you, and there's nothing I can do to change your affection for me. I want to live in light of that today. Amen.

Ever

No power in the sky above or in the earth below
—indeed, nothing in all creation will ever be able to
separate us from the love of God that is
revealed in Christ Jesus our Lord.

ROMANS 8:39

Jesus, *ever* means "never." Nothing *ever* can separate me from your love. This is a great comfort, one I need today when I wrongly believe that I could do all sorts of things that will separate me from you.

Remind me of the story of the prodigal son when I get ensnared in thinking like this. The father waited on tiptoes at the crest of the hill, waiting for his child to return. When he did, the father lavished love upon him, gave him his robe and ring, and instigated a great feast. This is a beautiful picture of the welcome you give me every day. Your love for me does not at all depend on me, just as the prodigal's position with the father had nothing to do with the prodigal and everything to do with the father's faithfulness.

Trials cannot separate your love from me. Temptations cannot undermine your affection. Satan and his evil forces, try as they might, cannot alter my right standing with you. No matter what the world throws my way, it cannot ruin your love. You are a faithful father. You cannot help but love your children.

Instead of taking your love for granted, let me live in response to your love by obeying you, praising you, and sharing your ways with others. May the reality that I'm loved infect the way I love others— even the difficult people in my life. Amen.

Affection

Love each other with genuine affection, and
take delight in honoring each other.

ROMANS 12:10

Jesus, teach me what it means to have genuine affection for those in my life. I admit that affection doesn't come naturally to me, and sometimes it frightens me. How can I tangibly demonstrate your love for others today? How can I listen, give an embrace, or empathize with a struggling friend? When I'm confused about how to go about loving those in my life, remind me of the way you lived on this earth, how you dignified the broken, listened to those whom no one listened to, welcomed children on your lap. You touched lepers and healed people with disease. You weren't afraid to get your hands dirty.

I want to have dirty hands and a clean heart, Jesus. Hands that get inconvenienced in serving others—all for your sake and your glory. I want my heart to reflect your affection for everyone, even those people who scare me, or ones whom I'm not naturally attracted to. Teach me what it means to have your vision, to see people no one sees, to help those who are helpless.

Instead of seeing service as drudgery or a "have-to," I want to learn the art of taking great delight in honoring others. Does that mean I write a note today? Give me a nudge about who needs that kind of encouragement. Does that mean I bring a meal to someone who needs nourishment? Help me to do that, not under compulsion, but with genuine affection. To serve you with joy is to serve others in like manner. Amen.

Presence

*Clothe yourself with the presence of the Lord Jesus Christ. And
don't let yourself think about ways to indulge your evil desires.*

ROMANS 13:14

Jesus, what a beautiful reminder for me today—to truly experience your presence. Teach me what it means to clothe myself in your presence, to walk moment by moment in your embrace. I realize it's a choice, that you don't want me to mindlessly go throughout my day in reaction to things, but that you want me to be proactively encountering you and your ways. Would you keep reminding me of this beautiful truth every day as I brush off sleep and put on my clothes?

I realize this is a choice on my part. It's a decision I make to think about you, to reorient my thoughts until they circumnavigate you. You are the Lord Jesus Christ, which means you are my master, my king, my everything. You deserve my allegiance and honor, my first thought of the day and the last.

I also know that the way my mind bends and where it settles is something within my control. I can let my thoughts wander to sin and stay defiantly there. And when my mind stays mired there, I tend to act out my thoughts—sin follows.

So today I choose you. I actively place my mind on how great you are. Wherever I go, whether I'm walking or driving, exercising or sitting still, working or resting—I will keep my thoughts centered on your goodness. Because when it's there, my mind won't have room for destructive, sinful thoughts. And for that, I'm grateful. Amen.

Build

We who are strong must be considerate of those who are sensitive
about things like this. We must not just please ourselves.
We should help others do what is right
and build them up in the Lord.

ROMANS 15:1-2

Jesus, thank you for making your body so diverse. I'm thankful that we're not all the same, nor do we all carry the same convictions. Some of my friends are new to discovering you, and some are veterans in the faith. As I see them both, remind me that my ruling choice is always love. Instead of asserting my way of seeing the world (through my lens), help me to see the world through their eyes. And develop a deep sense of empathy for those who differ from me.

Instead of judging a fellow believer for being weak in faith, remind me to pray for each one with compassion. And if I'm doing something in my freedom that undermines their tender faith, I want to stop. I don't want my freedom to hurt their relationship with you or their newfound trust. Instead of demanding they suddenly learn my way of doing things, I choose to be humble, to ask questions, and to model love.

Would you show me someone today who truly needs to be built up in their faith? I want to be an encouraging person. Slow me down enough to not merely be occupied by my own agenda so I can tangibly help a friend. Maybe that means stopping and praying with my friend in the moment, or sending an encouraging message, or meeting a need. Whatever it is, Lord, I want to be part of building up your body, not tearing it down. Amen.

Ambition

*My ambition has always been to preach the Good News where
the name of Christ has never been heard, rather than where
a church has already been started by someone else. I have
been following the plan spoken of in the Scriptures where it
says, "Those who have never been told about him will see,
and those who have never heard of him will understand."*

ROMANS 15:20-21

Jesus, I've often thought that the word *ambition* is a bad thing—
that those who are ambitious climb their way to the top, stepping on
others at all cost. But when I see it here, I'm reminded that ambition
can be a good thing, especially when it's connected to expanding your
kingdom. I admit, your kingdom is not always the first thing on my
mind when I wake. There have been far too many times where my own
kingdom has consumed my days.

I love that Paul wants to pioneer new work. He doesn't want to
interfere with already good work. In my context, Lord, show me where
there's a true need for your gospel, where it's not yet being preached or
lived out. May that truth inconvenience me, nag me at night, and gnaw
at my soul. I want Paul's ambition in this area, to be bravely obedient
to follow you down new pioneer paths—not for my gain, but for the
sake of your dynamically expanding kingdom.

Expand my view. I'm grateful I live in a time and a place where the
spiritual needs of the whole world are before me. Instead of letting that
immobilize me, let it ignite a holy fire—a desire in me to see your good
news spread around the globe. Amen.

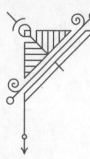

Imagined

That is what the Scriptures mean when they say, "No eye has seen, no ear has heard, and no mind has imagined what God has prepared for those who love him."

1 CORINTHIANS 2:9

Jesus, I need a renewed imagination. With media assaulting me day and night, with the glow of blue screens stealing my creativity, I've lost the part of me that dreams. I've been consumed by that which starves the soul. My imagination needs resurrection—and that resurrection must be orbiting around you.

I want my eyes to see into the future—the glory you have for me on heaven's shores. I want to make decisions in light of that day. But not merely so I gain reward, but because my heart toward you is what makes you smile.

I want my ears to be opened to the cries around me, but I also want to hear your heart. Instead of always listening to the voices that shout my shame, help me to hear your voice of love sung gloriously over me today. Expand my repertoire of hearing your voice. Enlarge my capacity to receive your love in this way.

I want my mind stretched and hewn, pliable in your hands. I want to have my imagination expanded so I'll see you as you are, not as I think you are. Where my imagination has seen me as utterly broken and unable to heal or grow, show me your tender ways, how you have been with me since my mother's womb. Your thoughts toward me are always love, but I've often imagined they are not. So please show me that you love me, and let my mind, heart, and soul follow suit. I want to live in light of your outrageous love. Amen.

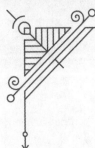

Slave

You say, "I am allowed to do anything"—
but not everything is good for you.
And even though "I am allowed to do anything,"
I must not become a slave to anything.

1 Corinthians 6:12

Jesus, I am so grateful for the freedom you bought me on the cross. Thank you that I no longer have to be enslaved to sin or legalism or pride. I love that I can freely move about my life with peace and joy—all because of your beautiful grace.

And yet, I don't want to abuse my privilege as a free child of God. Yes, I was once shackled to sin, but now that the handcuffs are off, give me a longing to pursue things that grow my heart, not recapture my affections for lesser things.

I want to first pursue you with everything within me. And then I want my life to consist of good things like the fruit of the Spirit. Oh, how I need your love, joy, peace, patience, kindness, gentleness, goodness, and self-control. All this fruit reveals your beautiful character in me. And if I have this fruit in abundance, I won't need to chase selfish desires or so-called freedom.

Please show me any place in my heart that is enslaved to sin, whether it be worshipping my reflection, chasing ambition, nursing bitterness, dismissing a friend, or pursuing my own pleasure. I want to, instead, be your slave. Amen.

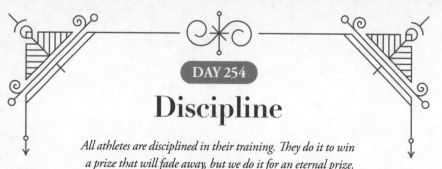

Discipline

*All athletes are disciplined in their training. They do it to win
a prize that will fade away, but we do it for an eternal prize.
So I run with purpose in every step. I am not just shadowboxing.*

1 CORINTHIANS 9:25-26

Jesus, I will admit—discipline makes me tired and stressed out. Help me have a healthier view of what discipline means. My daily choices reflect my relationship with you, and my habits make my life. So today would you show me where I've allowed bad habits to rule my days? And would you reveal where I need to pursue discipline as an athlete would?

I am not good at making daily good choices without a goal in mind. So set that prize before me. Help me keep it in mind. It's an eternal prize, as Paul says here, unfading and nonperishable. It's amazing to me as I look back on my life how many times I disciplined myself for things that would ultimately decay. Your Word says I need to work out my salvation with fear and trembling. Yes, Lord, keep me in that frame of mind—not that I'm working to earn it, but that living out my salvation means I joyfully choose to honor you in whatever I do.

I want to "run with purpose in every step." Teach me what that means. Help me redefine my purpose so it aligns with your grander purposes. Show me where I fit in your kingdom. Thank you that you've made me to live in this time period, this place, with these people around me. Help me to make the most of my space so that I can continue to run with endurance the course you've set for me to run. Amen.

Gifts

There are different kinds of spiritual gifts, but the same
Spirit is the source of them all. There are different kinds of
service, but we serve the same Lord. God works in different
ways, but it is the same God who does the work in all of us.

1 CORINTHIANS 12:4-6

Jesus, open my eyes to the beautiful diversity of your body today. Remind me that we all need each other, that if I'm a hand, I don't need to scorn a foot—that for a body to live and move, it needs all its moving parts, and each part has a specific role to play in movement and life.

Thank you for giving gifts to your people! Thank you for giving gifts to me. It almost seems like too much, since the gift of salvation is the best gift. But you are a generous God, and you have gifted me. Forgive me for downplaying the gifts you've given me. Help me not to envy the gifts of others, but to simply rejoice that we're all gifted uniquely in order to carry out your will on this earth.

I want to embrace the diversity of your church, while praising the unity that you bring, and the unchangeable nature of you. Thank you that while we are varied, you never change. You continue to be the head of this body, and you are doing marvelous things.

Show me how I can encourage a fellow believer today who is truly operating in light of the giftedness you've given. It may not be the way I serve you, but I see it as beautiful. I want to be a cheerleader in your church, not a critic.

Jesus, thank you for working through me. I am astounded that you would choose such a crazy thing—to display your power through my weakness. I'm humbled and grateful and in awe. Amen.

Nothing

*If I had the gift of prophecy, and if I understood all
of God's secret plans and possessed all knowledge,
and if I had such faith that I could move mountains,
but didn't love others, I would be nothing.*

1 CORINTHIANS 13:2

Jesus, I'll admit there are times when I long to understand all your secret plans. I am seldom prophetic, nor do I understand the mysteries of you. I have also lamented that I don't know more or enough to truly fathom this world and its intricacies. Knowledge is greatly praised in my world, and sometimes I feel my mind is too small for it. And when I watch those whose faith seems to move the earth, I want what they have—more like envy than a prayer.

All these things—prophecy, knowledge, and faith—are important, but they cannot compare to the greatest virtue: your love. You remind me here that when I pursue otherworldly insight or earthly knowledge, or even clothe myself with the greatest faith, it matters very little. In fact, it is nothing. I could possess all three and miss you.

I don't want that, Lord. Thank you for sharing this cautionary tale with me—that some who appear to be skilled and godly may be lacking the very essence of you, becoming counterfeit and a flimsy copy.

I want love. I long for my life to be marked by the cross, the place where your love poured out in selfless sacrifice. I want to be full of genuine kindness more than prophecy, knowledge, or faith. Let love be my ruling trait, Jesus. Amen.

Scriptures

*I passed on to you what was most important and what had
also been passed on to me. Christ died for our sins, just as
the Scriptures said. He was buried, and he was raised from
the dead on the third day, just as the Scriptures said.*

1 Corinthians 15:3-4

Jesus, your Word is powerful. Your Scriptures tell a grand story of redemption, from Genesis to Revelation—showing our beginning and our end. You, Jesus, are the culmination, the climax of that good book. Your story is the story all the stories hinge upon, and for that I'm grateful. Help me to find myself in the midst of your story, so that I can be a part of making history in the kingdom of God.

That history comes from the very real knowledge that you came to earth as a beautiful incarnation. You lived a sinless life, determined to follow the Father wherever he led you. His leading brought you to the cross, where you made the choice to be bloodied for us—a once-and-for-all sacrifice humankind can never repay. Three days later, you rose again and changed everything. This is the gospel I need to preach to myself daily because it truly is good news—not just for me, but also for a world desperate to live a new story.

I want to pass on this story, Jesus. Today I pray you would show me small and big ways to share this glorious good news, whether it be through acts of kindness, an apt word given at a perfect moment, a job well done, or sacrificing myself for the sake of another, I want to show the world what true transformation looks like, and that it originated in your origin story. Thank you, Jesus, for your indescribable, marvelous gift of life. Amen.

Perfume

*Thank God! He has made us his captives and continues
to lead us along in Christ's triumphal procession. Now he
uses us to spread the knowledge of Christ everywhere,
like a sweet perfume. Our lives are a Christ-like
fragrance rising up to God. But this fragrance is perceived
differently by those who are being saved and by those
who are perishing. To those who are perishing, we are
a dreadful smell of death and doom. But to those who
are being saved, we are a life-giving perfume.
And who is adequate for such a task as this?*

2 Corinthians 2:14-16

Jesus, you have done so much. You have accomplished the work the Father has set for you to do. And now you have asked me to join you in the triumphal procession—a parade of joy that shows just how great you are. You have set me free, and now you've given me the supreme joy of being a part of rescuing others. What a privilege.

Thank you that you have perfumed my life with yours. And that as I live my life for you, that perfume permeates the places I go. I don't have to make that happen; it simply occurs because your Spirit resides in me.

Instead of worrying about how people will respond to that perfume, help me be bold as I live my life for you. I understand some will see my life as an invitation to your grace, and others will recoil, wanting to flee from your offer of salvation. Help me not take the latter personally, but instead see it as confirmation that you are indeed at work through me.

The last question Paul asks is mine: Who is adequate for such a task as this? I feel that, Lord. I am inadequate, but you are my adequacy, and I rest in your ability today. Amen.

Reconciliation

And all of this is a gift from God, who brought us back to himself through Christ. And God has given us this task of reconciling people to him. For God was in Christ, reconciling the world to himself, no longer counting people's sins against them. And he gave us this wonderful message of reconciliation.

2 CORINTHIANS 5:18-19

Jesus, what a monumental task, reconciliation. I'm grateful I don't have to reconcile people to you, but that this is your work through me. Thank you for going first, for making a way for me to be reconciled to the Father because of your life, death, and resurrection. I am astounded by it all, and I sit here with great joy because you've chosen me. Thank you.

You have not counted my many sins against me. There is no bank in the sky adding up my infractions, making my balance sheet grossly imbalanced with sin. No, you have chosen to pardon my sins, and you no longer hold them against me. This is genuinely good news, and it has set me free from guilt and shame.

I want to share this news with others. Make me a minister of reconciliation today. Show me how to demonstrate your power and good news to those I come in contact with. I want to live as a reconciler because I know that it brings both you and me great joy.

Help me see the message of reconciliation not as a burden but as a wonder. Help me see it as an amazing privilege. After all, I have the privilege of letting people know they are not alone, that their sins have been dealt with decisively, and they no longer need to live as slaves. They are set free! May my message reflect that freedom today. Amen.

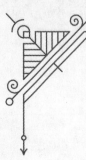

Serve

We serve God whether people honor us or despise us,
whether they slander us or praise us.
We are honest, but they call us impostors.
We are ignored, even though we are well known.
We live close to death, but we are still alive.
We have been beaten, but we have not been killed.

2 Corinthians 6:8-9

Jesus, let it be that I live for your approval and not the fickle opinion of the crowds. I want my integrity to be dependent on your goodness, not public applause. Please encourage me where my relationships have served to undermine instead of strengthen.

As I experience betrayal, dishonor, slander, or being ignored, let those times be a catalyst for empathy. Instead of wallowing in my own pain, remind me that there's a dying world out there of people who feel the same way I do right now.

Let me learn from the negative example of others' backbiting. May it instruct me to bless and not curse, to mend and not tear apart, to uplift instead of pull down.

I choose to forgive those who inadvertently hurt me. I choose to forgive those who meant to betray me. I choose to forgive those who said mean things about me behind my back. I choose to forgive those who assigned wrong motives to me. Because when I am forgiving others, I am most like you, Jesus. Amen.

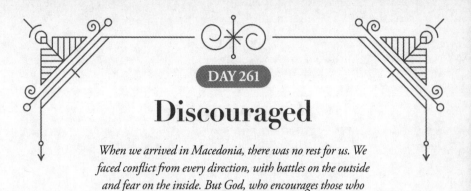

Discouraged

When we arrived in Macedonia, there was no rest for us. We
faced conflict from every direction, with battles on the outside
and fear on the inside. But God, who encourages those who
are discouraged, encouraged us by the arrival of Titus.

2 CORINTHIANS 7:5-6

Jesus, although I don't share Paul's story about ministry distress to that degree, I still resonate with his words here. I have had stretches of time where rest is elusive. Wherever I turn, conflict seems to erupt. Battles face me on the outside, and as a result, my inside world is full of fearful chaos. Oh, dear Lord, deliver me from this! Or give me a brand-new perspective so I can discern better how to navigate through.

You promise that you will encourage the discouraged. Would you send me a Titus this week who will help me sort through my heart and pray with passion toward wholeness? I don't merely want to cope with my restlessness and fear, I want to overcome it so I can be an agent of joy in this joyless world. But oh, how I need another friend who will battle alongside me. Your Word promises that when two or three are gathered together who love you, you will reside in the midst of them. That's what I want, dear Jesus.

After I sort through my fear, teasing it out and seeing it for what it is—a simple lack of faith—help me to turn my gaze outward, to those who have a similar struggle. Send me to be their Titus this week so I can participate in the lost art of encouragement. Amen.

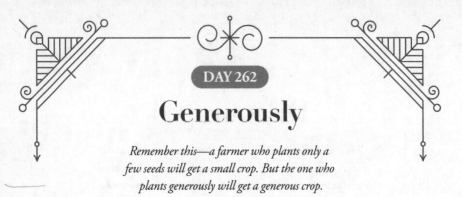

Generously

*Remember this—a farmer who plants only a
few seeds will get a small crop. But the one who
plants generously will get a generous crop.*

2 Corinthians 9:6

Jesus, I live in a stingy world, a world of hoarding and fear. And to be honest, there are times when I fret so much about having enough that I let that worry inform my giving. Instead of seeing this world as yours and realizing all I have is met in you, I somehow think it's more blessed to hoard than to give. Please forgive me. I don't want to live in this kind of narrow-minded stinginess.

So open my eyes today, Jesus, to the ways I've lacked generosity. I'm so grateful that you're tender with me, not pointing out my weaknesses so you can shame me, but instead offering me winsome hope and tangible care as I realize my need for you. I understand that in and of myself, I cannot give generously, but when I'm close to you, I won't be able to help but live that way.

Revolutionize my heart from the inside out. Make me into a disciple of yours whose wallet is fully converted. Would you be so kind as to show me a need this month that I can meet with absolute joy—even if it scares me? I want to let go of my vise grip on finances, fueled by worry, not faith.

The truth is, you are all I need. You see me, and you know me, and you will continue to provide for my needs. And how humbling is this? You will empower me to be part of your solution to provide for others who need help. Amen.

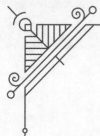

Boast

If I must boast, I would rather boast about
the things that show how weak I am.
God, the Father of our Lord Jesus, who is worthy
of eternal praise, knows I am not lying.

2 CORINTHIANS 11:30-31

Jesus, I don't want to boast about me, me, me. How tiring that gets, and how strange—because tasks accomplished in my own strength and for my own glory will eventually come to nothing. No, I want to be like the apostle Paul who, although he was full of great promise as a Pharisee and had an envied spiritual pedigree, realized that all his purported gifts counted for nothing. His sufficiency wasn't in himself; it was solidly in you.

And that's where I want to live today, Jesus. I want to find my worth at your footstool. I need to know I am sufficiently loved, fully alive, beautifully forgiven—all because of what you've done for me on the cross. You did everything. My response is to receive and dwell in that finished work.

I love the paradox that my weakness becomes your platform. When I move out of the way, you can perform your best. You don't need my cleverness. You don't even require that I have myself together. What you desire in my life to perform your utmost is simply my dependence, as well as recognizing that my weakness is a welcoming of your power.

So move me from simply being comfortable with my weakness to learning the power (and the paradox) of boasting in my weakness. I am not even sure how to do that, but I welcome your help. Amen.

With

Dear brothers and sisters, I close my letter with these last words:
Be joyful. Grow to maturity. Encourage each other.
Live in harmony and peace.
Then the God of love and peace will be with you.

2 CORINTHIANS 13:11

Jesus, I'm grateful for Paul's closing words here. They serve as a healthy framework for my day. Oh, how I want you to be with me today. I need your love and peace dwelling within me, informing my joy.

Teach me what it means to be joyful in and through this day. Instead of jumping to negative conclusions and allowing my mind to chase desperation rabbit trails, fill me with your renewed perspective. Instead of chronicling the bad moments, help me to count the blessings, and in that multiply my joy.

Instead of lagging behind and wallowing in my insecurity and smallness, I want to take another step toward spiritual maturity today. Show me one area I can grow in, by choosing rest over worry, faith over fear, peaceful over frazzled.

Bring a friend or family member who desperately needs tangible encouragement, and let my interaction with everyone be typified by harmony and peace, not arguments and stress. I ask all this by your strength, trusting you will bring this about. Amen.

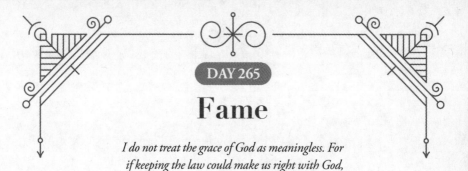

Fame

*I do not treat the grace of God as meaningless. For
if keeping the law could make us right with God,
then there was no need for Christ to die.*

GALATIANS 2:21

Jesus, *meaningless* is a strong word. I don't want to ever treat what you've done for me as if it is nothing. But I do that when I wrongly think there's something I must do to add to what you've already completed. I've often begun in the Spirit, only to take back control and end in my own strength. When I do that, I'm saying I can run things on my own, thank you very much.

Oh, how it must hurt you when I turn my back on your sufficiency and chase after my own. You offer everything I need for living this life in a godly manner, but I sometimes think it's all up to me. Forgive me. It's a pretty heavy statement that when I live independently of you, plugging along with my own resources, I am treating you and your grace as meaningless.

I don't want to add to your gospel. It is never Jesus plus a bunch of spiritual things I have to do. It is always Jesus in me, the hope of glory. So today, I choose to rest in your finished work on the cross. I welcome Sabbath rest to replace my work-as-you-go view of salvation. I choose to be like John the Baptist, who realized that he must decrease while you increased.

Help me live in light of Jesus plus nothing today. All you have done is amazing. I cannot complete it. Instead, I rest in your unchanging grace where I no longer have to worry about my future with you. It is utterly secure. Amen.

Vain

*How foolish can you be? After starting your new
lives in the Spirit, why are you now trying to
become perfect by your own human effort?
Have you experienced so much for nothing?
Surely it was not in vain, was it?*

GALATIANS 3:3-4

Jesus, I don't want to be foolish. I don't want to fool myself into thinking that salvation and sanctification rest on my shoulders. Instead, I want to explore what it means to truly live freely in the landscape of the Spirit—to dance in his strength, not my own. Widen my heart and mind to your ways, the way you perform what concerns me, how your sufficiency informs mine.

I acknowledge that my human effort is microscopic compared to the vastness of your capabilities. I could not rescue myself from sin. I could never have lived a perfect life for one day—let alone thirty-three years. I could not heal people from leprosy, cast out countless demons, feed 5000 from a simple lunch of bread and fish, or raise a friend from the dead. I could not carry the weight of everyone else's sins (of the whole world, then and now and the future). I could not die on the torturous cross. I could not resurrect in the aftermath of that act of supreme love. I am not you.

But you are gloriously you. You have done everything for me, yet somehow I want to diminish your work by "helping you out." No, today I choose to rest in your completed work on the cross. I choose to honor you, spend my day singing praise to you, and bow my heart in reverence before you. You did what I could never do, and as I humble myself before you, you continue to do amazing work in and through me. I welcome your work as I rest from mine. Amen.

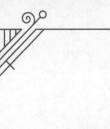

United

For you are all children of God through faith in Christ Jesus.
And all who have been united with Christ
in baptism have put on Christ,
like putting on new clothes.

GALATIANS 3:26-27

Jesus, as I try on new clothes, remind me of this truth: I have put on you. You are part of me; you are displayed in me; you are the hope I wear like a comfortable robe. Thank you for enabling me to be so close to you, as close as my clothing, as near as my breath.

Today I will rest in knowing I am your beloved child. Even if my own family of origin didn't perfectly reveal a healthy father-child relationship, elevate my gaze to your perfect fatherly ways. I don't want my own dysfunction to mar the way I view you. Show me where I've projected my own family's pain onto the way I think you work toward me. Instead, renew my mind with the truth of who you really are— compassionate, caring, empowering.

You give good gifts to your children. You discipline those you love, not with harsh words or capriciousness, but with tender purpose. You sent your Son to pay the price for my sin so I could have unfettered access to you. You promise that nothing can separate me from your love—not even my own waywardness. You are the good shepherd who pursues the one, leaving the ninety-nine. You simply love me as your child. You delight in me, and you listen when I'm afraid. Thank you for calling me your child. Help me live confidently in light of that truth. Amen.

Truly

So Christ has truly set us free.
Now make sure that you stay free,
and don't get tied up again in slavery to the law.

GALATIANS 5:1

Jesus, while it is entirely true that you set me free, I'm afraid I don't always live as one who experiences it. My own shame and fear hold me back. I sometimes think your grace and kindness are too good to be true. Or I believe the lies spoken over me that I'll never overcome that sin, and I'm destined to live a life of spiritual failure. The threat of this lives deep within me, and I'm afraid. Like a prisoner, I look for escape, but the cell is secure, and I cannot think my way out of it.

But you have gloriously set me free. You have the key to my prison and have unlocked it. And there I sit inside the cell, unaware of my freedom. Help me to realize I don't have to stay in that place. I am no longer enslaved to not being good enough. I don't have to believe the lie that I am less than. Instead, because of you, I have been given more than enough to live as free.

I have to admit that sometimes my cell feels quite comfortable. I know how to live with myself at the helm. Being on my own, flying in freedom with you, seems strangely scary. Help me today to live as your child, free from the prison, unshackled by me but tethered to you—my Emancipator. Amen.

Serve

You have been called to live in freedom, my brothers and sisters.
But don't use your freedom to satisfy your sinful nature.
Instead, use your freedom to serve one another in love.

GALATIANS 5:13

Jesus, I'm so grateful you haven't called me to rules. You haven't told me to figure life out on my own. Not only did you provide a way for me to have a relationship with you, but also you have empowered me, through the gift of your Spirit, to live with victory and freedom. I love freedom! I need freedom! I choose to cherish this unexpectedly sweet gift!

Show me what it means to live in freedom on this earth. Free me from obsessive thoughts, from spiraling downward in fear, from living as if you're not there. You are there. You are with me. You enliven me to understand freedom in so many areas. Set me free in the way I use your resources. Bring emancipation to the shackles of my past so that I no longer live in light of my victimhood, but move through my days with purpose and joy.

And as these verses remind me, may the freedom you bring me become irresistible. May it inform the way I love the people in my life. May I set other people free by the way I love them as you do. Amen.

Forgave

*He is so rich in kindness and grace that he purchased our freedom
with the blood of his Son and forgave our sins.*

EPHESIANS 1:7

Jesus, I sometimes conjure up my past and count my sins until they build a skyscraper beyond the clouds. My waywardness has overwhelmed me. I don't want to live shackled to my past choices, my stubborn rebellion. I sit here completely in need, dependent on your kindness and grace. Help me remind myself that my past story of woe need not inform today's reality.

You have purchased new freedom. It is finished. I no longer need to live identified as a sinner. Now, because of you, I am a saint in your kingdom. You have prepared good works for me to do—I simply need to walk in them. If I connect myself to the sinner identity, I will miss my new, enlivened identity as one who is absolutely loved by you.

You have forgiven me. Help me live in light of that absolute truth. The sins I've committed in the past? Forgiven. The wrong thoughts I have today? Forgiven. The choices I make tomorrow to live life independently of you? Forgiven. This is the bedrock truth I camp on. I don't want the truth of my forgiveness to enable me to sin more so that grace would abound. No! Instead, may your forgiveness permeate the way I live my life—in surrendered, dependent worship of you. You deserve nothing less. Amen.

Authority

*God has put all things under the authority of Christ and has
made him head over all things for the benefit of the church.
And the church is his body; it is made full and complete
by Christ, who fills all things everywhere with himself.*

EPHESIANS 1:22-23

Jesus, you have all the authority in this world, even when nations
crumble, genocide reigns, wars and rumors of wars haunt our daily
news feed, and politics grows more and more corrupt. You sit on the
throne above it all, above our fears and concerns.

And above all that, you are enthroned over the church, the beautiful head of your body. We are a messy lot, making up your hands and
arms to a world in need of embracing. Help us see ourselves as your
hug to this broken world.

Today I want to camp on the truth that you complete my heart,
even as the world shifts and shakes beneath me. Everything I need I
discover in your overflowing storehouse of love. I do not need to chase
after other things to fill my heart—instead, let my heart find my rest
in you alone.

I want to believe in your sufficiency that fills my insufficiency. I
want to be a willing cup to be filled with your refreshing presence. I
want to finally realize that I stand complete because of you. You are
everything, Lord Jesus. Amen.

Masterpiece

We are God's masterpiece. He has created us anew in Christ Jesus,
so we can do the good things he planned for us long ago.

EPHESIANS 2:10

Jesus, it's difficult for me to see myself as your masterpiece. But I can understand that you're an amazing artist because of the beauty of creation all around me. Translate that knowledge so it pertains to me. You make beautiful things, and I am one of those you have created. The next time I see a masterpiece, help me stop and consider that you have made me with the same dedicated care and time.

Part of my being your artistic rendering relies on your ability to create newness out of old. You have truly made me brand new. You have fashioned me from broken shards, reworking me into stained glass that tells the raucous story of your redemption. You take my ashes and craft them into statues of beauty. You who make everything from nothing know how to make new from decay.

Oh, Resurrected One, help me to lay down the things in my life that desperately need your resurrection power. I cannot fix my friend. I cannot make him see his erroneous ways. I have a hard time discerning your beauty within her. I scare easily, worry even more frequently, and I lack the kind of faith that helps me live with victory. All my worries and cares I lay at your artist feet. Take it all. Craft a heart that lets go of pain and embraces you. Help me be more and more beautiful by the quickness of my forgiveness and the constancy of my surrender. Amen.

Privilege

*By God's grace and mighty power,
I have been given the privilege of serving
him by spreading this Good News.*

EPHESIANS 3:7

Jesus, reorient my mind today. I want to move toward believing that sharing your gospel is a privilege, not a stressful task. It should burst forth from me, infectious, joyful. A privilege is something you receive when you're in special connection to someone with power, and I am certainly connected to you—the God who created the universe. You have done so much for me that I can scarcely articulate it. And all you've done has served to heal my heart and set my feet on a straight path.

Show me ways to be a part of sharing how good you are with others today. I want to speak of you as one speaks about a treasured friend. I want to live in a way that emulates the beauty you possess. I want to do my tasks today with holy awe, knowing that my work is not in vain and that you've dignified my labor. I want to represent you beautifully, to reveal your character to a world in deep need of good character.

All this comes about by your amazing grace and mighty power— all gifts I do not deserve, but relish nonetheless. Oh, how good you are to me. And how much your heart bends toward those who don't yet know you. I surrender my agenda today so I can bring a taste of your goodness to those starving for your affection (even if they don't realize they are). Amen.

Glory

*All glory to God, who is able, through his mighty power
at work within us, to accomplish infinitely more than we
might ask or think. Glory to him in the church and in Christ
Jesus through all generations forever and ever! Amen.*

EPHESIANS 3:20-21

Jesus, teach me what it means to live in light of your glory. You are greater than me, and you have done works I cannot comprehend. You are light, and in you there is no shifting shadow or variation. You have orchestrated the most beautiful exchange—your life for mine, so that I can live in newness of life. Thank you, Jesus.

I feel weak today. My resolve is thin, and my heart is battered. But you promise that your Spirit is within, and he loves to do good work in and through me. I need that power today—power to see things as you do, power to live life in your strength and not in mine, power to overcome the thoughts that steal my joy, power to love those who bother me or hurt my feelings. In and of myself, I am helpless to do all this, but you are more than capable. All you need is my constant, joy-filled surrender.

Elevate my capacity for doing more. Instead of shrinking back in fear at the tasks before me, help me to realize that when I'm partnered with you, all things are possible, even the impossible. You are the God of amazing possibilities, and I want to live today in light of that truth.

Expand my imagination so I'll be able to think greater thoughts of you and what you want to do on this earth. Forgive me for small faith, small thoughts, and a small heart. Do big work through me, and I will give you glory in the beautiful aftermath. Amen.

Head

*We will speak the truth in love, growing in every way more
and more like Christ, who is the head of his body, the church.*

EPHESIANS 4:15

Jesus, in my world, I tend to think it's all about you and me and what we do together. I view Christianity as a personal thing, not a corporate endeavor. Forgive me. Remind me of the importance of spending time with other people who love you, not forsaking my time with others out of fear of hurt, but giving them an open heart, available to love and be loved. You are the head of this glorious body of yours, and I hurt you if I actively avoid spending time with other people.

I also realize that my greatest growth comes in the context of relationship—with you, with others. I no longer want to have a heart that's closed off to you or others. Would you show me where I've chosen isolation over engagement? Would you heal me from past wounds so I can dare to move toward others again in a healthy way? I'm afraid, Lord, but I know you will be with me in every relationship I pursue, showing me how to live openhearted.

In my daily relationships, I do want to speak the truth in love—not truth at the expense of love with harsh words, nor love at the expense of truth. I want to be open, but with kindness, sharing your ways in a gentle way. Be the Lord of my daily interactions. Remind me to be quiet when it's necessary (and oh, that's quite often!). My prayer today is that I would be more and more like you in the way I love people. Amen.

Fighting

We are not fighting against flesh-and-blood enemies,
but against evil rulers and authorities of the unseen
world, against mighty powers in this dark world, and
against evil spirits in the heavenly places.

EPHESIANS 6:12

Jesus, I forget this truth. Forgive me. When arguments escalate, I tend to think my battle is against another person. I can so quickly move toward demonizing someone who has a different opinion than me. Or I can assign ill motives to them without them even realizing it. I can write off people who have hurt me, severing relationships prematurely. Oh, dear Jesus, help me.

In the midst of a personal battle with a loved one, shock me back to the present. Instead of looking at them as an enemy, remind me of my very real enemy, whose aim is to steal from me, kill my resolve and my relationships, and destroy my witness. Satan and his hordes are the real enemy, the ones who patrol the air and only want to mar your creation, Lord. With that firmly fixed in my mind, I know my prayers will change from, "Please change that person," to "Jesus, don't allow the enemy to deceive them anymore."

It's not hard to believe this world we live in has evil permeating the atmosphere, but sometimes that very evil causes me to want to hide. Shore me up. Keep me connected to you—secure and fearless. I don't want to live in defeat, cynical. Instead, remind me that you have won the victory. You dealt a death-knell blow to Satan when you cried your last words on the cross. The battle is real, but the victory is gloriously, most assuredly won. I choose to rest there. Amen.

Occasion

Pray in the Spirit at all times and on every occasion.
Stay alert and be persistent in your prayers
for all believers everywhere.

EPHESIANS 6:18

Jesus, this is a true mandate—one I want to take up daily, hourly, minute by minute. Teach me what it means to pray in the Spirit, invigorated by him, informed by his intelligence, fueled by a redemptive view of this world. I want to have a closer-than-my-breath relationship with you, where I share my heart and take the time to hear from you. In that circle of relationship, I know the world will change—not because of me, but because you are a God who loves to intersect this world and enact redemption. It's your heart, and I long for that to be my constant orientation.

No matter whom I encounter today, I want to be receptive to praying for those I meet—even if it means being uncomfortable or asking a stranger if I can pray. I know there have been many times when I've ignored that unction to pray, but today please empower me to jump outside of comfort and instead be an agent of comfort for others. After all, your Spirit is known as the Comforter, and what better way to bring comfort to those who hurt than to pray?

Help me obey the last part of this verse about alertness. Wake me up in the middle of the night to pray for those in desperate situations. Hearken my heart to bend toward prayer throughout today. And for those prayer requests that have lengthened to years, help me not to lose heart, but to continue praying persistently, knowing that your timing may differ from mine, but that you are faithful to answer. Amen.

Character

May you always be filled with the fruit of your salvation—
the righteous character produced in your life by Jesus
Christ—for this will bring much glory and praise to God.

PHILIPPIANS 1:11

Jesus, this is a world of people with dubious character—even in the church. So many people are stellar on the outside, well decorated for company, only to be dead men's bones on the inside, full of addictions and sin aplenty. I don't want to be that sort of follower. Instead, make my insides match my outsides. I want my heart to be fully redeemed, invigorated to make the kind of choices (by your strength) that make you smile. I want to hear, "Well done, good and faithful servant" when I finish my last breath on earth.

I want to be always filled with fruit—the kind of life that reveals all the beautiful things you have done. I know I can't playact my way through life, pretending to be good when my heart is far from you. I realize that my character comes directly as a result of your nearness to me, and my continued surrender. Oh, dear Jesus, I surrender again. I can't live this life without you. I need you to help me live as a person of character.

I do want my choices today to bring you praise, honor, and glory. I want to be like an obedient child who receives praise from a parent for a job well done. I want to welcome your discipline instead of running from it. Keep me from straying.

Would you help me long for godliness, Jesus? I know you have enabled me to die to sin and its lure in order to live for you. May the pull of righteous living be stronger than my desire to run my life without you. Amen.

Bold

I fully expect and hope that I will never be ashamed, but that I
will continue to be bold for Christ, as I have been in the past.
And I trust that my life will bring honor
to Christ, whether I live or die.
For to me, living means living for Christ, and dying is even better.

PHILIPPIANS 1:20-21

Jesus, I don't want to shrink back any longer. Give me boldness of action and speech; make me unconcerned with what other people think of me. Because when I live for the approval of others, I shrink, and my witness lessens. Instead, I want to live unashamedly for you because you faced the greatest kind of shame for me. Although the gospel may appear foolish to this world, I truly am not ashamed of it. I know I needed a Savior, and I'm utterly grateful for what you've done for me.

So let me live as if I truly believe that—full of guts and grit. Help me care more about what you think than fearing my reputation. Today I want to remember how fleeting life is, that I only have a few moments on this earth (in light of eternity) to make a difference in your kingdom. I want to make my life count, and I realize I cannot do this on my own. Like Paul, I need your strength to accomplish your kingdom goals.

I want to get to the place where I can confidently declare that for me to live is you, and to die is to gain more of you. You are everything to me, Jesus, and everything I have is yours. This includes my agenda. Hijack it today. I give you permission. Open new doors to ministry. Show me new people to love. Invigorate my heart with your kingdom perspective, and may I be bolder and bolder to share the gospel throughout my life. Amen.

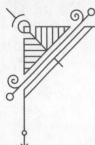

Humble

Don't be selfish; don't try to impress others.
Be humble, thinking of others as better than yourselves.
Don't look out only for your own interests,
but take an interest in others, too.

PHILIPPIANS 2:3-4

Jesus, I live in a world void of humility. Everyone wants to be known. Fame is possible these days, even if for a fleeting moment. We can star in our own movies, project our images to the whole world, and publish our words for the masses. We are megaphones for ourselves, our ways, our "truth." And all this fame-coddling has made us arrogant. Oh, please forgive us. Like Daniel prayed for his wayward nation, I confess on behalf of mine—we have lost humility, and we've worshipped the created rather than the Creator.

In this crazy world, you have called me to be utterly different. Replace my need for impressing others with deep humility. Instead of demanding that others serve me, praise me, and follow me, I pray I would bow the knee to you and humbly ask you whom you want me to serve today. Help me highlight the dignity of others, to praise their accomplishments, to genuinely encourage the part of others that clearly reveals how they bear your image.

I want to be like you, Jesus, who set aside your agenda for the sake of reconciling the world to yourself. You epitomized humility and sacrifice. In this world of celebrity (yes, even in the church), may I learn the beautiful art of going low, taking the last seat, and seeking to encourage others. Instead of spending my energy promoting myself, may I spend my life empowering others. Amen.

Focus

Forgetting the past and looking forward to what lies ahead,
I press on to reach the end of the race and receive the heavenly
prize for which God, through Christ Jesus, is calling us.

PHILIPPIANS 3:13-14

Jesus, what lies behind is hard to forget sometimes. Memories haunt me, inform my today. They seem like bullies, these recollections, and they certainly don't help me find the joy of today or anticipate the power of tomorrow. I don't know how to let go, but I trust that you will be able to give me the bravery I need to press forward.

Help me have single-hearted devotion to you today. I want to run a fierce race with zealous focus on the prize you have for me. I'm tired of living in retrospect; it gives me spiritual whiplash. I want to press on toward the next thing you have for me.

Keep heaven close to my mind today as I make decisions. Enable me to focus on the things that really matter in light of eternity. I will need your perseverance. I will need tenacity. I very much need your grit.

Be with me along this very long marathon. Remind me that this race you've called me to is not a sprint; it's not short term. Give me the courage I need to finish well, to reach the prize you hold out before me. Amen.

Citizens

We are citizens of heaven, where the Lord Jesus Christ lives.
And we are eagerly waiting for him to return as our Savior.
He will take our weak mortal bodies and change them
into glorious bodies like his own, using the same power
with which he will bring everything under his control.

PHILIPPIANS 3:20-21

Jesus, when the citizens around me clamor for fame or control, remind me afresh that my citizenship is not here, it's there—on the glorious shores of the hereafter. This is not my home. Forgive me for living as if it is, storing up treasures here as if the next life doesn't matter. Remind me that anything done in your strength for your kingdom will follow me beyond the grave. Reward will be mine to the extent that I live as if I'm wholly a citizen of heaven.

Instead of crafting my world as if you'll never come back, I want to constantly remember that what I see is not all there is. And as I gaze at the sky today, I want to fixate my mind on your glorious return. You will come to earth in the same manner you left, on the clouds, in order to gather your own to yourself. What an amazing thought!

I suffer in this body, Jesus. Things don't always work the way they should, and I know that one day this body will decay and degrade. One day I will breathe my last breath, and in a hiccup of a moment, I'll be in your presence. Oh, how I want my life to count here on this earth for the sake of eternity. So elevate my perspective away from the here and now to the final day and the hereafter. I await resurrection with baited breath and undeniable joy. Amen.

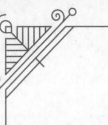

Joy

Always be full of joy in the Lord. I say it again—
rejoice! Let everyone see that you are considerate in
all you do. Remember, the Lord is coming soon.

PHILIPPIANS 4:4-5

Jesus, there's a lot of joy shared by Paul in this verse—it's effervescent. I want my life to overflow with that kind of anticipatory thankfulness. Joy is Paul's command, and I want to wholeheartedly follow it. Today instead of falling back into pessimism or its twin vice of cynicism, let me run to joy.

Remind me that you endured the cross, despising its shame because of the joy set before you. Teach me to set joy before me in a similar way so I can endure the temptations and trials of today.

Replace my mourning with laughter, my fear with faith, my worry with praise. I understand this is not just a ploy to force myself to be fake happy, but it's the kind of deep heart work you love to do within me. You are good at joy, and when you walked the earth, you exemplified it. So the closer I move toward you, the more of your joy will rub off, permeating my heart. That's my prayer, at least.

Let that joy inform the way I treat others today—with kind consideration. I want to treat people the way I like to be treated—with patience, happy banter, a listening ear, and kind words. Remind me that everyone is fighting an unseen battle, and each person is battle weary in their own way. We all need encouragement, and each day is an opportunity to grant it. Help me to love my family in light of your great love for me. Amen.

Contentment

*I have learned how to be content with whatever I have.
I know how to live on almost nothing or with everything.
I have learned the secret of living in every situation, whether
it is with a full stomach or empty, with plenty or little.
For I can do everything through Christ, who gives me strength.*

PHILIPPIANS 4:11-13

Jesus, what a countercultural thought—to be content in whatever circumstance I find myself. The currency of this world is discontent. There is always something more to own, always an additional mountain to climb, a bigger financial goal to reach, a greater level of recognition to fight for. Teach me this beautiful secret, Jesus, of living a life of contented peace, grateful for all you've brought my way.

The truth is, you are everything I need. In you, I have peace with my heavenly Father, strength to live each day, forgiven sins (past, present, future), healing from my wounds, and the kind of hope that cannot ever perish. You are sufficient. In you, I find purpose and love. I cannot hope for anything better.

But my mind often strays, and the vehicles it uses are envy and jealousy. I envy what others have. I am jealous of someone else's station in life. And that causes a root of discontentment to grow fast and deep like a noxious weed. Root this kind of greed out of me, teaching me the absolute power of radical contentment.

I realize I can only have that level of contentment through your power, Jesus. I lean into you today as I focus on my blessings. Amen.

Will

We have not stopped praying for you since we first heard about you. We ask God to give you complete knowledge of his will and to give you spiritual wisdom and understanding.

COLOSSIANS 1:9

Jesus, I get confused about your will sometimes, thinking it's outside of me, ready for me to pine over and discover. But your will is pretty clear as I read your Word. You want me to follow you wholeheartedly. You desire that I obey your commands by the strength your Spirit provides. You want me to treat others the way I'd like to be treated—to love you deeply so that I can also love others in the same way. I should welcome relationships and battle against bitterness. And I should freely give. In my work, I should labor with intent and integrity, while living with an open hand to bless many.

As I live that way, I understand you will not leave me alone as I try to discover the next path I should take. You are the light before me, the savior of my past, and the keeper of my future. You hold all things together. Even if I misstep, Jesus, you are not thwarted. Nothing can mar your sovereign plan. There's great joy in that.

Today I ask for spiritual wisdom and understanding. Open my eyes and heart to your Word so I can discern more freely. Breathe your Spirit into my broken relationships so I can be an agent of wisdom. I want to be someone whom people ask advice of, and I can only do that by the wisdom you provide. Amen.

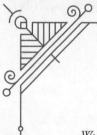

Power

We tell others about Christ, warning everyone and teaching everyone with all the wisdom God has given us. We want to present them to God, perfect in their relationship to Christ. That's why I work and struggle so hard, depending on Christ's mighty power that works within me.

COLOSSIANS 1:28-29

Jesus, thank you for Paul's example here of hard work and toil on behalf of your kingdom. It inspires me to persevere. It invigorates the tasks I do. Help me to keep eternity in mind when I go throughout my day. Give me perspective and purpose today.

But I have to admit: I am tired. My own strength just isn't enough to sustain me through the days, weeks, and months of my work, whether that be in the workforce or doing daily tasks at home. In short, I need strength because mine is waning.

The older I get, the slower I am. And I can't always hold my stress in check. Sometimes it grows like cancer, and my only solution is the couch and a mindless show.

Would you rejuvenate me today? When I get to the very end of my strength, would you meet me there in that seemingly helpless place? I understand the truth that your strength is made perfect in my weakness, but I am slow to truly live that way. Instead, I rely on my strength to the point of burnout, and then throw a prayer heavenward.

Instead of letting myself get to the end of my energy, I choose right now to trust you for power and energy and invigoration. Be the strength for my tasks, the power behind my efforts, and the hope in the midst of my trials. I love you for your strength, Jesus. Amen.

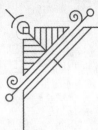

Roots

And now, just as you accepted Christ Jesus as your Lord,
you must continue to follow him. Let your roots grow
down into him, and let your lives be built on him.
Then your faith will grow strong in the truth you were taught,
and you will overflow with thankfulness.

COLOSSIANS 2:6-7

Jesus, thank you that our relationship doesn't hinge merely on one prayer I prayed on a specific date. No, it continues and evolves because you are with me as I work out my salvation with fear and trembling. I love following you, Jesus. I love the adventures you lead me on. It is the greatest privilege of my life to go where you lead me.

I want the kind of roots that tether me to your truth. Keep them growing deeper and deeper. I'm not so much concerned about the plant and fruits I will show the world because they will naturally happen as a result of roots dug deep. The deeper they go, the stronger my foundation, the greater the nutrients I'll receive to my soul.

Show me where I've satisfied myself with shallow roots. One of your parables warns me that shallow roots will yield faithlessness in the long run. Keep me grounded and hold me back so I can learn what it means to be faithful in small things, to bloom where you've planted me instead of chasing ahead and neglecting my roots.

I do want to be a person of truth—your truth, and as Paul encouraged, I want my life to overflow with thankfulness. Teach me the art of living that way, seeing the world through lenses of gratitude as I continue to stay rooted to you. Amen.

Capture

Don't let anyone capture you with empty philosophies and high-sounding nonsense that come from human thinking and from the spiritual powers of this world, rather than from Christ. For in Christ lives all the fullness of God in a human body.

COLOSSIANS 2:8-9

Jesus, there have been times when my mind is weak and my will is waning so much that I become quite open to capture. I'll admit that the world's way of thinking and doing things has an odd appeal to me. I love taking the easy way out. I enjoy chasing recognition. I like pursuing status and wealth. I wrongly think that all these things will inevitably bring me the kind of joy I'm longing for.

But the world's wisdom is like a chocolate bar dangling on a stick. I can never reach it. Although I try to touch the chocolate, it remains far. I continue to chase, but cannot find. Remind me that this world's wisdom is a treadmill to nowhere, a lesson in futility. It promises the world, but gives only heartache and deep fatigue.

Instead of filling myself up on the world's skewed "wisdom," I choose today to come to the fount of blessing—you, Jesus. You are the wisest, most intelligent person who walked this earth. You tell me the truth—that things will never satisfy, that making people idols only leads to heartache, that chasing the pleasure of sin may be fun for the moment, but will strangle my soul later. You are the fullness of love, the boundlessness of fulfillment, the power within me.

Keep my ears alert to your voice today, especially as the world shouts its truth from the media. I cannot rely on those half-truths any longer, nor do I want to fill my mind with things that keep me from pursuing you and you alone. Amen.

Think

*Since you have been raised to new life with Christ, set
your sights on the realities of heaven, where Christ
sits in the place of honor at God's right hand.
Think about the things of heaven, not the things of earth.
For you died to this life, and your real life
is hidden with Christ in God.*

COLOSSIANS 3:1-3

Jesus, I don't believe it's true that I can be so heavenly minded that I'm no earthly good. In fact, it's the opposite of that. When I fix my gaze on the reality of heaven, everything in my life begins to make sense. When I contemplate you seated in the place of power next to the Father, I am greatly encouraged. You are interceding for me there, and you are asking that your will would be done in and through my life just as it is done in heaven. What an amazing promise!

Forgive me for being so earthly minded that I'm no heavenly good. Instead, would you help me turn my head heavenward again, remembering all it took to get you there—life, death, resurrection, ascension? You have made a way for me, not just so I would be freed from my sin, but so I can become a freedom broker in this life for those still in bondage.

I have died to my old life, but sometimes I try to pick it up again. Keep me close to you. Hide me in the shelter of you so I truly understand your hope, power, and peace. I love you, Jesus. Amen.

Rule

Let the peace that comes from Christ rule in your hearts.
For as members of one body you are called to
live in peace. And always be thankful.

COLOSSIANS 3:15

Jesus, I don't relish living in turmoil. In fact, I try to avoid it at all costs. So I'm grateful for this reminder today to let your peace rule my heart. When I'm anxious and my peace is disturbed, I will return to this truth, that you will be the umpire of my life, helping me find peace in chaos, pain, or fear.

I also understand that my lack of peace often stems from my relationships. It's not that I'm fretting about having enough money as much as my peace gets sidelined by a harsh comment or a disdainful dismissal. In those cases, Jesus, help me to remember the power of peace. Teach me to be a peacemaker, even when I'd rather retaliate and prove my rightness. Help me take the lowest seat, not trying to force my agenda and my way of thinking to the detriment of my friend or family member. Help me to look for ways to strengthen the people in my life instead of constantly hoping they'll return the favor. I don't want to be someone whose life is spent keeping score.

I love that peace is tied to gratitude. The more I learn the art of thankfulness, the less expectations I put on others. I no longer need to force people to conform to my image in order to love them. I simply become thankful for the unique way you've made them. Help me grant others the same love you've granted me—that you love me as I am.

I choose to thank you today for all the relationships you've brought into my life—even the ones on the rocks. All of them have been part of my growth journey. I've learned better how to love. And I've seen my own selfishness. Thank you, Jesus. Amen.

Brought

For when we brought you the Good News, it was not
only with words but also with power, for the Holy Spirit
gave you full assurance that what we said was true.
And you know of our concern for you from the
way we lived when we were with you.

1 THESSALONIANS 1:5

Jesus, I'm so grateful for those who dared to bring me the good news about you. Where would I be without you? Thank you for sending faithful people my way so I could hear about your marvelous work on my behalf. Let their obedience inform the way I share you with others.

But don't let my message be simply words. No, Jesus, I also want to be open to the powerful ways you work. When you lived on this earth, you did many powerful miracles, works that pointed to the Father and his miraculous ways. People were astounded at not only your words, but also the power by which you delivered them. You healed many. So give me bigger prayers to pray today, where I actually believe you can heal people and bring great deliverance. Forgive me for praying small.

As I share you with others in words and power, I'm grateful there's a simple way to dignify the message—by living honestly before you. Help me conduct my life with integrity and joy. I want to choose the path of life, not destruction or manipulation. I pray my life would exemplify you, point to you, and show others what you are like. So please help me today to be understanding, quick to hear, open to patience, kind to a fault. I want to not only speak of you, tell of your power, or point to your good news, but I also want your Spirit within me to show this dying world that you are real. Amen.

Crown

What gives us hope and joy, and what will be our proud
reward and crown as we stand before our Lord Jesus when
he returns? It is you! Yes, you are our pride and joy.

1 THESSALONIANS 2:19-20

Jesus, I want to live a life full of relationships so I can confidently say this verse at the end of my life. I long to know that people are my proud reward and crown. Not stuff. Not accomplishments. Not purpose. Not looks. Not success. No, I want to have a heart that beats for others.

To do that, I need a healed heart. There are some who have hurt me so much that I'm afraid to engage again. I'd rather hide away in a cocoon, safely tucked inside, than to push through its gauzy layers to face the world outside. Heal me, Jesus. Set me free from past pain. I want to be a person of forgiveness and second chances, not one who chronicles everyone's sins day by day and holds them over folks.

To pour into others is my aim. But to do that, I need your Spirit within me. I know people fascinate you, and that you chose people when you lived here on earth. You went out of your way to find the broken, bleeding, and downcast. Give me eyes that look for folks like that. Enlarge the borders of my heart so I can welcome more people. Help me show hospitality to those who desperately need to know they are home and are loved.

And when I grow weary of giving, help me retain an eternal perspective as I see my relationships as crowns. They are the beauty I wear every day, and they will outlast this earth. When I'm giving to others, I am doing work that follows me to heaven. Amen.

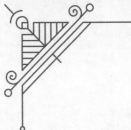

Strong

*So we have been greatly encouraged in the midst of
our troubles and suffering, dear brothers and sisters,
because you have remained strong in your faith. It gives us
new life to know that you are standing firm in the Lord.*

1 THESSALONIANS 3:7-8

Jesus, I want my life to be a great encouragement to others who are walking the walk of faith. May my faithfulness (powered by your Spirit) serve as salve to those who are actively choosing to love and follow you. Open my eyes to those around me who are facing troubles of any kind. Remind me to not live so much in my head that I don't see my friends who are suffering in their hearts.

Teach me how to have a strong faith. How do I exercise it so it grows? What does it mean to trust you with more and more areas of my life? Instead of turning automatically to fear, let me choose faith—to believe more in your ability to help me than in my inability to live this life on my own.

To stand firm is today's prayer. Instead of being swayed by worldly arguments and temptations aplenty, empower me to live what I believe, to stay connected to you, so that my life will be marked by fidelity, not fleeting feelings. You are so good to tutor me toward faithfulness, Jesus. I am rooted in you, and you have caused so much fruit and growth. Without you, I cannot stand firm. Without you, I can do nothing significant in the kingdom of God.

I pray for my friends who are suffering for your sake today. Give them hope. Enliven their faith. Empower them to stand strong and not back down. Deliver them from the plans of the evil one. Amen.

Presence

How we thank God for you! Because of you we have great joy as
we enter God's presence. Night and day we pray earnestly for you,
asking God to let us see you again to fill the gaps in your faith.

1 THESSALONIANS 3:9-10

Jesus, help me live in such a way that someone would write these words about me. I want to be someone who brings great joy to others, who is a true blessing to the people around me. In order to become that, I realize I need to stay very close to you. The nearer I am to you, the more loving and kindhearted I become. You are the epitome of irresistible love, and I long to embody that kind of presence in the lives of those around me.

But sometimes I get locked into myself, worrying more about me and nursing my own insecurity. When I get to that place, my life shrinks, and it becomes more about me seeking to have my needs filled and my life validated by others than pursuing the heart of others. Take me outside myself today. Replace my introspection with an outward focus—all through your power.

And would you make me a person of prayer who loves to pray for others? Not only right here, right now, but in the moment when I encounter someone with a need. Teach me the importance and power of praying consistently. Wake me up at night to intercede for those whose voices are growing hoarse from asking so much. I do want to be a person who prays as a lifestyle. Amen.

Pleases

*Finally, dear brothers and sisters, we urge you in the name of the
Lord Jesus to live in a way that pleases God, as we have taught you.
You live this way already, and we encourage you to do so even more.*

1 Thessalonians 4:1

Jesus, I do want to live in a way that pleases you, that makes you
smile. My deepest desire is to bring you joy. Instead of worrying about
how to orchestrate my life to make it the happiest, change the way I
view things so that my first thought is to live in a way that enlarges your
kingdom via your available strength.

I love that Paul spent hours and hours pouring his life into others.
He gave so much so that they would live exemplary lives. Would you
show me who I can teach what you've taught me? I want to be part of
your discipleship plan, helping others follow you closely. Make me a
believer who not only grows deep and wide, but one who takes that
hard-won wisdom and imparts it to those who are also on this journey. Teach me what it means to sacrifice my time for the sake of others who need to grow.

Show me people who need extra encouragement today—not simply the people who are discouraged or hurting, but the folks who are
doing great work for your kingdom and need to know they are seen.
Give me the words needed that will help them excel still more. And
when I'm in that place of growing weary of doing good, would you
prompt someone to encourage me? I know you love to use your body
of believers to empower each other, so I trust you to answer this prayer
in winsome, surprising ways. Amen.

Goal

*Make it your goal to live a quiet life, minding your own business
and working with your hands, just as we instructed you before.
Then people who are not believers will respect the way you live.*

1 Thessalonians 4:11-12

Jesus, there is so much talk and wisdom these days about goal setting and climbing higher toward our dreams. One of the things I've learned over the course of my life is that scurrying toward goals can sometimes leave me empty—reaching them, then looking to the next hill to climb. It can become a treadmill of stress, always producing, always moving toward the next thing.

So when I read this, my heart enlivens. You want me to live a simple life, pressing on without fanfare, attending to the work you have assigned to me. You are not after a splashy life. You aren't in the cacophony of self-promotion. You live in the quiet places of my life where I work with my hands to provide for my needs and the needs of others.

Dignify this work, Jesus. Help me to rest in the smallness of obedience, to be faithful in those small things so that later you can entrust me with much. Open my eyes to the needs of those around me so that I can share from the abundance you've brought me. Instead of being dependent on others, let me be dependent on you for everything, and give me joy as I work steadily, making my way in this world. I want to epitomize good work, self-discipline, and joy. Amen.

Tender

Warn those who are lazy. Encourage those who are timid. Take tender care of those who are weak. Be patient with everyone. See that no one pays back evil for evil, but always try to do good to each other and to all people.

1 THESSALONIANS 5:14-15

Jesus, thank you for this very practical guide to life. Although it's not second nature for me to admonish someone who appears lazy, if you would like me to, please help me do so with grace and tenderness.

Teach me the best way to encourage those who tend toward shyness. Help me to see them as you do—as valuable assets in your kingdom, with work specifically designed for them to accomplish. Those who are timid are often overlooked, so please refresh my vision to see folks who stay in the background.

For the weak in my life, I do want to be tender, not crushing a bending reed, but to be salve and refreshment to those who are hurting. Help me to laugh when they laugh, but to also mourn alongside them.

Would you reveal your patience toward me so I can return the favor toward those in my life? I am not by nature a patient person, so I know I need your Spirit's patience working in and through me.

Instead of retaliating in kind, teach me restraint. Help me to take a deep breath after I've been hurt, to be silent instead of lashing out. I want to be someone who loves well, who goes out of my way to help those in need. Show me how to do that today. Amen.

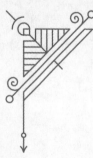

Flourishing

*Dear brothers and sisters, we can't help but thank God
for you, because your faith is flourishing and your love
for one another is growing. We proudly tell God's other
churches about your endurance and faithfulness in all
the persecutions and hardships you are suffering.*

2 Thessalonians 1:3-4

Jesus, what a blessing it is to know I'm part of your family. I have brothers and sisters, mothers and fathers in the faith, aunts and uncles aplenty. I am not alone. I am not an orphan, but beautifully adopted into your family. What an inheritance! What a legacy! I'm grateful beyond words.

In the midst of this great, big family, help me practice my faith—and may it be flourishing, nourished by good soil, with roots that go down deep, anchoring myself in you. I know that the proof of my faith is how well I love others—particularly those who differ from me. I confess my first instinct is to retaliate. Instead, keep me quiet, nestled close to you so that my first response is love. Help me to grow up to be the kind of family member who assumes positive intent, waits to shout my mind, and dignifies others by listening to them, asking life-giving questions.

The words Paul uses here are words I long to hear spoken over me. I want to be a follower of yours who endures and is faithful despite persecutions and hardships. This is the work of your Spirit within me, and I welcome it. Amen.

Fooled

*Don't be fooled by what they say. For that day will not come
until there is a great rebellion against God and the man of
lawlessness is revealed—the one who brings destruction.*

2 Thessalonians 2:3

Jesus, I know I live in a land of unclean lips, where people say all sorts of awful things and politicians bend toward corruption. Lawlessness abounds, and it will only get worse as your coming draws near. So help me be faithful in times like these. May your steadiness inform my reactions when the ground shifts beneath me.

Give me an alert mind, hungry for your wisdom. Help me to be so schooled in the teachings of your Word that I can instantly recognize a counterfeit. I realize that people can be wickedly persuasive, and that sharp tongues will deceive many. Lord, keep me close to your heart, near your mind, so that I can be a discerning believer where truth has become relative and people chase after philosophies that tickle their ears.

Help me recognize rebellion when it happens. I don't want to admire it, promote it, or stand idly by when others encourage the world to run from you. Empower me to stand on my own two feet, on your solid rock, steadfast in truth, rejoicing even in the midst of conflict. Oh, how I love you. Oh, how I need you. Especially when this world deviates toward a me-centered theology.

There will be destruction, Lord. I understand that. So help me to be a creative force of production, one who brings life, not death—promoting purpose, not decay. Keep me alert and strong. Amen.

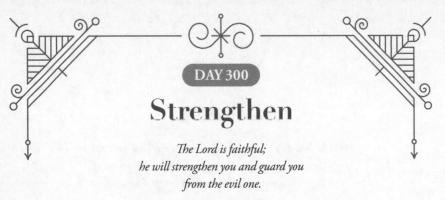

Strengthen

The Lord is faithful;
he will strengthen you and guard you
from the evil one.

2 Thessalonians 3:3

Jesus, I wish I always believed in your faithfulness. But I'm prone to panic when things seem out of control or my loved ones wander. I want to pitch a tent on the bedrock of your faithful love. Give me that kind of rock-solid faith that does not waver up and down like my emotions of late.

Thank you for giving me strength, the power to do all you have called me to. Thank you for noticing me when I feel my own control slipping. I am grateful that you rescue me when I can't seem to rescue myself.

Your Word says you guard me. Which means I don't have to stand guard over my life. Thank you that you are alert—more alert than a well-trained security guard or militia. You see what happened. You see what will happen. And you are worth my trust.

Today I pray you will help me be more alert to the schemes of the enemy. I need to remember his ways—to steal from, to kill, to destroy me. He is sneaky and lurking and clandestine. I want to be innocent of his ways, but not dismissive. Regarding him, I am grateful afresh that you are my guard. Keep my feet from chasing evil. Prevent me from lapsing into bitterness and unforgiveness. Help me to keep my anger in check. Free me from my addictions. Rest me close to your heart. Amen.

Full

May the Lord lead your hearts into a full
understanding and expression of the love of God and
the patient endurance that comes from Christ.

2 THESSALONIANS 3:5

Jesus, I don't always understand your love—for me, for others, for this world. Sometimes it feels like a vague concept, completely foreign to the soil of my life. There are days I don't live loved because it seems too good to be true. I don't always grasp how wide, how high, how deep your love is because I haven't experienced human love in that manner. Elevate the way I see love. Help me to perceive your love truly—not just as an abstract concept, not as an emotion, but as bedrock truth. You created me. You love me. Your Word confirms it—simple as that.

Forgive me for making it more complicated than that, Jesus. As Paul prayed, I long for your leading—that you would lead (gently!) my heart into a full expression of your love and patient endurance. What does that mean? What does that mean for me today when you seem far away, and I am left here on earth grasping at you, lonely and afraid?

But I am not overlooked. You are a good parent, and good parents care for their children. They nurture and protect them. They love them with arms wide open, even if their kids fail or run a thousand miles away. Help me to rest in that truth today. Instead of relying on how I feel, or how I would treat myself, let me be settled in knowing your love never stops. It always remains. It is truth. Although it's hard for me to grasp, I trust that you will give me the power to grasp it today. Why? Because I believe you want me to live loved as your beloved child. Amen.

Situation

Now may the Lord of peace himself give you his peace at all times and in every situation. The Lord be with you all.

2 Thessalonians 3:16

Jesus, thank you that you are with me in any situation. When I'm afraid, you are there offering me courage. When life speeds out of control, you bring calm to my heart. When someone hurts me, you remind me that you understand because when you walked the earth, others hurt you too. When I fret about money or provision, you keep me peaceful and trusting. When I panic, you enable me to take deep breaths until the chaos ends. When I experience rejection, when I feel insecure, you become my security.

I need you in every situation I face today. Thank you in advance that you are the Prince of peace who was, and is, and is to be. You are the God of my life, and you love to come to my rescue in every moment. You already know what I will face, and you provide peace in great measure, even when I don't realize it. Instead of giving in to panic today, remind me to stop and ask for your peace, to experience it fully in difficult moments.

Remind me that you are with me. As I sit here, this is truth. If I walk over there, this is truth. If I go about my day, this is truth. You are with me. You will never leave me. You will not turn away from me in disgust. You will walk alongside me, no matter what I face. Your presence is the constant truth I can count on. Amen.

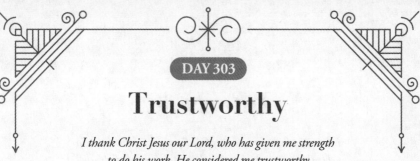

Trustworthy

I thank Christ Jesus our Lord, who has given me strength
to do his work. He considered me trustworthy
and appointed me to serve him.

1 TIMOTHY 1:12

Jesus, today my prayer is that I would be considered trustworthy. To be so means that I can be trusted to carry out the work you have given me. I won't look to my left or right. I won't seek the world's validation to my efforts. I won't neglect to count the cost. I won't question the direction you're leading me in, no matter how counterintuitive it seems. No, I determine to do what you want me to do. I give you my word—backed by the Spirit within me. Please appoint me to serve you—even in the hard places.

I don't want to have other motivations—for fame, glory, status, financial gain. I don't want to give to get. Instead, I want to be grateful for everything you've sent my way. I want my life to be an offering to you, consecrated, set apart, ready for service. These words seem lofty, but they are pedestrian, because they simply mean me walking out my devotion to you.

Help me to live my life with a full heart, no holding back. You have given me everything—healing, a new life, forgiveness, joy abounding. My response is to give you my everything—my heart, ambitions, faith, trust, and the manner in which I walk. You have done so much for me, and, in return, I want my life to be a worshipful offering to you. Thank you, Jesus.

Show me ways I can serve you today. But not only serve you; I want to worship you with the way I conduct my life. By your Spirit within me, I choose you. Amen.

Intercede

I urge you, first of all, to pray for all people. Ask God to help them; intercede on their behalf, and give thanks for them. Pray this way for kings and all who are in authority so that we can live peaceful and quiet lives marked by godliness and dignity. This is good and pleases God our Savior.

1 TIMOTHY 2:1-3

Jesus, thank you for all the people you've placed in my life. I'm grateful that I have the privilege to pray for so many. I don't want to see people as a burden to carry, but as folks whose pain and angst you will bear. So right now I place all of them in your hands for safekeeping. I entrust my friends and family to you. I lay the pain that others have inflicted on them at your throne because I know you can carry it far better than I can.

I lift up those in my local city government. May they be strong and loyal and work with integrity. Please empower my state legislature and the governor's office. May their rule of law mimic your ways. I pray for the president, the Congress, and the Supreme Court. Oh, dear Jesus, would you infuse your light in dark places? Work from the inside out in every government leader, because that's the kind of heart transformation that lasts.

I do want to live a peaceful and dignified life. Where there is chaos in my heart and mind, would you transform it to peace and joy? Where I've become lax about my spiritual life and the disciplines I pursue, remind me that my actions are not just for my sake, but they also bless the people of this world who so desperately need you. Oh, how I want to be an ambassador for your kingdom that you'll be proud of. I love the way you rule, Jesus. Amen.

Mystery

Without question, this is the great mystery of our faith:
Christ was revealed in a human body and vindicated by the Spirit.
He was seen by angels and announced to the nations.
He was believed in throughout the world
and taken to heaven in glory.

1 TIMOTHY 3:16

Jesus, you are a mystery to me. A beautiful conundrum. You're completely out of my scope of imagination, and yet you are real, and you performed amazing feats. You humbled yourself to become a human like me. You healed many and drove out evil spirits. You chose to obey your Father despite what it meant to your welfare. You carried all my sins, and the sin of all humanity, upon yourself. You died, then resurrected. And after many days of showing yourself to this ungrateful world, you ascended into heaven.

Yours is the greatest story ever told. I want to be part of your story, sharing it with many. I want to live a story worthy of yours, following after your ways. Lord, help me become humble and obedient. I want to look for opportunities to pray for people who are hurting and tormented. I want to bear the weight of others' pain. Teach me what it means to die to myself. Resurrect a brand-new story in me, while I let go of my old life and anticipate the new life you have for me. May my praise ascend to the heavens, full of joy and purpose.

I want to pattern my life after yours, Jesus. And yet, I know that to do so means to take the last place, to serve others wholeheartedly without need for reward, to find those who are unloved and offer your love. Empower me today. Amen.

Attention

*Give your complete attention to these matters. Throw yourself
into your tasks so that everyone will see your progress.
Keep a close watch on how you live and on your teaching.
Stay true to what is right for the sake of your own
salvation and the salvation of those who hear you.*

1 TIMOTHY 4:15-16

Jesus, teach me the art of focus. I am so distracted these days, wooed here and there by shiny things, the crazy Internet, and more tasks than hours in my day. When I'm living in the land of scattered, I can't seem to concentrate on what matters: you. I choose to slow down and make you my focus today. Be near, Jesus. Be near.

Give me the verve to heartily engage in my tasks, not so much that I neglect people, but with a good work ethic because I realize the days are evil, and you have called me to work hard. When I begin straying or my mind wanders to other things, refresh my outlook and empower me to complete what you've set before me.

I also want to be the kind of believer who doesn't simply say things about you, but lives those truths out loud. May my outward actions match my inward heart bearing. Keep me grounded in your Word so that the words I share don't steer people away from you, but beautifully toward you. Help me not to take your Word lightly, casually throwing it here and there without context. I want to be a diligent student of all your teaching, so that when I have the opportunity to teach, my words will bring life and hope and direction to all who hear. Amen.

Revealed

Remember, the sins of some people are obvious, leading
them to certain judgment. But there are others whose
sins will not be revealed until later. In the same way, the
good deeds of some people are obvious. And the good
deeds done in secret will someday come to light.

1 TIMOTHY 5:24-25

Jesus, what a powerful truth, but also quite frightening. What I
have hidden in the darkness will someday be brought to light. I don't
want to live in fear of that day. So in this moment, would you clean
house? Help me to find good people to confess my sins to, bringing
my darkness into light so I can be set free from my secrets and find forgiveness and guidance for my next steps. Oh, how I want to be faithful
to you in the way I conduct my life. From this point onward, no more
hiding. No more lying. No more secret dread. Just freedom and hope.

I'm heartened, though, that the opposite is true. Not only will my
dark deeds see the light of day under the gaze of your holy fire, but my
good deeds will come to light as well. As I forsake following my sin
nature and begin to reorient my life toward you, I pray for an increase
in work that pleases you. Instead of heralding myself and trying to do
good works so others will see, give me the joy of working behind the
scenes, blessing others in secret, giving anonymous gifts. I don't want
to trumpet myself. Instead, I want people to understand that you are a
God of secrets, and you provide for your children in sometimes covert,
mysterious ways. I want to be a part of that quiet revolution, Jesus.
Amen.

Godliness

True godliness with contentment is itself great wealth. After all, we brought nothing with us when we came into the world, and we can't take anything with us when we leave it. So if we have enough food and clothing, let us be content.

1 Timothy 6:6-8

Jesus, in this godless world, the word *godly* gets a bad rap. We see it as a haughty, holier-than-thou attitude, when really it's the opposite of that. To be godly is to act as you do—full of compassionate love, forgiveness, justice, and grace. So, dear Jesus, make me godly, to be more like you as the day commences, continues, and completes.

As you increase my ability to be like you in the world, make me countercultural. Replace my greedy heart with a heart of gratitude. I realize that chasing after wealth is a fool's game, and it is seldom satisfying. Instead, teach me to live radically content, happy with what you've brought my way, able to stop wanting more, more, more. This is a work of your Spirit, and I trust you to bring this about.

Keep my eyes from longing for what others have today. Instead of pining, I choose to praise you. Instead of focusing on what they have, help me focus on those who don't have enough. I would like to be the answer to *their* prayers today. Show me someone I can financially or tangibly bless. I wait with anticipation as you reveal who I can help. I am giddy with the thought of it.

Today I choose to list the blessings you have brought my way. You are good, good, good, and you have given me so much—not just things that fade away, or food that is quickly digested, but life, love, and a clean heart. Amen.

Entrusted

*I am suffering here in prison. But I am not ashamed of it, for I
know the one in whom I trust, and I am sure that he is able
to guard what I have entrusted to him until the day of his return.*

2 Timothy 1:12

Jesus, imprisonment is a harsh reality for some, but if I think that
way, I might just forget the prison I placed myself in before I followed
you. I was entrenched in my sin, devoid of hope, completely helpless
to live a good life. My past strangled me, shackling me to behaviors I
could not correct. But you have emancipated me from sin's prison. You
have set me gloriously free. And even when the apostle Paul sat suffering in a prison, he too was an emancipated person. No bars can hold
the Christian back from praising you and finding abundance today.
For that, I am grateful.

Once you set me free, you proved yourself faithful again and again.
You have been the most trustworthy one in my life. You have protected me from harm, shouldered my burdens, and walked alongside
me in deep valleys and high mountains. You have been my faithful
companion.

In light of that, like the apostle Paul, I am grateful that the life I've
entrusted to you will not be wasted. My work will not amount to nothing. The deeds I do, the praise I sing, the people I help—all this is noted
and will be rewarded. These are the things that neither moth nor rust
can ever destroy. They are kept in heaven for me and will serve as the
reward I willingly give back to you as praise on the other side. Amen.

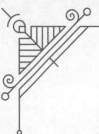

Pure

*If you keep yourself pure, you will be a special utensil for
honorable use. Your life will be clean, and you will be ready
for the Master to use you for every good work.*

2 TIMOTHY 2:21

Jesus, I live in an impure world. It surrounds me, tempts me, woos me toward itself. This world makes me want to be a part of its system mainly because so many people have found that pathway the easiest to follow, with less resistance. I have to fight to stay pure in this crooked generation. Help me to see folks who are lost not as terrible people, but as those who are lost, enslaved to themselves and their desires. May this make me pray all the more for my lost friends and family members, loving them well and pointing them to you.

Teach me what it means to live a pure life—undefiled, set free, delivered from the vise grip of sin. I love how I feel when my heart is clean, and I'm grateful for your cross that enabled such a luxury. I know that my purity is a direct result of your Spirit living inside me. Help me to honor the Spirit within, not grieving or quenching his promptings.

When you look down on this earth full of people going hither and yon, I would love to be one of the people you see as faithful. I want to be useful in your kingdom instead of constantly worrying about fashioning my own kingdom built on selfish desire and me-centeredness. Elevate my gaze from myself to you. As I seek your face, help me to face this world with bravery and purity. As I go about my day, remind me of the premium purity is in this impure world. Amen.

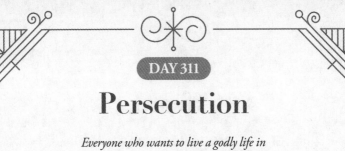

Persecution

Everyone who wants to live a godly life in
Christ Jesus will suffer persecution.

2 TIMOTHY 3:12

Jesus, this is one of those verses that pauses me. I'm mindful of my brothers and sisters around the world who suffer persecution daily. Right now I pray for them. Remind me throughout the day to lift the persecuted church up to your throne. Give them strength to choose you in the midst of dangerous and impossible situations. May their bravery inspire mine. And may I live in such a way that I don't take my own freedom for granted. Lord, if there is a tangible way I can help those who are persecuted, whether it be writing a letter, giving some of my resources, or praying deep into the night, reveal that to me. I don't want to put my head in the sand and pretend this is not real.

And for those not currently suffering persecution, help us to keep continually mindful of those who are. Prepare me to be faithful as persecution arises. Instead of being blindsided by it, teach me to live so closely to you today so that I can't help but be faithful to you when opposition presses in. I know that persecution is normative for many, and their faith grows by leaps and bounds because of it.

Would you grow me even when I'm not experiencing pushback? Would you teach me the power of faithfulness right here in the middle of my circumstances? I want to be considered faithful—strong enough (because of your strength) to be entrusted with ministry and loving others. And if it be your will, dear Jesus, would you please bring me in contact with a person who is suffering for their faith? It would be my privilege to encourage someone in that situation. Amen.

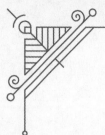

Afraid

But you should keep a clear mind in every situation.
Don't be afraid of suffering for the Lord.
Work at telling others the Good News,
and fully carry out the ministry God has given you.

2 TIMOTHY 4:5

Jesus, I do want to keep a clear mind, but this world sure slings dirt my way, muddying the way I see things. Bring clarity. Clarify what you want for me so I can follow you more strategically, no matter what situation I find myself in. For what I face today, bring wisdom tomorrow. Show me the path of life through the valley of dry bones. Reveal the way through strife. Teach me to be quiet when necessary, and to speak up when my words will salve wounds. Only you can give me that kind of discernment, so I trust in you.

When I'm afraid, bring me peace in the midst of chaos. I don't much like suffering, but you have proven to me that suffering helps me see things more clearly. If I bear up under it with your strength and perspective, I will grow much deeper in my relationship with you. In the midst of suffering, you will heal and grow me. I thank you in advance for that painful but fruitful work.

Even when I'm afraid to tell your good news, I know you will empower me to do so. Place people in my life who truly need to be set free. I know you are the remedy for their slavery. Like Timothy, I want to fully carry out the ministry you have given me. Help me to welcome that ministry instead of running away from it. Reveal a bigger picture of what that means today. Amen.

Appearing

My life has already been poured out as an offering to God. The time of my death is near. I have fought the good fight, I have finished the race, and I have remained faithful. And now the prize awaits me—the crown of righteousness, which the Lord, the righteous Judge, will give me on the day of his return. And the prize is not just for me but for all who eagerly look forward to his appearing.

2 TIMOTHY 4:6-8

Jesus, I want to be able to live these words Paul writes. He penned them from a sincere heart, backed by years of faithful service to you. In the same manner, I want to emulate him—to pour out my life for you like an offering. To live in such a way that living means you and dying means gain (because I get more of you). I want to fight against the spiritual forces of evil in this present darkness with the weapons you have graciously granted me. Even though the race is more like a marathon, help me to continue that race with joy, one step in front of the other, pressing closer to the finish line. Oh, dear Jesus, I want to be faithful to you—to begin well, yes. But also to finish well. I pray I wouldn't give up or give in as I age. Instead, may my life be a stronger witness the closer I get to seeing you in heaven.

Because of what you did on the cross, I know I can look forward to the crown of righteousness. Thank you. It will be my offering to you because that's what love does—it receives, then can't help but give back.

Today, teach me what it means to love your appearing—awaiting your future return or anticipating your very real presence in my life today. Amen.

Deliver

*The Lord will deliver me from every evil attack and
will bring me safely into his heavenly Kingdom. All
glory to God forever and ever! Amen.*

2 Timothy 4:18

Jesus, sometimes the spiritual attack against me feels overwhelmingly thick. I can't see my way out, but you know the way I take. You know best how to help me, to serve me in the darkness. You are my deliverer, and I choose to trust in your ability to deliver me today. Elevate my gaze from the battle around me on this earth to the fight that happens in the heavenlies.

Remind me that my weapons aren't my words that I spew toward others, but that my greatest strength comes from my surrendered life on my knees, praying and recognizing the real enemies that prowl, seeking to devour me. (They are not people; they are demonic.) In light of that, I don't want to demonize people and grant myself sainthood. They're not all evil, nor am I all good. Instead, help me see with your compassionate eyes those who hurt me. And keep me close to you as you battle the real enemy.

This is why you get all the glory in my life—because you solely are the Deliverer. You crushed Satan's power on the cross, and right now he lives as a wounded, angry predator. Thankfully, his wound is fatal, and he will inevitably be dealt with once and for all. You are the King of kings and the Lord of lords. You are victorious. You reign supreme—especially over the powers of darkness. Fight on my behalf, oh risen, victorious King! Amen.

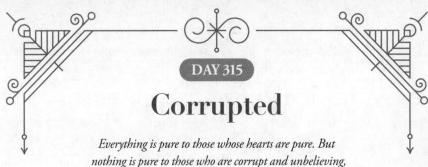

Corrupted

*Everything is pure to those whose hearts are pure. But
nothing is pure to those who are corrupt and unbelieving,
because their minds and consciences are corrupted.*

TITUS 1:15

Jesus, my heart's desire is to so know purity that corruption looks absolutely filthy to me. I confess there have been times when corrupted things look enticing and fun. But that's all a lie. Corruption only has the ability to tear down and destroy. But your Spirit does an opposite work—he builds up and gives me a new story.

Teach me what it means to live purely in a corrupted world. Help me to call sin what it is, and to rightly discern good from bad, right from wrong. May I be so steeped in your Word that I automatically recognize deception. I know the closer I am to you, who are purity embodied, the easier it will be for me to have wisdom as I navigate this world. Hold me close today, Jesus.

I pray for those people in my life who are enslaved to corruption. They are blind, and they have no idea that they are. Their consciences are darkened, and they can't naturally pursue you, Jesus. They are lost. Please seek and save them. Rescue them from the grip of the evil one. Show them the destination of their path—destruction, and place in them a longing for the light. Help them hit rock bottom so they will finally reach heavenward toward you. My heart breaks for the people in my life who move from destructive choice to devastating choice. Only you can free them. Only you can deliver. I trust you to do that, and I entrust my loved ones to you. Pursue them today. And if there's anything I can do to love them well, please show me. Amen.

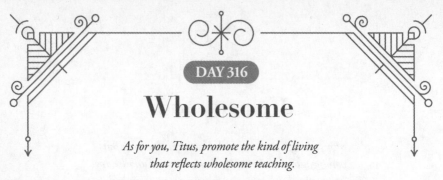

Wholesome

*As for you, Titus, promote the kind of living
that reflects wholesome teaching.*

Titus 2:1

Jesus, I'd love to understand how to "promote the kind of living that reflects wholesome teaching." I have a feeling that means that I have to live the words I share, keep my heart connected deeply to you, occupy my mind with your Word, and strive to live a life that exemplifies hospitality and love.

I love the word *wholesome*. It brings up images of healthy people enjoying laughter around a table, people comfortable in their own skin, relationships that bring true life, a home of peace, not chaos. I want to live that kind of life—wholly yours, wholly healthy. Would you highlight an area today where I'm not chasing wholesome living? Do I need to do an inventory of my relationships? Have I given in too much to bitterness and clung to my rightness in a situation? Have I neglected the important things in my pursuit of finite happiness?

Although I don't much see myself as a teacher, I realize that my life teaches many in the circle you've placed me in. I want to reflect and become the kind of person I'd like others to be as well. If I want my family members to forsake selfishness for generosity, am I doing the same? If I want my friends to listen well, am I returning the favor of a listening ear? If I want my daily interactions with strangers to be infused with your grace, am I reacting to them with impatience or kindness? Teach me, dear Jesus, and help my life to become a teachable moment for others—not for my own glory, but for yours. Amen.

Devotion

We are instructed to turn from godless living and sinful pleasures. We should live in this evil world with wisdom, righteousness, and devotion to God, while we look forward with hope to that wonderful day when the glory of our great God and Savior, Jesus Christ, will be revealed. He gave his life to free us from every kind of sin, to cleanse us, and to make us his very own people, totally committed to doing good deeds.

TITUS 2:12-14

Jesus, because devotion has meant a short period of time where I read an inspirational thought about you, I feel I've lost its true meaning. To live with devotion is not a compartmentalized task I squeeze into the margins of my life. No, it represents my whole life surrendered to you, allowing you to lead me where you want me. If I choose devotion to you, I will inevitably grow closer to you, and my life will have greater impact.

I know I become more like that which I worship. If I worship my own happiness at any cost, I begin to become more and more self-absorbed, and sin becomes entirely attractive to me. But if I turn away from pursuing my happiness and instead pursue your glory, I will joyfully forsake selfish living and become more like you in the process. Remind me that devotion and worship matter—but mostly in whom I am devoted to, and whom I choose to worship.

I understand I live in an evil world. I also know that I can either let the world shape me into its pattern, or I can pursue you wholeheartedly, allowing you to shape me into your beloved, peace-filled child. I choose the latter today. Amen.

Mercy

*When God our Savior revealed his kindness and love, he
saved us, not because of the righteous things we had done,
but because of his mercy. He washed away our sins, giving
us a new birth and new life through the Holy Spirit.*

TITUS 3:4-5

Jesus, teach me what mercy means. I am here praying to you today precisely because of your mercy. You didn't mete out punishment as I deserve. No. Instead, you chose the more difficult path—the path of surrender to your Father's painful agenda. You died for me because of your mercy. Your kindness compelled you to give up your life for my sake. I'm so grateful. Help me to preach this good news to myself every single day.

I have very little to offer you except my surrendered life as worship. Thank you that you accept this small act of sacrifice. Thank you that you love me, and that your love ushered in a clean life for me. I am no longer stained by sin's curse. You have washed away those sins, and they have gloriously slipped down the drain and are no more. I stand here today forgiven.

You have inaugurated a new life, a new birth, through your Spirit. When I doubt that, remind me how far I've come. When I slip back into bad thinking, refresh my mind with your Word. Deliver me from the pain of the past so I can joyfully anticipate life today, fully engaged, fully present, fully in the moment. This is the work of your Spirit in me, and I choose to welcome it right now.

When I consider all the freedom you've brought me, my next thought is this: Would you chase after my friend who is far from you, who is shackled in their own sin? They need to know your story of faithfulness and mercy. Amen.

Always

*I always thank my God when I pray for you, Philemon, because
I keep hearing about your faith in the Lord Jesus and your love
for all of God's people. And I am praying that you will put
into action the generosity that comes from your faith as you
understand and experience all the good things we have in Christ.
Your love has given me much joy and comfort, my brother, for
your kindness has often refreshed the hearts of God's people.*

PHILEMON 4-7

Jesus, I want to be the kind of person someone thanks God for.
Instead of pulling away from people and living insulated, push me out
of the nest into the next thing you have for me—which often involves
loving the people you've placed in my life. I cannot demonstrate my
faith in a vacuum, nor do I want to. But pain has gotten the best of me,
and I'm deeply afraid to poke my head back out in the world of relationships. Help!

I want to be more like Philemon, who dared to keep loving others.
His persistent faithfulness earned him commendation. He was generous and kind, and he brought joy to others.

Today I pray I would focus on this: How can I become joy, comfort,
and kindness for those in my life? Open my eyes to those who are lacking joy, and show me how to best encourage them. Reveal those who
are desperate for comfort, and shape me into the kind of person who
instinctively perceives someone's pain and knows how to bring tangible comfort. Show me someone starved for kindness, and enlighten me
as to how I can show direct kindness.

By your strength and grace, I will take little action steps toward
becoming more aware of other people's needs. Amen.

Beloved

He is no longer like a slave to you. He is more than a slave,
for he is a beloved brother, especially to me. Now
he will mean much more to you,
both as a man and as a brother in the Lord.

PHILEMON 16

Jesus, thank you for this passage about slavery and brotherhood. It's a poignant reminder to me that we are all the same in your eyes. An elite athlete is no more loved than a subsistence farmer. A famous singer is no more loved than a mother who sings lullabies over her baby. We are all precious to you, bought with a price, and wholly loved. In this world of hierarchies and merits, I lose sight of that truth. But you remind me that you are no respecter of persons. You love us all.

Keep me in that place today. As I see people or encounter them in different ways (online, through the mail, face-to-face, at work), remind me that each one is utterly valuable to you. They are made in your image, and you are immensely proud of them. Even if they're folks who deliberately hurt me, help me to understand that they have battles to fight that I know nothing about. Help me to be kind and merciful, particularly to the people who are having hard days.

Open my eyes to the breadth of your body, dear Jesus. Thank you for displaying your glory through all of us—and in such varied brilliance. Instead of being envious of someone else's gifts, settle me into gratitude. Instead of thinking less of someone who works quietly behind the scenes, make me a cheerleader. I'm so grateful for the diversity of your body. Amen.

Radiates

The Son radiates God's own glory and expresses the
very character of God, and he sustains everything
by the mighty power of his command.
When he had cleansed us from our sins, he sat down in the place
of honor at the right hand of the majestic God in heaven.

HEBREWS 1:3

Jesus, you radiate glory. I look forward to seeing you do that in the new heavens and the new earth, where we will need no sunlight because you will illuminate everything. You are God's expression to humanity, fully God, fully human—a mystery I have a hard time understanding. But that makes you all the more complex and beautiful. Enlarge my view of you, particularly when it comes to power. You hold all things together—this world, the seas, the land, the weather, my life, the lives of others. You are the great Sustainer of every living thing.

I long to have a life that radiates you to the people around me. I want to be like you—irresistibly loving, irrefutably kind, incredibly patient. Thank you that radiating isn't something I can conjure up, but it's your work in me. Your Spirit enlivens me, opens my heart to new relationships, and gives me the endurance I need to make it through each day joyfully. Thank you for holding me together, and for spinning my life into a beautiful story.

When life gets hectic (and it always does), bring me back to center. Help me picture you sitting at the right hand of God, having accomplished perfectly the work he had you do. You sit enthroned in glory. Everything is in subjection to you. You are my King, and you deserve my ardent love and allegiance. Amen.

Human

Because God's children are human beings—made of flesh and blood—the Son also became flesh and blood. For only as a human being could he die, and only by dying could he break the power of the devil, who had the power of death. Only in this way could he set free all who have lived their lives as slaves to the fear of dying.

HEBREWS 2:14-15

Jesus, your incarnation stuns me to silence. It's hard for me wrap my heart around the fact that you, who are everything, became as small as a zygote, then an embryo, then a squalling baby born in the humblest of places—a manger. Kings are not born this way. How can God become a person like this, in such a rudimentary, human way?

Remind me today of your flesh and blood. You skinned your knees. You experienced aches and heartache. You knew hunger and thirst. You experienced what it's like to be abandoned and forsaken. People hurled insults at you. You kept your word despite the persecution the religious leaders brought your way. You endured. You sweated. You labored.

And because of that, you have such a companionable understanding of me, of all of us. I'm grateful. You are the Savior I can confidently run to, tell you the frustrations of my day, reveal my heartache. You get it. You get me.

But your life on earth was more than mere empathy. It was warfare. You came to destroy death and the works of the devil. In a world full of death and evil, this brings me great comfort today. Thank you for setting my heart free from both. Amen.

House

Jesus deserves far more glory than Moses, just as a person who builds a house deserves more praise than the house itself.

HEBREWS 3:3

Jesus, while I'm grateful for the patriarchs who pointed the way toward you, you are much greater. Though I'm thankful for the righteous judges of the Old Testament who were a foreshadow of your righteousness, they are less than you. Though I'm comforted by the laments of the prophets of old and resonate with their messages, you are far greater than them, and their words pointed to you. You are greater than the greatest religious leaders, higher than the apostles, more worthy than the martyrs of old (and today). Of anyone who ever walked this earth, you are the greatest and you deserve all praise.

Show me where I've sold you short, where I've wrongly pursued others more than I've followed you. You deserve all my allegiance, my first thought when I wake up, my last thought as I drop to sleep. You are all and in all.

You have not only created this planet, but you have created every person too. You have created me. You are the builder of every living thing, and for that, you deserve honor and glory.

So let my life be an offering today of thanksgiving. You are strong. You are mighty. You are God. You are the deliverer of hope. You grant grace to many. You suffered and died for humanity. You sit on a throne, the righteous, wise King. I sit here in silence, pondering your greatness. Amen.

Word

The word of God is alive and powerful. It is sharper than the sharpest two-edged sword, cutting between soul and spirit, between joint and marrow. It exposes our innermost thoughts and desires.

HEBREWS 4:12

Jesus, I'm utterly grateful for your Word. Where would I be without its guidance, wisdom, and encouragement? Forgive me for living as if it doesn't have any bearing on my life and choices because it does. Help me immerse myself within its pages, not merely absorbing its universal message, but striving to obey it. I understand that knowledge of your Word can make me like a Pharisee—knowing much, but obeying little. I also understand that one ounce of obedience counts more than volumes of so-called knowledge. I know your Word through obeying it.

As I read it today, would you cut through me? Reveal what's underneath. Show me my soul. Reveal my heart and spirit. Shine a spotlight on where I'm pursuing you with my whole being. But I also give you permission to sift me, to show me where I need to repent, to turn away from behaviors and sins that lead me away from you. Your Word is able to do that, and I understand I must dig into it to mine its depths.

Jesus, I don't even know my innermost thoughts and desires, not overtly at least. Sometimes I'm locked away inside myself, a jumble of emotions and past pains. But your Word knows how to sort me out, and for that, I'm grateful. Your Word gives words to my predicament and it gives me a godly perspective on how to move on from here. Thank you for revealing yourself in the Word, and for training me to walk closely with you through it. Amen.

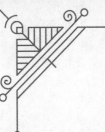

Naked

Nothing in all creation is hidden from God.
Everything is naked and exposed before his eyes, and
he is the one to whom we are accountable.

HEBREWS 4:13

Jesus, being exposed is scary. And in some weather, it's deadly. I know that my life is laid bare before you, but sometimes that scares me so I run away from you, thinking I can somehow hide. I'm like Adam and Eve that way, realizing I'm naked and ashamed, trying desperately to cover myself with plant leaves, only to have them fall while the rain drenches me. Thank you for what you did in the garden. You shed the blood of an innocent animal (a hint of what you would do in the future) in order to cover the first couple with warm animal skins. You covered their shame and nakedness.

That's my hope today. While it's not easy for me to pray this, I do pray that I would be comfortable being laid bare before you. Not for exposure's sake, but as an avenue of surrender. I want to experience being known fully, yet being covered and loved by you. I'm grateful you don't use exposure to shame me, but to heal me.

Show me where I've become a master of disguise, where I've run away from who I really am. I don't want to be an actor in a play I conduct called life. I want to be real, so much so that my outsides demonstrate what's going on in my heart. Because your love is compelling and covering, I can be set free to be myself. This is such a gift you've given me, delivering me from playacting toward a genuine, authentically lived life. Thank you, Jesus. Amen.

Priest

Since we have a great High Priest who has entered heaven, Jesus the Son of God, let us hold firmly to what we believe. This High Priest of ours understands our weaknesses, for he faced all of the same testings we do, yet he did not sin. So let us come boldly to the throne of our gracious God. There we will receive his mercy, and we will find grace to help us when we need it most.

HEBREWS 4:14-16

Jesus, I am so glad you're my faithful High Priest. You're not one who intercedes because you have to, but because you want to. I don't need to live in worry or shrink back in fear because you walked a path like mine when you encountered earth. You empathize with me, love me, and understand what it's like to live tethered to the ground. Thank you for choosing to incarnate yourself to earth, for resisting all the temptation thrown your way, yet not sinning.

Instead of shrinking back into myself, I choose today to remember your kindness, your deep understanding. You love me. You have mercy for me poured out, overflowing, fully available. Because of your audacious affection, I don't need to lurk away from your throne. Instead, like a beloved child of the king, I can run into the throne room and fling my cares (and myself) your way. I will not receive a harsh rebuke. You will not look at me with disdain. No, you welcome me, arms outstretched, ready for an embrace.

Today as my worries mount and my concerns multiply, I come to your throne of grace with boldness. Please give me the mercy I need. And infuse my life with grace so I can extend it to those I love today. Amen.

Strip

Since we are surrounded by such a huge crowd of witnesses to the life of faith, let us strip off every weight that slows us down, especially the sin that so easily trips us up. And let us run with endurance the race God has set before us.

HEBREWS 12:1

Jesus, today the race set before me seems impossibly long. I see the bend in the road, the hills to climb, the distance ahead—and I shrink back. I can't do this. Sometimes just moving through my life feels like supreme effort. I'm tired.

Maybe I'm tired because the world has flung so many things my way, and they've stuck to my torso, worming their way into my thoughts and heart. These weights make me heavy and cumbersome. I feel the weight of shame. I have carried the weight of not measuring up to impossible standards. Sin weighs me down, but I seem to be incapable of flinging it off. Broken relationships bear down on me. Harsh words strangle. Help me to see all these burdens clearly so I can take time today to strip them off. I don't want to carry so many weights, Jesus. Please set me free so I can run with endurance.

Teach me the art of single-minded focus. Keep the goal ever before me—the hope of complete restoration when I breathe my last. Being shaped into your image will take my lifetime, and I want to finish well. Like a runner who trains for a long race, I choose to strip away everything that weighs me down so I can complete the task in front of me.

But please, Lord, don't let me fall into drudgery. This race is not sad or depressing. No, it is a task of joy. For the joy set before me, help me run with unhindered well-being. Amen.

Careful

Be careful that you do not refuse to listen to the One who is
speaking. For if the people of Israel did not escape when they
refused to listen to Moses, the earthly messenger, we will certainly
not escape if we reject the One who speaks to us from heaven!

HEBREWS 12:25

Jesus, this verse scares me a bit. Because there have been days where I've nonchalantly gone about my business without even a glance heavenward. I seem to think I can exist without you, without your care, direction, or voice. Please forgive me.

I know you speak through your Word, so today I choose to nestle myself there, holed up in your truth. Let it settle into my marrow, informing my worth and my heart. I quiet myself as I read so your Word can read me, showing me where to repent, when to forgive, how to live. Your Word is living and active, and I'm grateful for that. It's not simply a book to read, then put down, but it is an alive epistle, enlivening me. I don't want to take it lightly, Jesus.

You also speak through nature. I've lost some important communication with you when I've cocooned myself in a cubicle or behind four walls. I know you're beckoning me outside to experience you through creation. Jesus, would you like to take a walk with me today?

You also speak in silence, but my world has become entirely too noisy. In this moment, I quiet myself. I stop asking you for things, and I simply sit still so I can hear from you. Amen.

Satisfied

*Don't love money; be satisfied with what
you have. For God has said,
"I will never fail you. I will never abandon you."*

HEBREWS 13:5

Jesus, what an interesting juxtaposition in this passage! I've long heard that you won't leave me or abandon me, and for that I'm grateful beyond words, but I haven't always understood this verse in context. Your offer to stay with me is written in the midst of money worries. And isn't that how I falter? When money problems arise (and seem to acquire teeth), I automatically wonder where you are, and whether or not you will come through in this situation.

As I look back on my life, I see your faithfulness. But like the Israelites when they forgot your power through the Exodus, or the apostles when they soon worried about food even after you'd fed 5000, I forget. In the moment of money worries, my fallback is to stress out. Sometimes I fear I love the security that money brings more than I love you. Please forgive me.

I'm grateful for good instruction here. To get through financial pressure, I simply need to subjugate money beneath you, proving I love you more than money. Then I need to take inventory around me and practice the lost art of contentment. Last, I must remind myself that you aren't going anywhere, that you are my God through abundance and lean times. You have been faithful. You are faithful. And you will be faithful. This is bedrock truth, a solid reality I can base my life on. What a relief that is! Amen.

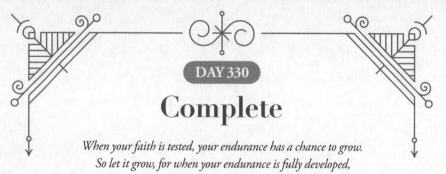

Complete

*When your faith is tested, your endurance has a chance to grow.
So let it grow, for when your endurance is fully developed,
you will be perfect and complete, needing nothing.*

JAMES 1:3-4

Jesus, often my endurance seems small. It certainly doesn't flourish, especially when I'm cultivating worry in my life. Instead of taking the next step, I stop, fret, and stay immobilized to the earth, unable to continue. Please rescue me from this habit. I need your Spirit to move in and through me, empowering me to endure.

I also realize that trials and suffering are what you use to grow my endurance. I wish it were different. I wish it could be that I grew great amounts during times of ease and plenty, but as I look back over my life, I see that's not the truth. I have grown more, learned to endure more, when life was messy and I had to reach for you or burrow down into myself. You are the reason I am where I am today. You have sustained me during times of intense trial.

Thank you for teaching me the art of endurance. It's my sincere prayer that my endurance will become fully developed, that I won't shrink back in fear when another trial assaults me, but that I will quietly put one more foot in front of the other because you have always proven yourself faithful, sustaining me in the past. You do not change, and your ability to sustain me remains. Thank you.

I do appreciate all you've done in my life. And it's amazing to me that you will bring me to new places where I'll experience completion and wholeness as a result of our lifetime together. In you, I am complete. In you, I endure. Amen.

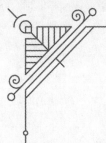

Light

Whatever is good and perfect is a gift coming
down to us from God our Father,
who created all the lights in the heavens.
He never changes or casts a shifting shadow.

JAMES 1:17

Jesus, help me remember the gifts you send from heaven. They are often shaped like the people in my life, the provisions you deliver, and the peace you give daily. Thank you for intersecting my life with so many gifts.

I'm amazed and grateful when I look at the stars, the sun, and the moon—those lights that remind me darkness cannot overcome this world. You made those lights because you are the Light, illuminating the bleakest night.

O Constant One, I'm so thankful you never change. You never shape shift. You are consistent, kind, open, and warm. You punish sin, yet accepted the punishment yourself so I could experience your unchanging ways day upon day.

In a world where darkness tries feebly to overcome the constant light, remind me of your abilities and steadfast ways. I trust you. Help my un-trust. And may it be that I truly become light in the dark corner of the world I live in, relying on your light in me. Help me to love well, representing your light and life-giving ways, as I seek to shine.

You are the true Light, and I am grateful. Amen.

Quick

You must all be quick to listen, slow to speak, and slow to
get angry. Human anger does not produce the righteousness
God desires. So get rid of all the filth and evil in your
lives, and humbly accept the word God has planted in
your hearts, for it has the power to save your souls.

JAMES 1:19-21

Jesus, help me inventory my relationships today—not to grow saddened by some or elated by others, but to evaluate how well I'm loving people. And the measure of that is my receptivity to listen. It's a lost art today. People want to shout one-sided rants on the Internet, cherishing their own opinions and marginalizing anyone who differs. This is not love, Jesus. This is selfishness.

I don't want to live in that selfish space anymore. Instead of demanding to be heard, I want to step back, look into my friends' eyes, and simply listen. Instead of thinking about what I want to say in return, let me retreat in silence, truly considering their words. Help me to mirror what they've said, to seek understanding with wise and insightful questions. Instead of forcing my understanding on them, help me to truly seek to understand the hearts of those I come in contact with. This is discipline, Lord. And it's discipline I sometimes lack.

Replace my red-hot anger with understanding. Instead of lashing out, help me to look inside and discover the why of my wrath. Help me to take a deep breath before I respond. Empower me to be meek, open, and sincere. Amen.

Love

It is good when you obey the royal law as found in the Scriptures: "Love your neighbor as yourself." But if you favor some people over others, you are committing a sin. You are guilty of breaking the law.

JAMES 2:8-9

Jesus, I want my life to exemplify the royal law—your law of love. To do that is a lifelong aim, one I struggle with, but one I want to improve on. I know first of all that I must love you above everything else. You should become my greatest affection, my everything, the one I chase like crazy. You are beautiful, and your love for me informs my love for you.

Your love will also empower me to do what seems like the impossible: to love myself. Jesus, I have a very hard time extending kindness my way. I would rather rule myself with harsh language and shame. Somehow I've forgotten that kindness leads us to repentance. Instead of being kind to myself, I yell. I treat myself like an enemy. Help me to see myself as a child beautifully loved by you. I want to learn to extend the kindness I give to strangers to myself. I know it hurts you when I hurt myself. Please, Jesus, set me free from self-loathing. Move me closer to a greater understanding of what it means to be loved by you.

As I learn this secret of loving myself, empower me to love others without a judgmental heart. Help me be *for* people, not against them. I want to learn the art of assuming positive intent. Would you show me someone today who desperately needs love? I want to practice the love you've shown me in the way I treat others. Amen.

Friendship

You adulterers!
Don't you realize that friendship with the
world makes you an enemy of God?
I say it again: If you want to be a friend of the world,
you make yourself an enemy of God.

JAMES 4:4

Jesus, I certainly don't want to be an adulterer—in love with the world while I take you for granted. But I've done it. I've let this world woo me toward itself. I've wrongly believed that wealth and power make me irresistible. I've bought into so many lies about my worth being based on how I look, who I know, and how much I've succeeded in. This world is about splash and flash, and I've let its shininess seduce me. I realize that when I chase after the world, I break your heart. Please, please forgive me.

I want a deep friendship with you, no longer enticed by the quick fix of the world's empty promises. That means I need discernment to see what is real, to long for what you provide—everlasting love over flash-in-the-pan enticements the world offers. It also means I have to actively turn away from everything this world promotes (that is not easy) and turn toward you. In that space of dependence on you, I'll finally experience the peace and freedom you freely offer your children.

I don't want to be your enemy anymore. I don't want to be pursuing empty idols—trinkets that suffice for a moment, but leave me desperately wanting more. Bring me today to the fount of living water, the place where my soul will be completely filled up, not wanting more. Jesus, I want to live my life in finding satisfaction and satiation in you alone. Amen.

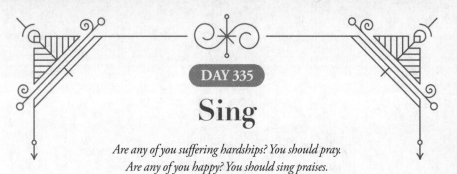

Sing

Are any of you suffering hardships? You should pray.
Are any of you happy? You should sing praises.

JAMES 5:13

Jesus, I'm praying. I'm believing that you are with me right here in the circle of friendship as I lift up my worries and cares to you. Only you know everything that's going on inside of me. Only you know how far I've come, where I've stumbled, and what secrets I keep. Only you. I lay me down. I lay my agenda at your feet. I give you my hurts, regrets, and ongoing struggles with sin, and I ask you to take it all. In that place of deep surrender, I ask for perspective and joy.

And as that joy materializes, not from myself but from your vast reserves, I will choose to sing. I will sing of your greatness. I will sing of the ways you've rescued me from enemies too strong, and even from my self-destructive ways. You have followed me throughout my life, empowering me once I knew you, and you have set me free in so many ways. I can't help but sing of your deliverance, your provision, and your insight. You have overflowed me with gratitude for all you've done.

I still have questions. I still struggle. I still don't understand many mysteries. And I wish I lived surrendered every single day. But through it all, I will pray, and I will praise. Both are necessary to my health. And both build our relationship.

Keep me close to you today, because your close proximity is my good. You are everything I need. You are my sustainer, my friend, and my helper. Amen.

Glad

Be truly glad. There is wonderful joy ahead, even though
you must endure many trials for a little while. These
trials will show that your faith is genuine.
It is being tested as fire tests and purifies gold—though
your faith is far more precious than mere gold. So when
your faith remains strong through many trials, it will
bring you much praise and glory and honor
on the day when Jesus Christ is revealed to the whole world.

1 Peter 1:6-7

Jesus, teach me what it means to be truly glad. Especially as I face upcoming trials. The natural way I want to respond is dread, and dread and gladness are two entirely different traits. Would you infuse me with your gladness? Give me the kind of perspective I need to endure whatever trials come my way. Show me, through this trial, that my faith is genuine—it's not just wishful thinking.

I don't much like the furnace, Lord. But I realize that whatever I face has the potential to refine my soul, inform my gladness, and build my trust—all through your faithful teaching. With that perspective, I don't have to be terrified of what may come. Instead, I make it my aim to hold close to you because you will be with me throughout every trauma.

I do long to see my faith be like gold—shining as a testament to your faithfulness in my life. Oh, may you find me faithful, no matter what—entrusting my life to you even when questions mount and the pathway seems dim. That's what trust is. That's what faith is. It's believing even when I don't see the outcome yet. Hold me, Jesus, through everything I face today. Amen.

Neighbors

Be careful to live properly among your unbelieving neighbors.
Then even if they accuse you of doing wrong, they
will see your honorable behavior,
and they will give honor to God when he judges the world.

1 Peter 2:12

Jesus, when I consider the story of the Good Samaritan and the clever way you answered the man who asked, "Who is my neighbor?" I get a little overwhelmed. In a world where I can have relationships with people from all over the world, your command to love my neighbor feels impossible. How do I discern who to pour my life into? Perhaps it's mostly geography? Or maybe depth of relationship that helps me with this conundrum?

But as I read this verse, things become clear. My neighbor, in this instance, is someone who sees me regularly, someone who can notice my habits, who isn't fooled by a false veneer. It's someone who truly knows me in proximity. So in light of all that, Jesus, help me to live a life of integrity around the people I interact with daily—at home, at work, in my neighborhood. I want to be known as someone who loves you well and takes care of relationships.

It's my greatest desire that you would be honored where I live. It's amazing to me that you've invited me to participate in your honor by giving me tasks to do. You've strategically placed me exactly where I am to love specific people and do particular work. Instead of lamenting that I'm not doing something flashy for your kingdom, I rejoice in the amazing way you've placed me right here. Help me bloom here, to be faithfully yours. Amen.

Sympathize

*All of you should be of one mind. Sympathize with
each other. Love each other as brothers and sisters. Be
tenderhearted, and keep a humble attitude. Don't repay
evil for evil. Don't retaliate with insults when people insult
you. Instead, pay them back with a blessing. That is what
God has called you to do, and he will grant you his blessing.*

1 PETER 3:8-9

Jesus, these words are such a perfect framework for life. Thank you
for inspiring Peter to record relational instructions. Teach me what it
means to be of one mind with the people in my life. I know that can't
mean uniformity, but it must mean that in our diversity, we all choose
to love each other.

Today let me meet my friends and family with a sympathetic heart,
one that longs to understand instead of demanding to be understood.
Instead of fighting like brothers and sisters, help me to place people's
needs above my own, to prefer and serve those you've surrounded me
with. Tender my heart toward those who struggle. Instead of letting
myself get exasperated, remind me of my own need for tender compassion. Let that inform the way I interact with the people in my life.

I don't want to live in a way that says I've got all the answers. Instead,
keep me close to you, humble and dependent. Then humility will be
the hallmark of my conversations.

Jesus, if I face pushback today, help me go to you first instead of
relying on an automatic response. I don't want to retaliate. Instead,
refocus my heart toward understanding and reconciliation. Amen.

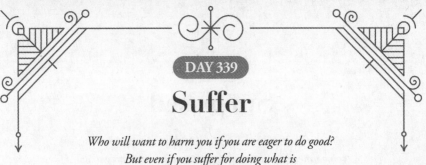

Suffer

Who will want to harm you if you are eager to do good?
But even if you suffer for doing what is
right, God will reward you for it.
So don't worry or be afraid of their threats.

1 PETER 3:13-14

Jesus, it isn't always the case that I suffer for doing what is right. As I look back on my life, I can see so many times when I've suffered because of my own sinful choices. Those consequences were necessary—because you are a loving savior who disciplines his children. Thank you for loving me that much.

But when I suffer for doing what is right, there's a part of me that yells, "Not fair!" In that space, I can nullify all that "right" I did by pushing against the unfair consequence. Instead, let me lean in, dear Jesus. Empower me to have the long view in mind, that suffering gives me great rewards, and it helps my soul prosper. I know that, in the moment, suffering for doing what is right doesn't feel great. But as it plays itself out, I will be stronger because of it. Keep me dependent on you during that time.

So as I suffer, give me your perspective. Instead of shrinking back from the threats of others, help me to entrust myself to you, knowing that you experienced the exact same kind of suffering on earth. You were misunderstood. You were betrayed (and you did nothing to deserve it). You were delivered over to death—an innocent man dying for a sinful people. You are my example, Jesus, of what it means to suffer well. May I experience a deeper understanding of who you are through the things I suffer. Amen.

Surprised

*Dear friends, don't be surprised at the fiery trials you are
going through, as if something strange were happening to you.
Instead, be very glad—for these trials make you partners with
Christ in his suffering, so that you will have the wonderful
joy of seeing his glory when it is revealed to all the world.*

1 PETER 4:12-13

Jesus, I've often wanted to be a partner with you in my life, but to be a partner of suffering? I haven't longed for that. To be honest, I run away from it. But as I look back on my life, I realize that the closest I've felt to you were the times when all I had was you as I suffered seemingly alone. You were there. You taught me so much through that season of suffering. While I won't be masochistic and beckon suffering my way, I will pray that when it comes, I will have a deeper understanding of its value. I no longer need to orchestrate my life in such a way as to avoid suffering at any cost. While I may not welcome it (because it's hard), I can be at peace with it.

It's interesting to me that when trials come, Jesus, I'm often taken by surprise. Keep me aware of the way the world works so that the next trial that flies my way doesn't sideline me. May it cause me to press into you, accessing your massive reserve of endurance, patience, and perseverance. My world may turn upside down, but you will remain faithful and blessedly the same.

This verse speaks of wonderful joy. Oh, how I want to experience that kind of joy as I endure the next trial. And may it be that I taste a little more of your glory—not to boast, but to enhance the way I praise you even more. You are glorious, and you are worthy of all my praise. Amen.

Work

Dear brothers and sisters, work hard to prove that you really are among those God has called and chosen. Do these things, and you will never fall away. Then God will give you a grand entrance into the eternal Kingdom of our Lord and Savior Jesus Christ.

2 PETER 1:10-11

Jesus, help me not to take your kingdom lightly. I don't want to flit and flitter around my days, unaware of your presence, while doggedly building my own kingdom. No, I want to work—for you—because you have done the incalculable for me. You have bought me with a price—the price of your life. You have secured my future and given me your Spirit as a down payment on my eternal home. You have set me free from a difficult past. You have healed my heart in so many ways. So let my response be reverent worship and deeds that reveal my changed heart—all this as my act of gratitude toward you.

When I look back on the times I've fallen away from you, I shudder. My heart was bitter, and my mind stayed on dark thoughts. My shame overwhelmed me, and my once-alive heart grew cold. Jesus, please remind me of those times when I'm tempted to turn my back on you. Instead, may I work (with the strength you provide) all the harder, building your kingdom. Because when I'm about your work, I don't have time or energy to run from you.

What a beautiful thought that you will provide me a grand entrance into your eternal kingdom. It's too much—this promise. I don't deserve it. I don't deserve you. But you love me anyway, and for that I am grateful. Amen.

False

There were also false prophets in Israel, just as there will be false teachers among you. They will cleverly teach destructive heresies and even deny the Master who bought them. In this way, they will bring sudden destruction on themselves.

2 PETER 2:1

Jesus, this is a loud world I live in, and everyone has something to share. It's hard amid the cacophony of voices to discern what is true and what is false. But your Spirit resides in me—a beautiful mystery—and he is able to help me uncover false teaching. Your Word will also be my guide as I hear messages over the airwaves—I can always test what I hear through its unchanging standard. Thank you for not leaving me alone to fend for myself in a sea of philosophies.

Remind me of this verse when it seems to me like people who distort your Word are flourishing and have no recompense for their actions and teaching. It seems like false teachers profit from their words. They deceive many, often cheating people of what little money they have, and live lavish lifestyles. But your Word promises that you see them. You are well aware of their teaching and antics. No one can deceive you, and all man's secrets are laid bare under your holy gaze.

Thank you for warning me about false teachers, Jesus. I'm grateful to be aware. Keep me alert whenever I hear something that tickles my ears but doesn't resonate with your heart. Help me be bold in exposing teaching that does not honor you, but with gentleness and kindness—and in person, if possible. This is a world full of lies, Jesus, and I so desperately appreciate your truth. Amen.

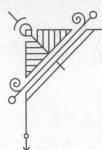

Slow

*The Lord isn't really being slow about his
promise, as some people think.
No, he is being patient for your sake.
He does not want anyone to be destroyed,
but wants everyone to repent.*

2 PETER 3:9

Jesus, I admit that I often think you're too slow. Forgive me for the doubt and impatience that typify my days. Perhaps it's because I live in a culture of convenience, and I'm accustomed to getting whatever I want in my perfect timing—so much so that I forget the beauty of your actual, perfect timing.

Thank you that you exercise patience for my sake. I want to return the favor and be patient for your sake. As I pray this, I'm reminded of your great patience toward me when I was far from you. Thank you for rescuing me.

Help me remember your ways when I grow impatient for my friends and family members to repent before you. I can't determine the moment they will bend the knee, but I certainly can pray that you will intersect their lives in surprising ways. Send other believers into their lives. Speak to them through powerful dreams. Give each person a longing for you that they can't understand. Keep them thirsty for your kingdom.

I choose today to rest in knowing you've got this whole world in the palm of your hand. Please build your kingdom, and start with me. Amen.

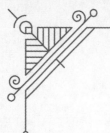

New

We are looking forward to the new heavens
and new earth he has promised,
a world filled with God's righteousness.

2 PETER 3:13

Jesus, the old heavens and the old earth hold several charms. It's hard for me to imagine anything better than a starry sky or a majestic mountain range afire at sunset. But when I look at the state of things—terrorism, starvation, wars, inhumanity, human trafficking—I long for what is next. I look forward to a place where everything's finally made right and your justice reigns beautifully on the earth.

Remind me when the news alarms me that this is not all there is. Evil will not ultimately triumph over good. People who oppress others for financial or sexual gain will not inevitably get away with it. You see it all, and for that I'm grateful. I'm also thankful that meting out justice is not on my shoulders. I cannot discern a human heart. I cannot even figure out my own. But everyone and everything is laid bare before you. Only you are qualified to judge humankind.

So let me live in light of that awesome truth. It frightens me a bit, if I'm honest. I know my heart isn't always pure. In fact, it likes to stray. Nevertheless, because of what you've done on the cross, I can be set free, wiped clean, made holy. I can look forward with confidence to the day when the new heavens and the new earth come because I know you will welcome me. Jesus, you are the way I find peace in this world and the next. Thank you for making a way. Amen.

Existed

We proclaim to you the one who existed from the beginning,
whom we have heard and seen. We saw him with our own eyes
and touched him with our own hands. He is the Word of life.

1 John 1:1

Jesus, when I'm tempted to believe Christianity is a myth, bring me back to this truth. You existed. History records your life. You had a beginning through the Virgin Mary (even though you have always existed), and you had an end (even though your death wasn't the true end of you). The apostles saw you and touched you. Books recorded your works, though they couldn't contain all the miracles you performed. The way we record time hinges on your life, death, and resurrection.

Teach me what it means that you are the Word of life. You are the very thought of God. You were with the Father and the Spirit during creation. You have always existed, and you always will exist. You are all powerful, all knowing, all seeing. You hold all things together. You are holy and pure. You demonstrate compassion. Your life was a walking miracle, defying the laws of gravity (walking on water), and circumventing physical disease (you healed it all). You are greater than Satan and his demonic horde, and one day you will vanquish him forever. You are King of kings and Lord of lords. And beyond all that amazingness, you actually love me. You set me free. You gave me hope, perspective, and life. Thank you, dear Jesus. Thank you. Amen.

Hate

Anyone who hates a fellow believer
is still living and walking in darkness.
Such a person does not know the way to go,
having been blinded by the darkness.

1 JOHN 2:11

Jesus, I know this world is dark. But I forget that the darkness is a result of lovelessness, of indifference, of hate. Please search my life and heart, even in the chaos that lives there, for any trace of hatred for others. When I'm dismissive, convict me. When I write someone out of my life because they've hurt me, help me to see their worth and glory. When I nurse hostility toward someone who seems like an enemy, reprimand me, reminding me that I, too, was once your enemy.

I know this even means my family, those whose long-term hurts are harder to forgive. Help me to prefer my family over my own selfish agenda. When I'm tempted to rage, replace that with a servant's heart. When I'm miffed, help me to take a few breaths before responding.

Today I want to be quick to listen, slow to speak. As I live and move throughout the day, remind me of the importance of not letting the sun go down on my anger. I want to keep short accounts with others so I'm not tormented at night, rehashing old arguments. Oh, how I want to be like you, Jesus, when you walked this earth, loving everyone, telling the truth, and forgiving those who betrayed you. You truly are the light that dispels hatred and darkness. Amen.

Fading

*And this world is fading away, along with
everything that people crave.
But anyone who does what pleases God will live forever.*

1 John 2:17

Jesus, help me to understand the frailty of this world I live in. Nothing lasts forever except you, your Word, and people. And yet I crave so much more—to my sadness. I want stability and safety. I long for harmony at any cost. I think more money will solve my problems. Or if I could only conquer this health problem, then I will be happy. Instead, teach me to find my joy only in you, only by your strength.

Give me the mind-set that helps me think about how my chase of the temporal messes with my ultimate enjoyment of the eternal. I want to store up treasures in heaven, where nothing can destroy them. Forgive me for treasuring what the world offers because that treasure fades away or ends up in a trash heap.

Doing what you want me to do brings me the deepest joy. It may not be flashy, but it's good. Keep me close to you today so I can sense your heartbeat and do your beckoning. Keep me alert to your calling. Instead of being distracted by the things of this world, I want to distract myself with eternity. In quiet moments today, help me to stop, gather my thoughts, and consider you—the Author and Perfecter of my faith. In that place of contemplating you, keeping my mind and heart on you, I will find the kind of joy that cannot be taken away. Amen.

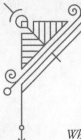

Destroy

When people keep on sinning, it shows that they belong to the devil,
who has been sinning since the beginning.
But the Son of God came to destroy the works of the devil.

1 JOHN 3:8

Jesus, I'm not usually someone who likes the word *destroy*, but in this case, it makes me rejoice! I don't know what it will be like to be set free from the evil one and his insidious influence on this world, but I can imagine it will be completely liberating. Thank you that when you walked the earth, you messed with Satan, destroyed his work (which was really all about destroying people), and crushed him on the head—rendering him fatally wounded. Thank you that one day he will be forever destroyed for his rebellion against you and his crimes against humanity.

I am grateful I belong to you. What a privilege to belong to someone so powerful, so good, so righteous. I can scarcely thank you enough for ushering me into your family. Your death was the means for my adoption. With you I belong. With you, I can extinguish the fiery darts of the evil one. With you as the truth, I can uncover the lies whispered to me in the dead of night. With you alongside me, I can finally be set free from those lies and live within the truth.

Protect me from the evil one, Lord. When sin entices me and promises me "happiness," remind me that happiness like that is fleeting and it leaves a terrible spiritual aftertaste. I've been set free from sin, and I don't want to be enslaved by it anymore. Amen.

Afraid

*Such love has no fear, because perfect love expels all fear.
If we are afraid, it is for fear of punishment, and this
shows that we have not fully experienced his perfect
love. We love each other because he loved us first.*

1 JOHN 4:18-19

Jesus, why is it that love scares me? I read verses like this, and intellectually I understand that I should not be afraid, but I am. I'm afraid to be loved, to be known, to be accepted for who I am. Override my feelings today, Jesus. Remind me of the simple truth that you love me, and you're not bent on punishing me as I approach you. You are not the FBI agent in the sky, ready to arrest me for various sins.

Perhaps I have not fully experienced your perfect love enough to understand this. Maybe I have projected my own imperfect parents on you and assumed you act the way they do. Or maybe I've been hurt by church leaders, and I think you'll act in a similar unbecoming fashion. Forgive me for that. I want to see and experience you for who you are, not as who I think you are.

Surprise me today with the kind of love that breaks through my fears. Instead of slinking away, may I invite you to stay. Instead of letting fear be my automatic fallback, teach me to trust your love, to lean into it, to let it inform my worth. When I've experienced your wild love in the past, it has absolutely influenced me to be more loving toward those you've placed in my life. I'm grateful for that.

Today I choose to settle into your love. I trust that you are bigger than my fear, and that you will kindly heal the wounded places of my heart. You are better than any human being who has ever hurt me, Jesus. Amen.

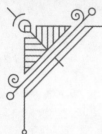

Pleases

We are confident that he hears us whenever we ask
for anything that pleases him. And since we know
he hears us when we make our requests,
we also know that he will give us what we ask for.

1 JOHN 5:14-15

Jesus, teach me to pray in such a way that I constantly ask for what pleases you. Instead of a laundry list of everything I want, help me to reevaluate and seek after the things that make you smile. Build into me godly character. Teach me to choose integrity over self-aggrandizement. Keep me alert to the needs of the "least of these." Take my focus away from myself so I can become an empathetic follower of you, ready to encourage the downtrodden. Give me a carefree yet dependent view of you and money. In other words, let me entrust my finances to you, while I hold them loosely. Give me courage to say the things you want me to say without shrinking back. And keep me very close to your heart and Word.

Thank you for hearing me as I pray these prayers. You love to answer, and that truth has been evident throughout my life. You have chosen to grow me up. You have given me new venues to proclaim you. You have strengthened me when I walked in weakness. You have ignited bravery in me when all I wanted to do was shrink and become small. You have provided good relationships for me. You have sustained me in lean times, teaching me dependence. This is why I love to pray, Jesus, because you love to answer. Amen.

Peace

*Grace, mercy, and peace, which come from God the Father
and from Jesus Christ—the Son of the Father—will
continue to be with us who live in truth and love.*

2 John 3

Jesus, would you unpack these traits in me today? Grace, mercy, and peace.

Jesus, I need grace to treat others with respect, particularly those who seem bent on hurting my feelings. I need grace to live and move throughout my day, pardoning those who disappoint me. Grace is something I must have when I'm dealing with myself. As I learn to pardon others, give me that same dose of grace to afford myself the same kindness. Help me treat myself as I would a best friend. And as I look over this day in the quietness of the night, help me evaluate it with grace-filled vision.

There is so little mercy in this world, Jesus. Instead, there is harshness and many claims to be right. In the middle of the cacophony of voices, let mine be a merciful voice, taking a look at every angle of a problem instead of immediately assigning blame. Teach me what it tangibly means to be a person of mercy. Would you send me someone today with whom I can practice this lost art?

Peace, Jesus. I need peace. When circumstances crowd into my life and threaten to mar my peace, help me retreat into the solidity of your peace. Your peace is not dependent on circumstances. Instead, it thrives when my expectations aren't met. You are the Prince of peace, and for that I'm grateful. When I'm prone to give in to panic, I pray you would settle my soul, help me take another breath, and rest in your calmness. Amen.

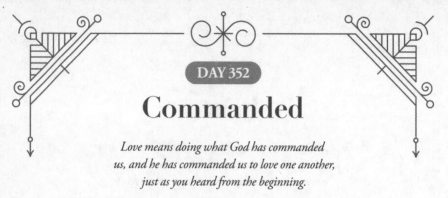

Commanded

*Love means doing what God has commanded
us, and he has commanded us to love one another,
just as you heard from the beginning.*

2 JOHN 6

Jesus, when I think about love, I don't always think of a command or obedience. Would you stretch my understanding of love in light of this? To truly love you is really quite simple. To love you is to obey you. And to obey you is to love others. I love how rudimentary this is—so much so that anyone can understand it. The commandments are summarized in loving you and loving others.

Today I look back over my week and think on the times I turned my back on you. You nudged me to do something small, and I dismissed it and walked away. Please forgive me. Instead of being addicted to my own agenda, I want to become more interruptible by your Spirit, to respond in the moment with joy and quick obedience. I want a heart like that. Because the truth is, I love you. And I want you to know I love you. I'm grateful that I can't do anything to make you love me more— that has been settled. It's that your abounding love has informed the way I live. I'm grateful, so I choose to live my life with gratitude for all you've done.

Keep me alert to the needs of others in my life. Instead of scheming about how I can manipulate or nag others to meet my needs, keep me outwardly focused, resting in the way you've already met my need. From that full heart, help me pour my heart out to others, to love them well, and to meet the needs of the people in my life. Amen.

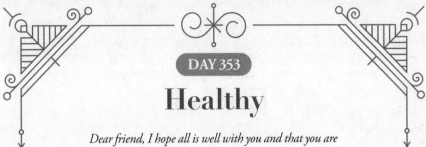

Healthy

*Dear friend, I hope all is well with you and that you are
as healthy in body as you are strong in spirit.*

3 JOHN 2

Jesus, this would be an amazing sentence to put in a greeting card.
I pray I would harbor these hopes for my loved ones. I lift up those in
my life who are struggling with unrelenting health issues. Give them
supernatural strength. Help them to see the eternal purpose in suffering. When those I love come near to death's door, surround them with
the kind of peace that stays, the kind that makes no sense but is beautifully orchestrated by you. If it be your will, would you bring profound
healing to those who are battling illness today? When you walked this
earth, you healed many, many people of diseases. Enlarge my faith so I
will pray with trust that you have the ability to heal even today.

Jesus, I give you those people who are struggling in their spirit
today—those beaten down by the world's expectations, those who
are suffering under too much weight. Relieve their grief. Shepherd
them through the grieving process so they can come through on the
other end with their heart intact and their spirit enriched. Give them
hope when hopelessness seems like the logical choice. Lift their head
when theirs drops because of another trial. Sustain them with specific encouragement, and if you want me to be part of that encouragement, let me know. For those stuck in trauma's grip, be the safe place
they need to process it. For those broken by the words of others, speak
words of unending life over them.

As I've interceded for others in their health and spirits, I pray the
same for myself as well. Heal me—body and spirit—today. Oh, how
I need you. Amen.

Example

Dear friend, don't let this bad example influence you. Follow only what is good. Remember that those who do good prove that they are God's children, and those who do evil prove that they do not know God.

3 JOHN 11

Jesus, forgive me for being sidelined by the bad behavior of others, particularly those who say they follow you. It trips me up, especially when leaders break their integrity, or people pretend to be one way when they're really another way. This is disheartening, Lord. Help my disappointment in others' inconsistencies and penchant for sin inform the way I live. Help me to live the kind of life that inspires others instead of causing them to stumble. I know I'm not a perfect follower of you, but I want to be better than I was yesterday, and I desperately need the power of your Spirit to live that way.

When the bad things of this world shout for my attention, instead I choose to follow what is good. Like Mary, who sat at your feet when the world whirred around her, help me to choose the most important person—you—as I work throughout my day. Teach me what it means to live a life of good works—not deeds I do to try to impress you or "win" my salvation (that's impossible), but a heart that can't help but do good works because of the revolutionary work you've done in me. Your goodness informs mine, and for that I'm grateful.

Keep me alert, Jesus, to those who masquerade as followers of you but really participate in deeds of darkness. I need your discernment. Your Word reminds me not to even eat with people like this, so please keep me alert to who they are. Amen.

Salvation

Dear friends, I had been eagerly planning to write to you about the salvation we all share. But now I find that I must write about something else, urging you to defend the faith that God has entrusted once for all time to his holy people.

JUDE 3

Jesus, what a gift your salvation is. I sometimes forget the value of it. Before I knew you, my life was chaos, and it lacked any sort of peace. I had no assurance of anything. I was forced to gain my esteem from the fickle ways of the world, which meant I was constantly disappointed and stressed out. My heart was restless and searching, never finding what it needed. But then I found you, and your peace flooded me with joy. It's a beautiful salvation, and you are to thank.

I live in a world that doesn't value this great salvation, though. I run into people throughout my days who don't give you a second thought. You're not on their radar, and they are living lives devoid of your beauty. They trample over others to get to the top, only to find their goal empty. They addict themselves to many things in their desperation to fill that aching spot, only to grab at more things to fill them. They wear an amazing facade, but because they live far from you, their Creator, they are desperate for love.

So Jesus, give me guts and bravery to share the hope I have in you. Keep me close to you as I do this. I don't want to shove you into people's lives. Instead, make my words winsome, inviting. Help me to share you in a way that invites conversation and open-ended questions. Keep me alert to the needs of the people around me, so I can also pray for them in the moment. Help me meet needs as I share your gospel, Jesus. Amen.

Build

You, dear friends, must build each other up in your most holy faith, pray in the power of the Holy Spirit, and await the mercy of our Lord Jesus Christ, who will bring you eternal life. In this way, you will keep yourselves safe in God's love.

JUDE 20-21

Jesus, as I survey the people in my life, I know many are struggling. They need to be built up in their faith. How can I do that today? What does it mean to build my brothers and sisters up? Open my heart and mind to Scripture I can share that will bring new perspective, Jesus. Empower me to meet specific needs, including monetary ones. Help me to stop in the moment and text a prayer to a friend, or if I'm with someone, to pray right then instead of saying, "I will pray for you." When I think of what others need, remind me of what I need, then enable me to give what I know encourages me when I'm struggling.

I choose right now to pray in the power of the Holy Spirit. Instead of praying faithlessly, I choose to pray believing that the Spirit will intercede in any and every situation that burdens me. I choose to believe that you will answer and that your answers are supernatural. Instead of praying under the weight of worries, help me pray as if the worries are already being shouldered by you.

Help me live in anticipation of what you will do. Teach me the power of waiting. I look forward to new levels of your mercy displayed in my life and in the lives around me. You have pardoned me, and for that I'm eternally grateful. In all this, Lord, would you refocus me on this simple fact? I am your loved child, and you hold me in the palm of your hand. Amen.

Glorious

*Now all glory to God, who is able to keep you from falling away
and will bring you with great joy into his glorious presence
without a single fault.
All glory to him who alone is God, our Savior
through Jesus Christ our Lord.
All glory, majesty, power, and authority are his before all time,
and in the present, and beyond all time! Amen.*

JUDE 24-25

Jesus, teach me what glory means. I understand glory is what you radiate; it's the essence of who you are. It's your reputation, your renown. And when I live in light of it, I'm a better follower, more aware of eternal things, less preoccupied with myself.

Thank you for being so attentive to my walk with you. You are truly able to come to my rescue when I am nearly swayed by the world's enticement and logic. I don't want to fall away. I don't want to be another statistic of someone walking away from the faith. I don't want to live a prodigal's life. So keep me close to you—not just by the skin of my teeth, but with anticipatory joy for the life I have right now.

I am imperfect. I sin. I mangle my relationships, and I hurt you. But you are present and available when I get to these distasteful predicaments. You are a confession prayer away, near to me when I call on you and ask for forgiveness. When I'm in close connection with you, I can breathe a sigh of relief because I realize my sins are forgiven and forgotten. In that knowledge comes deep joy. Because of what you've accomplished on the cross, I can enter into the glorious presence of the Father without spot or blemish. This is beautiful, sacrificial work on your part. I owe you my life—and it's something I willingly surrender to you. I give you all glory for your majesty, power, and authority. Amen.

Living

When I saw him, I fell at his feet as if I were dead. But he laid his right hand on me and said, "Don't be afraid! I am the First and the Last. I am the living one. I died, but look—I am alive forever and ever! And I hold the keys of death and the grave."

REVELATION 1:17-18

Jesus, you are great. I am small. You are life. I am someone you created. You are powerful. I am weak. You are God. I am not. Help me bend in to those truths. You are greater than my biggest expectation, stronger than my greatest feats, better than my best efforts, more loving than any loving act I can imagine. I pray today in utter awe of you. And if I were John in this situation, I would mimic his stance—falling at your feet as if I were dead.

Help me not lose sight of your awesome power. Help me not relegate you to best friend status and treat you like a chum. You are the God of the universe. In you everything holds together. You are both Creator and Redeemer. You are the King of kings and the Lord of lords. I sit here stunned to silence at your majesty.

Even so, Jesus, you stoop to touch my head and remind me of your affection. You choose to welcome me into your family. You made the way for that welcome through the beautiful sacrifice you made. Here you remind me that you are the First and the Last, the Alpha and the Omega, the "in the beginning" and the "happily ever after." You are everything. You are *my* everything.

Thank you that you've been entrusted with the keys of death and the grave. You are the only one worthy of such a responsibility. Thank you that I don't have to fear death or the grave because I have a relationship with you. Oh, how I love you, Jesus. Oh, how I worship you right now. Amen.

Complaint

I have this complaint against you.
You don't love me or each other as you did at
first! Look how far you have fallen!
Turn back to me and do the works you did at
first. If you don't repent, I will come and remove your
lampstand from its place among the churches.

REVELATION 2:4-5

Jesus, what a sobering complaint you had against the Laodiceans—their fervent love had diminished. They lost their first love—you—and that lack of love affected the way they loved others too. I don't want you to have to complain about me in similar terms, but I have to admit that when I look back to the moment I met you and the subsequent months, I had deep fervor for you. My love for you was ecstatic, and I couldn't help but share you with anyone and everyone I met. My enthusiasm could not be contained.

But now, in my maturity, I've lost some of that spark. Our relationship has become mundane, and my effervescence has fizzled. Forgive me. Help me to return to that place of first love, to turn away from other things that have stolen my affections. I don't want to worship control or safe living. I don't want to live for rudimentary things. I don't want to chase after money or health or relationships if it means I stop chasing after you. I want you to be my first affection, the first thought of my day, the first in my allegiance as I consider how to live.

Jesus, I repent. I turn away from living a life of ease, and I turn toward the wild adventure of following you. If I need to slow down and recalibrate my heart, give me the space to do that. Amen.

Door

I know all the things you do, and I have opened a door
for you that no one can close. You have little strength,
yet you obeyed my word and did not deny me.

REVELATION 3:8

Jesus, I'm grateful for the doors you have opened for me. The best door you opened is yourself. You are the way, the truth, and the life. You are the avenue, the pathway I have taken to know the heart of my Father. That certainly is a door I don't want to take for granted.

Show me the other doors you have opened for me. Help me to be brave enough, empowered by the Spirit, to walk through them no matter how uncertain or unfamiliar they may be. They represent a new pathway you have for me, a new avenue of faith. Help me retain my trust as I step out into the unknown, tightly clutching your hand.

I'm grateful that this church you're addressing has little strength, and yet with that little strength, they were able to obey you. They did not deny you. Perhaps that little strength is the ability to put their trust ultimately in your strength. It was an act of their will to believe that you are stronger when they are weaker. I want to live that way too. You are not calling me to be great and mighty. You are already those things. You are calling me instead to dependence, to walk out like Peter did on the water with no ability to stand, fully trusting in your ability to defy gravity for his sake. Keep me settled into that place, Jesus. I may have little strength, but I serve a strong God.

Thank you that you also chronicle everything I've done. Nothing is wasted. No act of obedience is lost for eternity. No, you know my heart, and you see everything I've done in the quiet. Thank you. Amen.

Gold

You say, "I am rich. I have everything I want. I don't need a thing!"
And you don't realize that you are wretched and miserable and
poor and blind and naked. So I advise you to buy gold from me—
gold that has been purified by fire. Then you will be rich. Also
buy white garments from me so you will not be shamed by your
nakedness, and ointment for your eyes so you will be able to see.

REVELATION 3:17-18

Jesus, how hard it is for those who are rich to enter into your kingdom. It's a narrow pathway, and we can't buy our way in. But oh, the shiny lure of money is a slippery idol. Instead of praying for my health as my very first response to illness, I call a doctor (because money will solve this). Instead of running to you for joy and fulfillment, I run to a store (because new possessions will satiate my need). Instead of volunteering to help someone, I throw money at a problem (because that's the same as doing, right?).

I confess that money has often been my god. I've wrongly believed that if I simply had more of it, I would be happier and all my problems would be solved. Oh, please forgive me, Jesus. I've been rich in money but poor in faith. Instead of thinking money will save me, teach me afresh that you deserve that only spot as Savior in my life. Teach me what it means to buy your gold, refined in the fire, the kind that lasts. I don't want to chase after something that will inevitably burn up and count for nothing in eternity. Instead, Jesus, I want to live for you, doing the kinds of works that will follow me to the other side. Amen.

Holy

*Each of these living beings had six wings, and their wings
were covered all over with eyes, inside and out. Day
after day and night after night they keep on saying,
"Holy, holy, holy is the Lord God, the Almighty—the one
who always was, who is, and who is still to come."*

REVELATION 4:8

Jesus, I can scarcely picture this scene—and I've seen a lot of really good movies with amazing visual effects. What will it be like to see these six-winged creatures, covered with eyes, proclaiming your holiness? It shows me that everything you created was designed to praise your goodness. I am no different. May these words become my anthem today and every day.

I know that when a word is repeated twice, it's meant to express just how important it is. But three times? That's the utmost exclamation point. You are holiness personified. You are utterly *other* than me. You are different, set apart, wholly unique in your righteousness. You are good, and no one else compares to that goodness. My mind cannot comprehend everything you are.

Your Word says you have always existed. You were. You are. You will be. You exist in the present tense, and time does not constrain you. You are great. You are powerful. You are mighty. You are God. And for that, I worship you with everything I have within me. Amen.

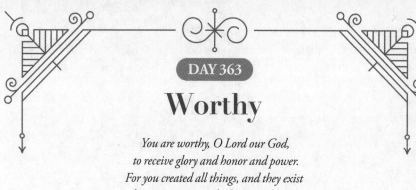

Worthy

You are worthy, O Lord our God,
to receive glory and honor and power.
For you created all things, and they exist
because you created what you pleased.

REVELATION 4:11

Jesus, you are worthy because you are worth everything. You are the Creator of all I see, the strength of my life, the reason I live. I give you glory—because you deserve it. I give you honor—because you embody it. I praise your power—because it is otherworldly and amazing.

Tucked into this verse is something I need to internalize: You create what you please, which means it pleased you to create me. I know I'm not the center of the universe. The world doesn't revolve around me. I will not give in to narcissism. But on the other hand, I don't want to live a defeated life, believing wrongly in my worthlessness. Because I am created in your image, I have worth. I carry a snapshot of your glory within me. May that simple truth inform the way I live. And as I revel in that, remind me again that any other person who lives and breathes is also allotted the name of image bearer. You were pleased to create them too. Teach me to love in light of that.

May today be one where I count my blessings, particularly existence blessings. I can read. I can write. I have eyes and ears and a body that lives. I am breathing. I can think. All of this is a gift from you. Amen.

Deeds

I heard a voice from heaven saying,
"Write this down:
Blessed are those who die in the Lord from now on.
Yes, says the Spirit, they are blessed indeed,
for they will rest from their hard work;
for their good deeds follow them!"

REVELATION 14:13

Jesus, sometimes my work feels like penance or drudgery. I am tired and bewildered. But I choose right now to take comfort in knowing that you count my deeds. You see my work. Nothing is wasted in the kingdom of God, and for that I am grateful.

I look forward to the day when all this labor is completed, and I will finally experience deep, abiding rest. Even now, before that long rest begins, thank you for the promise of still water and green pastures. But in the meantime, when my to-do list grows longer than my imagination, please grant me perspective.

Keep me close to your heartbeat today. No matter what task is placed in front of me, help me carry on a continual dialogue with you, so we can do these things together. Give me a heart of praise as I carry out the work for the day, grateful for hands that tinker, a mind that thinks, a body that works.

I make a determination to experience your joy and peace in my job today, no matter how tedious it seems or how unnoticed I feel. Amen.

Shout

I heard a loud shout from the throne, saying,
"Look, God's home is now among his people!
He will live with them, and they will be his people.
God himself will be with them.
He will wipe every tear from their eyes,
and there will be no more death or sorrow or crying or pain.
All these things are gone forever."

REVELATION 21:3-4

Jesus, amen to this. I look forward to this day, when all the wrongs will be righted and you will make this world aright. The new heavens and the new earth will be stunningly beautiful, illuminated by you. There will be no need for sunshine anymore because your glory will radiate light. I will no longer feel distant from you, but all day every day I will live in your presence. All my relationships will be settled, and all my tears will be dealt with.

Help me to live in light of this reality. Keep me close to you, worshipping you today because that will be my eternal occupation in heaven. When mourning or grief overwhelms my soul, readjust my orientation, and remind me of the next life. Help this vision of a place without tears to keep me enduring when the tears turn to rivers.

When I'm battling chronic pain (or my loved one is), remind me that this momentary pain will end. It's accruing for me a weight of glory. How I suffer on this earth matters in the next life. Help me to be faithful, to continue to follow you through droughts and deserts because someday I'll be in the presence of living water When I feel like quitting, give me the strength I need to finish well, to run this race you've given me with endurance. And as I run and fall and get back up again, sustain me with your joy. Amen.

Come

The Spirit and the bride say, "Come."
Let anyone who hears this say, "Come."
Let anyone who is thirsty come.
Let anyone who desires drink freely from the water of life.

REVELATION 22:17

Jesus, what a beautiful beckoning this is. You simply call me to yourself. You entreat me with one word: *Come.* I am thirsty. I thirst for so much, but mostly I thirst for you. So I come to you and take a good, long drink, fully satisfied because you are the fountain of life, the living water my soul needs. You fulfill every need, and you welcome me to you.

Sometimes, though, I don't acknowledge my thirst. I walk around feeling weak without acknowledging that I haven't approached your fountain for a long time. I've become proficient in becoming my own strength, living on my terms, outside of dependence upon you. Please forgive me. While my will sometimes rebels and thinks I am sufficient in myself, my soul knows full well that you are my sustenance. You are what my soul truly needs. So in this moment, I stop. And I come. I accept your invitation, because I so desperately need it, and I've grown weary of manufacturing my own strength.

May your invitation inform my life from this day forward. Slake my thirst. Overflow me with your presence. Instead of proving my sufficiency by running ragged, may I instead prove my dependence by drinking deeply. Thank you, Jesus, for your indescribable gift—your life, your death, your resurrection—that enable me to immerse myself in you and receive the love you have for me. It's a love that has utterly transformed my life. Amen.

ACKNOWLEDGMENTS

Jesus, I'll start with you because you mean the world to me (you mean *more* than the world to me). I'm living joyfully because of your rescue. Thank you for lifting me from the pit, setting my feet on solid ground, and putting a song of praise in my lungs. This book is my continued worship to you.

Kathleen Kerr, you're the best type of editorial cheerleader there is, and beyond that, you believed in this book, and then you absorbed it and made it better. Thank you, also, to the great team of people at Harvest House who have helped this devotion find its rightful place in reader's hands: LaRae Weikert, Betty Fletcher, Bob Hawkins Jr., Emily Weigel, Jeff Weatherell, Gene Skinner, Margie Brown, Ken Lorenz, and so many hands, eyes, and hearts that helped this book launch.

To my agent, David Van Diest, and his amazing wife, Sarah, you placed this book in its proper home, talked me off a few literary ledges, and have faithfully prayed for my ministry and career. Thank you.

Leslie Wilson and D'Ann Mateer (my Aaron and Hur), thank you for being in this crazy industry with me as confidants and editors. This book sings because of your feedback. Lisa Whittle, I'm so grateful for your evenhanded listening and your commiseration as I navigate publishing alongside you. To my prayer team of 13 years now, the impact of this devotional is directly related to your intercession. To all my sweet Restory newsletter recipients who made this book happen by asking (forcing!) me to write it, thank you. You're why I picked up the pen to write out my prayers because I so loved praying for you on the page. Your feedback fueled the heart of this book.

Thank you, Mom, for loving me, and Mark (may you rest in peace) for ushering in sweet reconciliation.

Lake Pointe Church, you've been a beautiful support and encouragement throughout my writing and speaking ministry. I'm grateful.

Patrick, you are my backbone, and you have my heart. Sophie, your prayers mean everything to me—your friendship too. Aidan, thank you for inspiring my prayers. Julia, your example of empathy humbles me and helps me look at the world with new eyes. I love you all.